Modern Cryptography and Computational Number Theory

Modern Cryptography and Computational Number Theory

Edited by Megan Cosgrove

CLANRYE INTERNATIONAL

www.clanryointornational.com

Clanrye International,
750 Third Avenue, 9th Floor,
New York, NY 10017, USA

ISBN: 978-1-63240-707-8

Cataloging-in-Publication Data

Modern cryptography and computational number theory / edited by Megan Cosgrove.
    p. cm.
Includes bibliographical references and index.
ISBN 978-1-63240-707-8
1. Data encryption (Computer science). 2. Cryptography. 3. Number theory.
I. Cosgrove, Megan.
QA76.9.A25 M63 2018
005.82--dc23

For information on all Clanrye International publications
visit our website at www.clanryeinternational.com

Contents

Preface

The process of securing communication and encoding all types of electronic and computer communication is known as cryptography. It is used to secure information from the third parties. The main concepts on which modern cryptography is based are authentication, non-repudiation, confidentiality and data integrity. Cryptography uses elements of mathematics especially the computational number theory to encrypt the messages. This book studies, analyses and upholds the pillars of cryptography and its utmost significance in modern times. The topics covered in it deal with the core aspects of the area. This textbook is a complete source of knowledge on the present status of this important field.

A foreword of all chapters of the book is provided below:

Chapter 1 - Number theory mainly focuses on the study of integers. It studies the properties of rational numbers and prime numbers. The subdivisions studied under this subject are analytic number theory, Diophantine geometry and algebraic number theory among others. The chapter on computational number theory offers an insightful focus, keeping in mind the complex subject matter; **Chapter 2 -** Primality tests are used in various fields like mathematics and cryptography. They can be categorized into deterministic tests and probabilistic tests. Miller–Rabin primality test and Solovay–Strassen primality test are some of the significant and important topics related to computational number theory. The following section unfolds its crucial aspects in a critical yet systematic manner; **Chapter 3 -** Cryptography helps in securing communication from third parties. Topics like data integrity, authentication and data confidentiality are central in cryptography. Public-key cryptography is especially used in the creation of cryptosystems. The topics discussed in the section are of great importance to broaden the existing knowledge on public key cryptography; **Chapter 4 -** Elliptic curves are very important for the subject of number theory. Elliptical curve cryptography is based on the theory of elliptic curves. It is used to make cryptographic keys more efficient and faster. These keys are generated through the properties of elliptic curve equations. This chapter discusses elliptic curves based cryptography in a critical manner providing key analysis to the subject matter; **Chapter 5 -** A digital signature comprises of three algorithms. These three algorithms are key generations, signature verifying algorithm and signing algorithm. Digital signature is usually used for financial transactions, software distribution and contract management software. This chapter has been carefully written to provide an easy understanding of the varied facets of digital signatures and ciphering.

At the end, I would like to thank all the people associated with this book devoting their precious time and providing their valuable contributions to this book. I would also like to express my gratitude to my fellow colleagues who encouraged me throughout the process.

Editor

Introduction to Computational Number Theory

Number theory mainly focuses on the study of integers. It studies the properties of rational numbers and prime numbers. The subdivisions studied under this subject are analytic number theory, Diophantine geometry and algebraic number theory among others. The chapter on computational number theory offers an insightful focus, keeping in mind the complex subject matter.

Computational Number Theory

In mathematics and computer science, computational number theory, also known as algorithmic number theory, is the study of algorithms for performing number theoretic computations.

Number Theory

A Lehmer sieve, which is a primitive digital computer once used for finding primes and solving simple Diophantine equations.

Number theory or, in older usage, arithmetic is a branch of pure mathematics devoted primarily to the study of the integers. It is sometimes called "The Queen of Mathematics" because of its foundational place in the discipline. Number theorists study prime numbers as well as the properties of objects made out of integers (e.g., rational numbers) or defined as generalizations of the integers (e.g., algebraic integers).

Integers can be considered either in themselves or as solutions to equations (Diophantine geometry). Questions in number theory are often best understood through the study of analytical objects (e.g., the Riemann zeta function) that encode properties of the integers, primes or other number-theoretic objects in some fashion (analytic number theory). One may also study real numbers in relation to rational numbers, e.g., as approximated by the latter (Diophantine approximation).

The older term for number theory is *arithmetic*. By the early twentieth century, it had been superseded by "number theory". (The word "arithmetic" is used by the general public to mean "elementary calculations"; it has also acquired other meanings in mathematical logic, as in *Peano arithmetic*, and computer science, as in *floating point arithmetic*.) The use of the term *arithmetic* for *number theory* regained some ground in the second half of the 20th century, arguably in part due to French influence. In particular, *arithmetical* is preferred as an adjective to *number-theoretic*.

Dawn of Arithmetic

The first historical find of an arithmetical nature is a fragment of a table: the broken clay tablet Plimpton 322 (Larsa, Mesopotamia, ca. 1800 BCE) contains a list of "Pythagorean triples", i.e., integers (a, b, c) such that $a^2 + b^2 = c^2$. The triples are too many and too large to have been obtained by brute force. The heading over the first column reads: "The *takiltum* of the diagonal which has been subtracted such that the width..."

The Plimpton 322 tablet

The table's layout suggests that it was constructed by means of what amounts, in modern language, to the identity

$$\left(\frac{1}{2}\left(x - \frac{1}{x}\right)\right)^2 + 1 = \left(\frac{1}{2}\left(x + \frac{1}{x}\right)\right)^2,$$

which is implicit in routine Old Babylonian exercises. If some other method was used, the triples were first constructed and then reordered by c/a, presumably for actual use as a "table", i.e., with a view to applications.

It is not known what these applications may have been, or whether there could have been any; Babylonian astronomy, for example, became prominent only later. It has been suggested instead that the table was a source of numerical examples for school problems.

While Babylonian number theory—or what survives of Babylonian mathematics that can be called thus—consists of this single, striking fragment, Babylonian algebra (in the secondary-school sense of "algebra") was exceptionally well developed. Late Neoplatonic sources state that Pythagoras learned mathematics from the Babylonians. Much earlier sources state that Thales and Pythagoras traveled and studied in Egypt.

Euclid IX 21—34 is very probably Pythagorean; it is very simple material ("odd times even is even", "if an odd number measures [= divides] an even number, then it also measures [= divides] half of it"), but it is all that is needed to prove that $\sqrt{2}$ is irrational. Pythagorean mystics gave great importance to the odd and the even. The discovery that $\sqrt{2}$ is irrational is credited to the early Pythagoreans (pre-Theodorus). By revealing (in modern terms) that numbers could be irrational, this discovery seems to have provoked the first foundational crisis in mathematical history; its proof or its divulgation are sometimes credited to Hippasus, who was expelled or split from the Pythagorean sect. This forced a distinction between *numbers* (integers and the rationals—the subjects of arithmetic), on the one hand, and *lengths* and *proportions* (which we would identify with real numbers, whether rational or not), on the other hand.

The Pythagorean tradition spoke also of so-called polygonal or figurate numbers. While square numbers, cubic numbers, etc., are seen now as more natural than triangular numbers, pentagonal numbers, etc., the study of the sums of triangular and pentagonal numbers would prove fruitful in the early modern period (17th to early 19th century).

We know of no clearly arithmetical material in ancient Egyptian or Vedic sources, though there is some algebra in both. The Chinese remainder theorem appears as an exercise in *Sunzi Suanjing* (3rd, 4th or 5th century CE.)

There is also some numerical mysticism in Chinese mathematics, but, unlike that of the Pythagoreans, it seems to have led nowhere. Like the Pythagoreans' perfect numbers, magic squares have passed from superstition into recreation.

Classical Greece and the Early Hellenistic Period

Aside from a few fragments, the mathematics of Classical Greece is known to us either through the reports of contemporary non-mathematicians or through mathematical works from the early Hellenistic period. In the case of number theory, this means, by and large, *Plato* and *Euclid*, respectively.

While Asian mathematics influenced Greek and Hellenistic learning, it seems to be the case that Greek mathematics is also an indigenous tradition.

Eusebius, PE X, chapter 4 mentions of Pythagoras:

"In fact the said Pythagoras, while busily studying the wisdom of each nation, visited Babylon, and Egypt, and all Persia, being instructed by the Magi and the priests: and in addition to these he is related to have studied under the Brahmans (these are Indian philosophers); and from some he gathered astrology, from others geometry, and arithmetic and music from others, and different things from different nations, and only from the wise men of Greece did he get nothing, wedded as they were to a poverty and dearth of wisdom: so on the contrary he himself became the author of instruction to the Greeks in the learning which he had procured from abroad."

Aristotle claimed that the philosophy of Plato closely followed the teachings of the Pythagoreans, and Cicero repeats this claim: *Platonem ferunt didicisse Pythagorea omnia* ("They say Plato learned all things Pythagorean").

Plato had a keen interest in mathematics, and distinguished clearly between arithmetic and calculation. (By *arithmetic* he meant, in part, theorising on number, rather than what *arithmetic* or *number theory* have come to mean.) It is through one of Plato's dialogues—namely, *Theaetetus*—that we know that Theodorus had proven that $\sqrt{3}, \sqrt{5}, ..., \sqrt{17}$ are irrational. Theaetetus was, like Plato, a disciple of Theodorus's; he worked on distinguishing different kinds of incommensurables, and was thus arguably a pioneer in the study of number systems. (Book X of Euclid's Elements is described by Pappus as being largely based on Theaetetus's work.)

Euclid devoted part of his *Elements* to prime numbers and divisibility, topics that belong unambiguously to number theory and are basic to it (Books VII to IX of Euclid's Elements). In particular, he gave an algorithm for computing the greatest common divisor of two numbers (the Euclidean algorithm; *Elements*, Prop. VII.2) and the first known proof of the infinitude of primes (*Elements*, Prop. IX.20).

In 1773, Lessing published an epigram he had found in a manuscript during his work as a librarian; it claimed to be a letter sent by Archimedes to Eratosthenes. The epigram proposed what has become known as Archimedes' cattle problem; its solution (absent from the manuscript) requires solving an indeterminate quadratic equation (which reduces to what would later be misnamed Pell's equation). As far as we know, such equations were first successfully treated by the Indian school. It is not known whether Archimedes himself had a method of solution.

Diophantus

Title page of the 1621 edition of Diophantus' *Arithmetica*, translated into Latin by Claude Gaspard Bachet de Méziriac.

Very little is known about Diophantus of Alexandria; he probably lived in the third century CE, that is, about five hundred years after Euclid. Six out of the thirteen books of Diophantus's *Arithmetica* survive in the original Greek; four more books survive in an Arabic translation. The *Arithmetica* is a collection of worked-out problems where the task is invariably to find rational solutions to a system of polynomial equations, usually of the form $f(x, y) = z^2$ or $f(x, y, z) = w^2$. Thus, nowadays, we speak of *Diophantine equations* when we speak of polynomial equations to which rational or integer solutions must be found.

One may say that Diophantus was studying rational points — i.e., points whose coordinates are rational — on curves and algebraic varieties; however, unlike the Greeks of the Classical period, who did what we would now call basic algebra in geometrical terms, Diophantus did what we would now call basic algebraic geometry in purely algebraic terms. In modern language, what Diophantus did was to find rational parametrizations of varieties; that is, given an equation of the form (say) $f(x_1, x_2, x_3) = 0$, his aim was to find (in essence) three rational functions g_1, g_2, g_3 such that, for all values of r and s, setting $x_i = g_i(r, s)$ for $i = 1, 2, 3$ gives a solution to $f(x_1, x_2, x_3) = 0$.

Diophantus also studied the equations of some non-rational curves, for which no rational parametrisation is possible. He managed to find some rational points on these curves (elliptic curves, as it happens, in what seems to be their first known occurrence) by means of what amounts to a tangent construction: translated into coordinate geometry (which did not exist in Diophantus's time), his method would be visualised as drawing a tangent to a curve at a known rational point, and then finding the other point of intersection of the tangent with the curve; that other point is a new rational point. (Diophantus also resorted to what could be called a special case of a secant construction.)

While Diophantus was concerned largely with rational solutions, he assumed some results on integer numbers, in particular that every integer is the sum of four squares (though he never stated as much explicitly).

Āryabhata, Brahmagupta, Bhāskara

While Greek astronomy probably influenced Indian learning, to the point of introducing trigonometry, it seems to be the case that Indian mathematics is otherwise an indigenous tradition; in particular, there is no evidence that Euclid's Elements reached India before the 18th century.

Āryabhata (476–550 CE) showed that pairs of simultaneous congruences $n \equiv a_1 \bmod m_1$, $n \equiv a_2 \bmod m_2$ could be solved by a method he called *kuṭṭaka*, or *pulveriser*; this is a procedure close to (a generalisation of) the Euclidean algorithm, which was probably discovered independently in India. Āryabhata seems to have had in mind applications to astronomical calculations.

Brahmagupta (628 CE) started the systematic study of indefinite quadratic equations—in particular, the misnamed Pell equation, in which Archimedes may have first been interested, and which did not start to be solved in the West until the time of Fermat and Euler. Later Sanskrit authors would follow, using Brahmagupta's technical terminology. A general procedure (the chakravala, or "cyclic method") for solving Pell's equation was finally found by Jayadeva (cited in the eleventh century; his work is otherwise lost); the earliest surviving exposition appears in Bhāskara II's Bīja-gaṇita (twelfth century).

Indian mathematics remained largely unknown in Europe until the late eighteenth century; Brahmagupta and Bhāskara's work was translated into English in 1817 by Henry Colebrooke.

Arithmetic in the Islamic Golden Age

Al-Haytham seen by the West: frontispice of *Selenographia*, showing Alhasen [*sic*] representing knowledge through reason, and Galileo representing knowledge through the senses.

In the early ninth century, the caliph Al-Ma'mun ordered translations of many Greek mathematical works and at least one Sanskrit work (the *Sindhind*, which may or may not be Brahmagupta's Brāhmasphuṭasiddhānta). Diophantus's main work, the *Arithmetica*, was translated into Arabic by Qusta ibn Luqa (820–912). Part of the treatise *al-Fakhri* (by al-Karajī, 953 – ca. 1029) builds on it to some extent. According to Rashed Roshdi, Al-Karajī's contemporary Ibn al-Haytham knew what would later be called Wilson's theorem.

Western Europe in the Middle Ages

Other than a treatise on squares in arithmetic progression by Fibonacci — who lived and studied in north Africa and Constantinople during his formative years, ca. 1175–1200 — no number theory to speak of was done in western Europe during the Middle Ages. Matters started to change in Europe in the late Renaissance, thanks to a renewed study of the works of Greek antiquity. A catalyst was the textual emendation and translation into Latin of Diophantus's *Arithmetica* (Bachet, 1621, following a first attempt by Xylander, 1575).

Early Modern Number Theory

Fermat

Pierre de Fermat (1601–1665) never published his writings; in particular, his work on number theory is contained almost entirely in letters to mathematicians and in private marginal notes. He wrote down nearly no proofs in number theory; he had no models in the area. He did make repeated use of mathematical induction, introducing the method of infinite descent.

Pierre de Fermat

One of Fermat's first interests was perfect numbers (which appear in Euclid, *Elements* IX) and amicable numbers; this led him to work on integer divisors, which were from the beginning among the subjects of the correspondence (1636 onwards) that put him in touch with the mathematical community of the day. He had already studied Bachet's edition of Diophantus carefully; by 1643, his interests had shifted largely to Diophantine problems and sums of squares (also treated by Diophantus).

Fermat's achievements in arithmetic include:

- Fermat's little theorem (1640), stating that, if a is not divisible by a prime p, then $a^{p-1} \equiv 1 \bmod p$.

- If a and b are coprime, then $a^2 + b^2$ is not divisible by any prime congruent to −1 modulo 4; and every prime congruent to 1 modulo 4 can be written in the form $a^2 + b^2$. These two statements also date from 1640; in 1659, Fermat stated to Huygens that he had proven the latter statement by the method of infinite descent. Fermat and Frenicle also did some work (some of it erroneous) on other quadratic forms.

- Fermat posed the problem of solving $x^2 - Ny^2 = 1$ as a challenge to English mathematicians (1657). The problem was solved in a few months by Wallis and Brouncker. Fermat considered their solution valid, but pointed out they had provided an algorithm without a proof (as had Jayadeva and Bhaskara, though Fermat would never know this.) He states that a proof can be found by descent.

- Fermat developed methods for (doing what in our terms amounts to) finding points on curves of genus 0 and 1. As in Diophantus, there are many special procedures and what amounts to a tangent construction, but no use of a secant construction.

- Fermat states and proves (by descent) in the appendix to *Observations on Diophantus* (Obs. XLV) that $x^4 + y^4 = z^4$ has no non-trivial solutions in the integers. Fermat also mentioned to his correspondents that $x^3 + y^3 = z^3$ has no non-trivial solutions, and that this could be proven by descent. The first known proof is due to Euler (1753; indeed by descent).

Fermat's claim ("Fermat's last theorem") to have shown there are no solutions to $x^n + y^n = z^n$ for all $n \geq 3$ (the only known proof of which is beyond his methods) appears only in his annotations on the margin of his copy of Diophantus; he never claimed this to others and thus would have had no need to retract it if he found any mistake in his supposed proof.

Euler

Leonhard Euler

The interest of Leonhard Euler (1707–1783) in number theory was first spurred in 1729, when a friend of his, the amateur Goldbach, pointed him towards some of Fermat's work on the subject. This has been called the "rebirth" of modern number theory, after Fermat's relative lack of success in getting his contemporaries' attention for the subject. Euler's work on number theory includes the following:

- *Proofs for Fermat's statements.* This includes Fermat's little theorem (generalised by Euler to non-prime moduli); the fact that $p = x^2 + y^2$ if and only if $p \equiv 1 \bmod 4$; initial work towards a proof that every integer is the sum of four squares (the first complete proof is by Joseph-Louis Lagrange (1770), soon improved by Euler himself); the lack of non-zero integer solutions to $x^4 + y^4 = z^2$ (implying the case *n=4* of Fermat's last theorem, the case *n=3* of which Euler also proved by a related method).

- *Pell's equation*, first misnamed by Euler. He wrote on the link between continued fractions and Pell's equation.

- *First steps towards analytic number theory.* In his work of sums of four squares, partitions, pentagonal numbers, and the distribution of prime numbers, Euler pioneered the use of what can be seen as analysis (in particular, infinite series) in number theory. Since he lived before the development of complex analysis, most of his work is restricted to the formal manipulation of power series. He did, however, do some very notable (though not fully rigorous) early work on what would later be called the Riemann zeta function.

- *Quadratic forms.* Following Fermat's lead, Euler did further research on the question of which primes can be expressed in the form $x^2 + Ny^2$, some of it prefiguring quadratic reciprocity.

- *Diophantine equations.* Euler worked on some Diophantine equations of genus 0 and 1. In particular, he studied Diophantus's work; he tried to systematise it, but the time was not yet ripe for such an endeavour – algebraic geometry was still in its infancy. He did notice there was a connection between Diophantine problems and elliptic integrals, whose study he had himself initiated.

Lagrange, Legendre and Gauss

Carl Friedrich Gauss's Disquisitiones Arithmeticae, first edition

Joseph-Louis Lagrange (1736–1813) was the first to give full proofs of some of Fermat's and Euler's work and observations – for instance, the four-square theorem and the basic theory of the misnamed "Pell's equation" (for which an algorithmic solution was found by Fermat and his contemporaries, and also by Jayadeva and Bhaskara II before them.) He also studied quadratic forms in full generality (as opposed to $mX^2 + nY^2$) — defining their equivalence relation, showing how to put them in reduced form, etc.

Adrien-Marie Legendre (1752–1833) was the first to state the law of quadratic reciprocity. He also conjectured what amounts to the prime number theorem and Dirichlet's theorem on arithmetic progressions. He gave a full treatment of the equation $ax^2 + by^2 + cz^2 = 0$ and worked on quadratic forms along the lines later developed fully by Gauss. In his old age, he was the first to prove "Fermat's last theorem" for $n = 5$ (completing work by Peter Gustav Lejeune Dirichlet, and crediting both him and Sophie Germain).

Carl Friedrich Gauss

In his *Disquisitiones Arithmeticae* (1798), Carl Friedrich Gauss (1777–1855) proved the law of quadratic reciprocity and developed the theory of quadratic forms (in particular, defining their composition). He also introduced some basic notation (congruences) and devoted a section to computational matters, including primality tests. The last section of the *Disquisitiones* established a link between roots of unity and number theory:

The theory of the division of the circle...which is treated in sec. 7 does not belong by itself to arithmetic, but its principles can only be drawn from higher arithmetic.

In this way, Gauss arguably made a first foray towards both Évariste Galois's work and algebraic number theory.

Maturity and Division into Subfields

Ernst Kummer

Peter Gustav Lejeune Dirichlet

Starting early in the nineteenth century, the following developments gradually took place:

- The rise to self-consciousness of number theory (or *higher arithmetic*) as a field of study.

- The development of much of modern mathematics necessary for basic modern number theory: complex analysis, group theory, Galois theory—accompanied by greater rigor in analysis and abstraction in algebra.

- The rough subdivision of number theory into its modern subfields—in particular, analytic and algebraic number theory.

Algebraic number theory may be said to start with the study of reciprocity and cyclotomy, but truly came into its own with the development of abstract algebra and early ideal theory and valuation theory. A conventional starting point for analytic number theory is Dirichlet's theorem on arithmetic progressions (1837), whose proof introduced L-functions and involved some asymptotic analysis and a limiting process on a real variable. The first use of analytic ideas in number theory actually goes back to Euler (1730s), who used formal power series and non-rigorous (or implicit) limiting arguments. The use of *complex* analysis in number theory comes later: the work of Bernhard Riemann (1859) on the zeta function is the canonical starting point; Jacobi's four-square theorem (1839), which predates it, belongs to an initially different strand that has by now taken a leading role in analytic number theory (modular forms).

Main Subdivisions

Elementary Tools

The term *elementary* generally denotes a method that does not use complex analysis. For example, the prime number theorem was first proven using complex analysis in 1896, but an elementary proof was found only in 1949 by Erdős and Selberg. The term is somewhat ambiguous: for example, proofs based on complex Tauberian theorems (e.g. Wiener–Ikehara) are often seen as quite enlightening but not elementary, in spite of using Fourier analysis, rather than complex analysis as such. Here as elsewhere, an *elementary* proof may be longer and more difficult for most readers than a non-elementary one.

Number theory has the reputation of being a field many of whose results can be stated to the layperson. At the same time, the proofs of these results are not particularly accessible, in part because the range of tools they use is, if anything, unusually broad within mathematics.

Analytic Number Theory

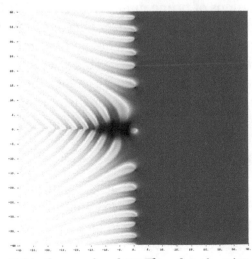

Riemann zeta function ζ(s) in the complex plane. The color of a point s gives the value of ζ(s): dark colors denote values close to zero and hue gives the value's argument.

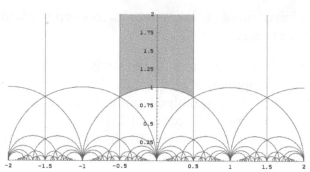

The action of the modular group on the upper half plane. The region in grey is the standard fundamental domain.

Analytic number theory may be defined

- in terms of its tools, as the study of the integers by means of tools from real and complex analysis; or

- in terms of its concerns, as the study within number theory of estimates on size and density, as opposed to identities.

Some subjects generally considered to be part of analytic number theory, e.g., sieve theory, are better covered by the second rather than the first definition: some of sieve theory, for instance, uses little analysis, yet it does belong to analytic number theory.

The following are examples of problems in analytic number theory: the prime number theorem, the Goldbach conjecture (or the twin prime conjecture, or the Hardy–Littlewood conjectures), the Waring problem and the Riemann hypothesis. Some of the most important tools of analytic number theory are the circle method, sieve methods and L-functions (or, rather, the study of their properties). The theory of modular forms (and, more generally, automorphic forms) also occupies an increasingly central place in the toolbox of analytic number theory.

One may ask analytic questions about algebraic numbers, and use analytic means to answer such questions; it is thus that algebraic and analytic number theory intersect. For example, one may define prime ideals (generalizations of prime numbers in the field of algebraic numbers) and ask how many prime ideals there are up to a certain size. This question can be answered by means of an examination of Dedekind zeta functions, which are generalizations of the Riemann zeta function, a key analytic object at the roots of the subject. This is an example of a general procedure in analytic number theory: deriving information about the distribution of a sequence (here, prime ideals or prime numbers) from the analytic behavior of an appropriately constructed complex-valued function.

Algebraic Number Theory

An *algebraic number* is any complex number that is a solution to some polynomial equation $f(x) = 0$ with rational coefficients; for example, every solution of x of $x^5 + (11/2)x^3 - 7x^2 + 9 = 0$ (say) is an algebraic number. Fields of algebraic numbers are also called *algebraic number fields*, or shortly *number fields*. Algebraic number theory studies algebraic number fields. Thus, analytic and algebraic number theory can and do overlap: the former is defined by its methods, the latter by its objects of study.

It could be argued that the simplest kind of number fields (viz., quadratic fields) were already studied by Gauss, as the discussion of quadratic forms in *Disquisitiones arithmeticae* can be restated in terms of ideals and norms in quadratic fields. (A *quadratic field* consists of all numbers of the form $a + b\sqrt{d}$, where a and b are rational numbers and d is a fixed rational number whose square root is not rational.) For that matter, the 11th-century chakravala method amounts—in modern terms—to an algorithm for finding the units of a real quadratic number field. However, neither Bhāskara nor Gauss knew of number fields as such.

The grounds of the subject as we know it were set in the late nineteenth century, when *ideal numbers*, the *theory of ideals* and *valuation theory* were developed; these are three complementary ways of dealing with the lack of unique factorisation in algebraic number fields. (For example, in the field generated by the rationals and $\sqrt{-5}$, the number 6 can be factorised both as $6 = 2 \cdot 3$ and $6 = (1 + \sqrt{-5})(1 - \sqrt{-5})$; all of $2, 3, 1 + \sqrt{-5}$, and $1 - \sqrt{-5}$ are irreducible, and thus, in a naïve sense, analogous to primes among the integers.) The initial impetus for the development of ideal numbers (by Kummer) seems to have come from the study of higher reciprocity laws, i.e., generalisations of quadratic reciprocity.

Number fields are often studied as extensions of smaller number fields: a field L is said to be an *extension* of a field K if L contains K. (For example, the complex numbers C are an extension of the reals R, and the reals R are an extension of the rationals Q.) Classifying the possible extensions of a given number field is a difficult and partially open problem. Abelian extensions—that is, extensions L of K such that the Galois group $\mathrm{Gal}(L/K)$ of L over K is an abelian group—are relatively well understood. Their classification was the object of the programme of class field theory, which was initiated in the late 19th century (partly by Kronecker and Eisenstein) and carried out largely in 1900–1950.

An example of an active area of research in algebraic number theory is Iwasawa theory. The Langlands program, one of the main current large-scale research plans in mathematics, is sometimes described as an attempt to generalise class field theory to non-abelian extensions of number fields.

Diophantine Geometry

The central problem of *Diophantine geometry* is to determine when a Diophantine equation has solutions, and if it does, how many. The approach taken is to think of the solutions of an equation as a geometric object.

For example, an equation in two variables defines a curve in the plane. More generally, an equation, or system of equations, in two or more variables defines a curve, a surface or some other such object in n-dimensional space. In Diophantine geometry, one asks whether there are any *rational points* (points all of whose coordinates are rationals) or *integral points* (points all of whose coordinates are integers) on the curve or surface. If there are any such points, the next step is to ask how many there are and how they are distributed. A basic question in this direction is: are there finitely or infinitely many rational points on a given curve (or surface)? What about integer points?

An example here may be helpful. Consider the Pythagorean equation $x^2 + y^2 = 1$; we would like to study its rational solutions, i.e., its solutions (x, y) such that x and y are both rational. This is the same as asking for all integer solutions to $a^2 + b^2 = c^2$; any solution to the latter equation gives us a solution $x = a/c, y = b/c$ to the former. It is also the same as asking for all points with rational coordinates on the curve described by $x^2 + y^2 = 1$. (This curve happens to be a circle of radius 1 around the origin.)

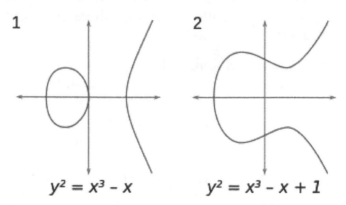

1

2

$y^2 = x^3 - x$ $y^2 = x^3 - x + 1$

Two examples of an elliptic curve, i.e., a curve of genus 1 having at least one rational point.
(Either graph can be seen as a slice of a torus in four-dimensional space.)

The rephrasing of questions on equations in terms of points on curves turns out to be felicitous. The finiteness or not of the number of rational or integer points on an algebraic curve—that is, rational or integer solutions to an equation $f(x, y) = 0$, where f is a polynomial in two variables—turns out to depend crucially on the *genus* of the curve. The *genus* can be defined as follows: allow the variables in $f(x, y) = 0$ to be complex numbers; then $f(x, y) = 0$ defines a 2-dimensional surface in (projective) 4-dimensional space (since two complex variables can be decomposed into four real variables, i.e., four dimensions). Count the number of (doughnut) holes in the surface; call this number the *genus* of $f(x, y) = 0$. Other geometrical notions turn out to be just as crucial.

There is also the closely linked area of Diophantine approximations: given a number x, how well can it be approximated by rationals? (We are looking for approximations that are good relative to the amount of space that it takes to write the rational: call a/q (with $\gcd(a, q) = 1$)) a good ap proximation to x if $|x - a/q| < \dfrac{1}{q^c}$, where c is large.) This question is of special interest if x is an algebraic number. If x cannot be well approximated, then some equations do not have integer or rational solutions. Moreover, several concepts (especially that of height) turn out to be crucial both in Diophantine geometry and in the study of Diophantine approximations. This question is also of special interest in transcendental number theory: if a number can be better approximated than any algebraic number, then it is a transcendental number. It is by this argument that π and e have been shown to be transcendental.

Diophantine geometry should not be confused with the geometry of numbers, which is a collection of graphical methods for answering certain questions in algebraic number theory. *Arithmetic geometry*, on the other hand, is a contemporary term for much the same domain as that covered by the term *Diophantine geometry*. The term *arithmetic geometry* is arguably used most often when one wishes to emphasise the connections to modern algebraic geometry (as in, for instance, Faltings' theorem) rather than to techniques in Diophantine approximations.

Recent Approaches and Subfields

The areas below date as such from no earlier than the mid-twentieth century, even if they are based on older material. For example, as is explained below, the matter of algorithms in number theory is very old, in some sense older than the concept of proof; at the same time, the modern study of computability dates only from the 1930s and 1940s, and computational complexity theory from the 1970s.

Probabilistic Number Theory

Take a number at random between one and a million. How likely is it to be prime? This is just another way of asking how many primes there are between one and a million. Further: how many prime divisors will it have, on average? How many divisors will it have altogether, and with what likelihood? What is the probability that it will have many more or many fewer divisors or prime divisors than the average?

Much of probabilistic number theory can be seen as an important special case of the study of variables that are almost, but not quite, mutually independent. For example, the event that a random integer between one and a million be divisible by two and the event that it be divisible by three are almost independent, but not quite.

It is sometimes said that probabilistic combinatorics uses the fact that whatever happens with probability greater than 0 must happen sometimes; one may say with equal justice that many applications of probabilistic number theory hinge on the fact that whatever is unusual must be rare. If certain algebraic objects (say, rational or integer solutions to certain equations) can be shown to be in the tail of certain sensibly defined distributions, it follows that there must be few of them; this is a very concrete non-probabilistic statement following from a probabilistic one.

At times, a non-rigorous, probabilistic approach leads to a number of heuristic algorithms and open problems, notably Cramér's conjecture.

Arithmetic Combinatorics

Let A be a set of N integers. Consider the set $A + A = \{ m + n \mid m, n \in A \}$ consisting of all sums of two elements of A. Is $A + A$ much larger than A? Barely larger? If $A + A$ is barely larger than A, must A have plenty of arithmetic structure, for example, does A resemble an arithmetic progression?

If we begin from a fairly "thick" infinite set A, does it contain many elements in arithmetic progression: $a, a + b, a + 2b, a + 3b, \ldots, a + 10b$, say? Should it be possible to write large integers as sums of elements of A?

These questions are characteristic of *arithmetic combinatorics*. This is a presently coalescing field; it subsumes *additive number theory* (which concerns itself with certain very specific sets of arithmetic significance, such as the primes or the squares) and, arguably, some of the *geometry of numbers*, together with some rapidly developing new material. Its focus on issues of growth and distribution accounts in part for its developing links with ergodic theory, finite group theory, model theory, and other fields. The term *additive combinatorics* is also used; however, the sets A being studied need not be sets of integers, but rather subsets of non-commutative groups, for which the multiplication symbol, not the addition symbol, is traditionally used; they can also be subsets of rings, in which case the growth of $A + A$ and $A.A$ may be compared.

Computations in Number Theory

While the word *algorithm* goes back only to certain readers of al-Khwārizmī, careful descriptions of methods of solution are older than proofs: such methods (that is, algorithms) are as old as any recognisable mathematics—ancient Egyptian, Babylonian, Vedic, Chinese—whereas proofs appeared only with the Greeks of the classical period. An interesting early case is that of what we now call the Euclidean algorithm. In its basic form (namely, as an algorithm for computing the greatest common divisor) it appears as Proposition 2 of Book VII in *Elements*, together with a proof of correctness. However, in the form that is often used in number theory (namely, as an algorithm for finding integer solutions to an equation $ax + by = c$, or, what is the same, for finding the quantities whose existence is assured by the Chinese remainder theorem) it first appears in the works of Āryabhata (5th–6th century CE) as an algorithm called *kuṭṭaka* ("pulveriser"), without a proof of correctness.

There are two main questions: "can we compute this?" and "can we compute it rapidly?". Anybody can test whether a number is prime or, if it is not, split it into prime factors; doing so rapidly is another matter. We now know fast algorithms for testing primality, but, in spite of much work (both theoretical and practical), no truly fast algorithm for factoring.

The difficulty of a computation can be useful: modern protocols for encrypting messages (e.g., RSA) depend on functions that are known to all, but whose inverses (a) are known only to a chosen few, and (b) would take one too long a time to figure out on one's own. For example, these functions can be such that their inverses can be computed only if certain large integers are factorized. While many difficult computational problems outside number theory are known, most working encryption protocols nowadays are based on the difficulty of a few number-theoretical problems.

On a different note — some things may not be computable at all; in fact, this can be proven in some instances. For instance, in 1970, it was proven, as a solution to Hilbert's 10th problem, that there is no Turing machine which can solve all Diophantine equations. In particular, this means that, given a computably enumerable set of axioms, there are Diophantine equations for which there is no proof, starting from the axioms, of whether the set of equations has or does not have integer solutions. (We would necessarily be speaking of Diophantine equations for which there are no integer solutions, since, given a Diophantine equation with at least one solution, the solution itself provides a proof of the fact that a solution exists. We cannot prove, of course, that a particular Diophantine equation is of this kind, since this would imply that it has no solutions.)

Applications

The number-theorist Leonard Dickson (1874–1954) said "Thank God that number theory is unsullied by any application". Such a view is no longer applicable to number theory. In 1974, Donald Knuth said "...virtually every theorem in elementary number theory arises in a natural, motivated way in connection with the problem of making computers do high-speed numerical calculations". Elementary number theory is taught in discrete mathematics courses for computer scientists; and, on the other hand, number theory also has applications to the continuous in numerical analysis. As well as the well-known applications to cryptography, there are also applications to many other areas of mathematics.

Prizes

The American Mathematical Society awards the *Cole Prize in Number Theory*. Moreover number theory is one of the three mathematical subdisciplines rewarded by the *Fermat Prize*.

Elementary Number-Theory

Brief review of notions from elementary number theory concerning the set

$$Z = \{..., -2, -1, 0, 1, 2...\} \; of \; integers \; and$$
$$N = \{0, 1, 2, ...\} \; of \; natural \; numbers.$$
$$Z_n = \{0, 1, 2... \, n-1\}$$
$$Z_n^{\,+} = \{1, 2... \, n-1.\}$$

Common divisors and greatest common divisors (GCD):

Let $a, b \; \in Z$

$d \in Z \wedge d \mid a \wedge d \mid b \Rightarrow d \mid ax + by \; [x, y \in Z]$

Let d = gcd (a, b)

$d' \mid a \; \wedge \; d' \mid b \Rightarrow d' \mid d$ [d'is common divisor of a and b]

The following are elementary properties of the gcd function:

gcd(a , b) = gcd(b , a)

gcd(a , b) = gcd(- a , b)

gcd(a , b) = gcd(| a |, | b |)

gcd(a , 0) = | a |

gcd(a , ka) = | a | for any k ∈ Z .

Theorem 1

If a and b are any integers then gcd(a,b) is the smallest positive element of the set {ax + by : x, y ∈ Z}

Proof:

Let s be the smallest positive element of the set:{ ax + by : x , y ∈Z}

Let $q = \lfloor a \, / s \rfloor \; and \; s = ax + by$

a mod s = a − qs = a - q (ax + by) = a (1 - qx) + b (- qy)

a mod s < s and a mod s is a linear combination of a and b . Thus a mod s = 0 ⇒ s | a

Using analogous reasoning we can show s | b. Thus $s \leq gcd\ (a,b)$.

Let d = gcd (a,b) ⇒ d | a and d | b. Thus d | s and s >0 ⇒ d ≤ s. We have shown before d ≥ s and thus we have established that d=s.

Corollary 1:

For any integers a and b, if d | a and d | b then d | gcd(a, b).

Relatively Prime Integers

Two integers a, b are said to be relatively prime if their only common divisor is 1, that is, if gcd(a, b) = 1.

Theorem 2

For any integers a, b, and p, if both gcd(a, p) = 1 and gcd(b, p) = 1, then gcd(ab, p) = 1.

Proof :

gcd(a, p) = 1 ⇒ ∃ x, y ∈ Z such that ax + py = 1

gcd(b, p) = 1 ⇒ ∃ x′ y′ ∈ Z such that bx′ + py′ = 1

Multiplying these equations and rearranging, we have

ab(x x′) + p(ybx′ + y′ax + pyy′) = 1.

Thus linear combination of a, b and p is equal to 1

Thus we have gcd (ab, p) = 1

Theorem 3

For all primes p and all integers a, b if p | ab ⇒ p | a or p | b .

Proof:

Assume otherwise, i.e., p | a and p | b. Since p is prime only 2 factors are there for p i.e. 1 & p. Therefore gcd(a, p) =1 and gcd(b, p) =1 then gcd (ab, p)=1 ⇒ p | ab.

Unique factorization

A composite integer a can be written in exactly one way as a product of the form:

$$a\ = P_1^{e_1} P_2^{e_2} ... P_k^{e_k}$$

Where pi's are primes ∀i ∈ (1..k) such that $P_1 < P_2 < P_3 ----- < p$

and $e_i \in \mathbf{Z}^+\ (\ i = 1, 2, ----- k\ )$

Theorem 4 (GCD Recursion theorem)

For any non negative integer a and positive integer b gcd (a, b)= gcd (b, a mod b)

Proof:

We will show gcd (b, a mod b) | gcd (a, b) and gcd (a, b) | gcd (b, a mod b). Let d = gcd (b, a mod b). Thus d | b and d | (a mod b).

Now $a = \left\lfloor \dfrac{a}{b} \right\rfloor b + a \bmod b$. Hence a is a linear combination of b and a mod b and so $d \mid a$.

Therefore d | a and d | b ⇒ d | gcd (a, b) from Corollary 1.

Let $d = gcd(a, b) \Rightarrow d \mid a$ and $d \mid b$. Now $a \bmod b = a - \left\lfloor \dfrac{a}{b} \right\rfloor b$ and that implies a mod b is a linear

combination of a and b. Thus $d \mid (a \bmod b) \Rightarrow d \mid b$ and $d \mid (a \bmod b) \Rightarrow d \mid gcd(b, a \bmod b)$ from Corollary 1.

Theory of Computation

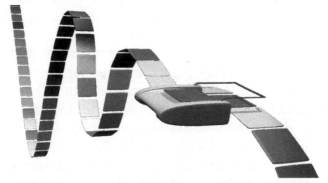

An artistic representation of a Turing machine. Turing machines
are frequently used as theoretical models for computing.

In theoretical computer science and mathematics, the theory of computation is the branch that deals with how efficiently problems can be solved on a model of computation, using an algorithm. The field is divided into three major branches: automata theory and language, computability theory, and computational complexity theory, which are linked by the question: *"What are the fundamental capabilities and limitations of computers?"*.

In order to perform a rigorous study of computation, computer scientists work with a mathematical abstraction of computers called a model of computation. There are several models in use, but the most commonly examined is the Turing machine. Computer scientists study the Turing machine because it is simple to formulate, can be analyzed and used to prove results, and because it represents what many consider the most powerful possible "reasonable" model of computation. It might seem that the potentially infinite memory capacity is an unrealizable attribute, but any decidable problem solved by a Turing machine will always require only a finite amount of memory.

So in principle, any problem that can be solved (decided) by a Turing machine can be solved by a computer that has a finite amount of memory.

History

The theory of computation can be considered the creation of models of all kinds in the field of computer science. Therefore, mathematics and logic are used. In the last century it became an independent academic discipline and was separated from mathematics.

Some pioneers of the theory of computation were Alonzo Church, Kurt Gödel, Alan Turing, Stephen Kleene, John von Neumann and Claude Shannon.

Branches

Automata Theory

Grammar	Languages	Automaton	Production rules (constraints)
Type-0	Recursively enumerable	Turing machine	$\alpha \rightarrow \beta$ (no restrictions)
Type-1	Context-sensitive	Linear-bounded non-deterministic Turing machine	$\alpha A \beta \rightarrow \alpha \gamma \beta$
Type-2	Context-free	Non-deterministic pushdown automaton	$A \rightarrow \gamma$
Type-3	Regular	Finite state automaton	$A \rightarrow a$ and $A \rightarrow aB$

Automata theory is the study of abstract machines (or more appropriately, abstract 'mathematical' machines or systems) and the computational problems that can be solved using these machines. These abstract machines are called automata. Automata comes from the Greek word which means that something is doing something by itself. Automata theory is also closely related to formal language theory, as the automata are often classified by the class of formal languages they are able to recognize. An automaton can be a finite representation of a formal language that may be an infinite set. Automata are used as theoretical models for computing machines, and are used for proofs about computability.

Formal Language Theory

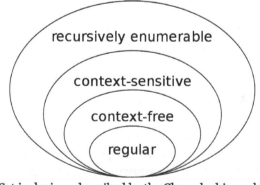

Set inclusions described by the Chomsky hierarchy

Language theory is a branch of mathematics concerned with describing languages as a set of operations over an alphabet. It is closely linked with automata theory, as automata are used to generate and recognize formal languages. There are several classes of formal languages, each allowing more complex language specification than the one before it, i.e. Chomsky hierarchy, and each corresponding to a class of automata which recognizes it. Because automata are used as models for computation, formal languages are the preferred mode of specification for any problem that must be computed.

Computability Theory

Computability theory deals primarily with the question of the extent to which a problem is solvable on a computer. The statement that the halting problem cannot be solved by a Turing machine is one of the most important results in computability theory, as it is an example of a concrete problem that is both easy to formulate and impossible to solve using a Turing machine. Much of computability theory builds on the halting problem result.

Another important step in computability theory was Rice's theorem, which states that for all non-trivial properties of partial functions, it is undecidable whether a Turing machine computes a partial function with that property.

Computability theory is closely related to the branch of mathematical logic called recursion theory, which removes the restriction of studying only models of computation which are reducible to the Turing model. Many mathematicians and computational theorists who study recursion theory will refer to it as computability theory.

Computational Complexity Theory

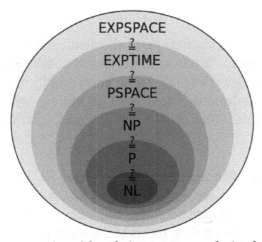

A representation of the relation among complexity classes

Complexity theory considers not only whether a problem can be solved at all on a computer, but also how efficiently the problem can be solved. Two major aspects are considered: time complexity and space complexity, which are respectively how many steps does it take to perform a computation, and how much memory is required to perform that computation.

In order to analyze how much time and space a given algorithm requires, computer scientists express the time or space required to solve the problem as a function of the size of the input problem.

For example, finding a particular number in a long list of numbers becomes harder as the list of numbers grows larger. If we say there are n numbers in the list, then if the list is not sorted or indexed in any way we may have to look at every number in order to find the number we're seeking. We thus say that in order to solve this problem, the computer needs to perform a number of steps that grows linearly in the size of the problem.

To simplify this problem, computer scientists have adopted Big O notation, which allows functions to be compared in a way that ensures that particular aspects of a machine's construction do not need to be considered, but rather only the asymptotic behavior as problems become large. So in our previous example we might say that the problem requires $O(n)$ steps to solve.

Perhaps the most important open problem in all of computer science is the question of whether a certain broad class of problems denoted NP can be solved efficiently. This is discussed further at Complexity classes P and NP, and P versus NP problem is one of the seven Millennium Prize Problems stated by the Clay Mathematics Institute in 2000. The Official Problem Description was given by Turing Award winner Stephen Cook.

Models of Computation

Aside from a Turing machine, other equivalent models of computation are in use.

Lambda calculus

> A computation consists of an initial lambda expression (or two if you want to separate the function and its input) plus a finite sequence of lambda terms, each deduced from the preceding term by one application of Beta reduction.

Combinatory logic

> is a concept which has many similarities to λ-calculus, but also important differences exist (e.g. fixed point combinator Y has normal form in combinatory logic but not in λ-calculus). Combinatory logic was developed with great ambitions: understanding the nature of paradoxes, making foundations of mathematics more economic (conceptually), eliminating the notion of variables (thus clarifying their role in mathematics).

μ-recursive functions

> a computation consists of a mu-recursive function, *i.e.* its defining sequence, any input value(s) and a sequence of recursive functions appearing in the defining sequence with inputs and outputs. Thus, if in the defining sequence of a recursive function $f(x)$ the functions $g(x)$ and $h(x, y)$ appear, then terms of the form 'g(5)=7' or 'h(3,2)=10' might appear. Each entry in this sequence needs to be an application of a basic function or follow from the entries above by using composition, primitive recursion or μ recursion. For instance if $f(x) = h(x, g(x))$, then for 'f(5)=3' to appear, terms like 'g(5)=6' and 'h(5,6)=3' must occur above. The computation terminates only if the final term gives the value of the recursive function applied to the inputs.

Markov algorithm

> a string rewriting system that uses grammar-like rules to operate on strings of symbols.

Register machine

> is a theoretically interesting idealization of a computer. There are several variants. In most
> of them, each register can hold a natural number (of unlimited size), and the instructions
> are simple (and few in number), e.g. only decrementation (combined with condition-
> al jump) and incrementation exist (and halting). The lack of the infinite (or dynamically
> growing) external store (seen at Turing machines) can be understood by replacing its role
> with Gödel numbering techniques: the fact that each register holds a natural number al-
> lows the possibility of representing a complicated thing (e.g. a sequence, or a matrix etc.)
> by an appropriate huge natural number — unambiguity of both representation and inter-
> pretation can be established by number theoretical foundations of these techniques.

In addition to the general computational models, some simpler computational models are useful
for special, restricted applications. Regular expressions, for example, specify string patterns in
many contexts, from office productivity software to programming languages. Another formalism
mathematically equivalent to regular expressions, Finite automata are used in circuit design and
in some kinds of problem-solving. Context-free grammars specify programming language syntax.
Non-deterministic pushdown automata are another formalism equivalent to context-free grammars. Primitive recursive functions are a defined subclass of the recursive functions.

Different models of computation have the ability to do different tasks. One way to measure the
power of a computational model is to study the class of formal languages that the model can generate; in such a way to the Chomsky hierarchy of languages is obtained.

Computational Complexity Theory

Computational complexity theory is a branch of the theory of computation in theoretical computer
science that focuses on classifying computational problems according to their inherent difficulty,
and relating those classes to each other. A computational problem is understood to be a task that is
in principle amenable to being solved by a computer, which is equivalent to stating that the problem may be solved by mechanical application of mathematical steps, such as an algorithm.

A problem is regarded as inherently difficult if its solution requires significant resources, whatever the algorithm used. The theory formalizes this intuition, by introducing mathematical models
of computation to study these problems and quantifying the amount of resources needed to solve
them, such as time and storage. Other complexity measures are also used, such as the amount of
communication (used in communication complexity), the number of gates in a circuit (used in circuit
complexity) and the number of processors (used in parallel computing). One of the roles of computational complexity theory is to determine the practical limits on what computers can and cannot do.

Closely related fields in theoretical computer science are analysis of algorithms and computability
theory. A key distinction between analysis of algorithms and computational complexity theory is
that the former is devoted to analyzing the amount of resources needed by a particular algorithm
to solve a problem, whereas the latter asks a more general question about all possible algorithms
that could be used to solve the same problem. More precisely, computational complexity theory

tries to classify problems that can or cannot be solved with appropriately restricted resources. In turn, imposing restrictions on the available resources is what distinguishes computational complexity from computability theory: the latter theory asks what kind of problems can, in principle, be solved algorithmically.

Computational Problems

A traveling salesman tour through Germany's 15 largest cities.

Problem Instances

A computational problem can be viewed as an infinite collection of *instances* together with a *solution* for every instance. The input string for a computational problem is referred to as a problem instance, and should not be confused with the problem itself. In computational complexity theory, a problem refers to the abstract question to be solved. In contrast, an instance of this problem is a rather concrete utterance, which can serve as the input for a decision problem. For example, consider the problem of primality testing. The instance is a number and the solution is "yes" if the number is prime and "no" otherwise (in this case "no"). Stated another way, the *instance* is a particular input to the problem, and the *solution* is the output corresponding to the given input.

To further highlight the difference between a problem and an instance, consider the following instance of the decision version of the traveling salesman problem: Is there a route of at most 2000 kilometres passing through all of Germany's 15 largest cities? The quantitative answer to this particular problem instance is of little use for solving other instances of the problem, such as asking for a round trip through all sites in Milan whose total length is at most 10 km. For this reason, complexity theory addresses computational problems and not particular problem instances.

Representing Problem Instances

When considering computational problems, a problem instance is a string over an alphabet. Usually, the alphabet is taken to be the binary alphabet (i.e., the set {0,1}), and thus the strings are bitstrings. As in a real-world computer, mathematical objects other than bitstrings must be suitably encoded. For example, integers can be represented in binary notation, and graphs can be encoded directly via their adjacency matrices, or by encoding their adjacency lists in binary.

Even though some proofs of complexity-theoretic theorems regularly assume some concrete choice of input encoding, one tries to keep the discussion abstract enough to be independent of the choice of encoding. This can be achieved by ensuring that different representations can be transformed into each other efficiently.

Decision Problems as Formal Languages

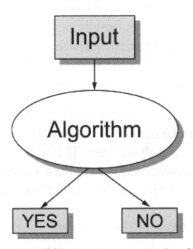

A decision problem has only two possible outputs, *yes* or *no* (or alternately 1 or 0) on any input.

Decision problems are one of the central objects of study in computational complexity theory. A decision problem is a special type of computational problem whose answer is either *yes* or *no*, or alternately either 1 or 0. A decision problem can be viewed as a formal language, where the members of the language are instances whose output is yes, and the non-members are those instances whose output is no. The objective is to decide, with the aid of an algorithm, whether a given input string is a member of the formal language under consideration. If the algorithm deciding this problem returns the answer *yes*, the algorithm is said to accept the input string, otherwise it is said to reject the input.

An example of a decision problem is the following. The input is an arbitrary graph. The problem consists in deciding whether the given graph is connected, or not. The formal language associated with this decision problem is then the set of all connected graphs—of course, to obtain a precise definition of this language, one has to decide how graphs are encoded as binary strings.

Function Problems

A function problem is a computational problem where a single output (of a total function) is expected for every input, but the output is more complex than that of a decision problem, that is, it isn't just yes or no. Notable examples include the traveling salesman problem and the integer factorization problem.

It is tempting to think that the notion of function problems is much richer than the notion of decision problems. However, this is not really the case, since function problems can be recast as decision problems. For example, the multiplication of two integers can be expressed as the set of triples (a, b, c) such that the relation $a \times b = c$ holds. Deciding whether a given triple is a member of this set corresponds to solving the problem of multiplying two numbers.

Measuring the Size of an Instance

To measure the difficulty of solving a computational problem, one may wish to see how much time the best algorithm requires to solve the problem. However, the running time may, in general, depend on the instance. In particular, larger instances will require more time to solve. Thus the time required to solve a problem (or the space required, or any measure of complexity) is calculated as a function of the size of the instance. This is usually taken to be the size of the input in bits. Complexity theory is interested in how algorithms scale with an increase in the input size. For instance, in the problem of finding whether a graph is connected, how much more time does it take to solve a problem for a graph with $2n$ vertices compared to the time taken for a graph with n vertices?

If the input size is n, the time taken can be expressed as a function of n. Since the time taken on different inputs of the same size can be different, the worst-case time complexity $T(n)$ is defined to be the maximum time taken over all inputs of size n. If $T(n)$ is a polynomial in n, then the algorithm is said to be a polynomial time algorithm. Cobham's thesis says that a problem can be solved with a feasible amount of resources if it admits a polynomial time algorithm.

Machine Models and Complexity Measures

Turing Machine

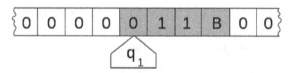

An illustration of a Turing machine

A Turing machine is a mathematical model of a general computing machine. It is a theoretical device that manipulates symbols contained on a strip of tape. Turing machines are not intended as a practical computing technology, but rather as a thought experiment representing a computing machine—anything from an advanced supercomputer to a mathematician with a pencil and paper. It is believed that if a problem can be solved by an algorithm, there exists a Turing machine that solves the problem. Indeed, this is the statement of the Church–Turing thesis. Furthermore, it is known that everything that can be computed on other models of computation known to us today, such as a RAM machine, Conway's Game of Life, cellular automata or any programming language can be computed on a Turing machine. Since Turing machines are easy to analyze mathematically, and are believed to be as powerful as any other model of computation, the Turing machine is the most commonly used model in complexity theory.

Many types of Turing machines are used to define complexity classes, such as deterministic Turing machines, probabilistic Turing machines, non-deterministic Turing machines, quantum Turing machines, symmetric Turing machines and alternating Turing machines. They are all equally powerful in principle, but when resources (such as time or space) are bounded, some of these may be more powerful than others.

A deterministic Turing machine is the most basic Turing machine, which uses a fixed set of rules to determine its future actions. A probabilistic Turing machine is a deterministic Turing machine with an extra supply of random bits. The ability to make probabilistic decisions often helps algorithms solve problems more efficiently. Algorithms that use random bits are called randomized algorithms. A non-deterministic Turing machine is a deterministic Turing machine with an added feature of non-determinism, which allows a Turing machine to have multiple possible future actions from a given state. One way to view non-determinism is that the Turing machine branches into many possible computational paths at each step, and if it solves the problem in any of these branches, it is said to have solved the problem. Clearly, this model is not meant to be a physically realizable model, it is just a theoretically interesting abstract machine that gives rise to particularly interesting complexity classes.

Other Machine Models

Many machine models different from the standard multi-tape Turing machines have been proposed in the literature, for example random access machines. Perhaps surprisingly, each of these models can be converted to another without providing any extra computational power. The time and memory consumption of these alternate models may vary. What all these models have in common is that the machines operate deterministically.

However, some computational problems are easier to analyze in terms of more unusual resources. For example, a non-deterministic Turing machine is a computational model that is allowed to branch out to check many different possibilities at once. The non-deterministic Turing machine has very little to do with how we physically want to compute algorithms, but its branching exactly captures many of the mathematical models we want to analyze, so that non-deterministic time is a very important resource in analyzing computational problems.

Complexity Measures

For a precise definition of what it means to solve a problem using a given amount of time and space, a computational model such as the deterministic Turing machine is used. The *time required* by a deterministic Turing machine M on input x is the total number of state transitions, or steps, the machine makes before it halts and outputs the answer ("yes" or "no"). A Turing machine M is said to operate within time $f(n)$, if the time required by M on each input of length n is at most $f(n)$. A decision problem A can be solved in time $f(n)$ if there exists a Turing machine operating in time $f(n)$ that solves the problem. Since complexity theory is interested in classifying problems based on their difficulty, one defines sets of problems based on some criteria. For instance, the set of problems solvable within time $f(n)$ on a deterministic Turing machine is then denoted by DTIME($f(n)$).

Analogous definitions can be made for space requirements. Although time and space are the most well-known complexity resources, any complexity measure can be viewed as a computational resource. Complexity measures are very generally defined by the Blum complexity axioms. Other complexity measures used in complexity theory include communication complexity, circuit complexity, and decision tree complexity.

The complexity of an algorithm is often expressed using big O notation.

Best, Worst and Average Case Complexity

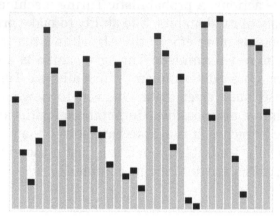

Visualization of the quicksort algorithm that has average case performance $\Theta(n \log n)$.

The best, worst and average case complexity refer to three different ways of measuring the time complexity (or any other complexity measure) of different inputs of the same size. Since some inputs of size n may be faster to solve than others, we define the following complexities:

- Best-case complexity: This is the complexity of solving the problem for the best input of size n.

- Worst-case complexity: This is the complexity of solving the problem for the worst input of size n.

- Average-case complexity: This is the complexity of solving the problem on an average. This complexity is only defined with respect to a probability distribution over the inputs. For instance, if all inputs of the same size are assumed to be equally likely to appear, the average case complexity can be defined with respect to the uniform distribution over all inputs of size n.

For example, consider the deterministic sorting algorithm quicksort. This solves the problem of sorting a list of integers that is given as the input. The worst-case is when the input is sorted or sorted in reverse order, and the algorithm takes time $O(n^2)$ for this case. If we assume that all possible permutations of the input list are equally likely, the average time taken for sorting is $O(n \log n)$. The best case occurs when each pivoting divides the list in half, also needing $O(n \log n)$ time.

Upper and Lower Bounds on the Complexity of Problems

To classify the computation time (or similar resources, such as space consumption), one is interested in proving upper and lower bounds on the minimum amount of time required by the most efficient algorithm solving a given problem. The complexity of an algorithm is usually taken to be its worst-case complexity, unless specified otherwise. Analyzing a particular algorithm falls under the field of analysis of algorithms. To show an upper bound $T(n)$ on the time complexity of a problem, one needs to show only that there is a particular algorithm with running time at most $T(n)$. However, proving lower bounds is much more difficult, since lower bounds make a statement about all possible algorithms that solve a given problem. The phrase "all possible algorithms" includes not just the algorithms known today, but any algorithm that might be discovered in the future. To show a lower bound of $T(n)$ for a problem requires showing that no algorithm can have time complexity lower than $T(n)$.

Upper and lower bounds are usually stated using the big O notation, which hides constant factors and smaller terms. This makes the bounds independent of the specific details of the computational model used. For instance, if $T(n) = 7n^2 + 15n + 40$, in big O notation one would write $T(n) = O(n^2)$.

Complexity Classes

Defining Complexity Classes

A complexity class is a set of problems of related complexity. Simpler complexity classes are defined by the following factors:

- The type of computational problem: The most commonly used problems are decision problems. However, complexity classes can be defined based on function problems, counting problems, optimization problems, promise problems, etc.

- The model of computation: The most common model of computation is the deterministic Turing machine, but many complexity classes are based on non-deterministic Turing machines, Boolean circuits, quantum Turing machines, monotone circuits, etc.

- The resource (or resources) that are being bounded and the bounds: These two properties are usually stated together, such as "polynomial time", "logarithmic space", "constant depth", etc.

Of course, some complexity classes have complicated definitions that do not fit into this framework. Thus, a typical complexity class has a definition like the following:

> The set of decision problems solvable by a deterministic Turing machine within time $f(n)$. (This complexity class is known as DTIME($f(n)$).)

But bounding the computation time above by some concrete function $f(n)$ often yields complexity classes that depend on the chosen machine model. For instance, the language $\{xx \mid x$ is any binary string$\}$ can be solved in linear time on a multi-tape Turing machine, but necessarily requires quadratic time in the model of single-tape Turing machines. If we allow polynomial variations in running time, Cobham-Edmonds thesis states that "the time complexities in any two reasonable and general models of computation are polynomially related" (Goldreich 2008, Chapter 1.2). This forms the basis for the complexity class P, which is the set of decision problems solvable by a deterministic Turing machine within polynomial time. The corresponding set of function problems is FP.

Important Complexity Classes

Many important complexity classes can be defined by bounding the time or space used by the algorithm. Some important complexity classes of decision problems defined in this manner are the following:

Complexity class	Model of computation	Resource constraint
Deterministic time		
DTIME($f(n)$)	Deterministic Turing machine	Time $f(n)$
P	Deterministic Turing machine	Time poly(n)
EXPTIME	Deterministic Turing machine	Time $2^{\text{poly}(n)}$
Non-deterministic time		
NTIME($f(n)$)	Non-deterministic Turing machine	Time $f(n)$
NP	Non-deterministic Turing machine	Time poly(n)
NEXPTIME	Non-deterministic Turing machine	Time $2^{\text{poly}(n)}$

Complexity class	Model of computation	Resource constraint
Deterministic space		
DSPACE($f(n)$)	Deterministic Turing machine	Space $f(n)$
L	Deterministic Turing machine	Space O($\log n$)
PSPACE	Deterministic Turing machine	Space poly(n)
EXPSPACE	Deterministic Turing machine	Space $2^{\text{poly}(n)}$
Non-deterministic space		
NSPACE($f(n)$)	Non-deterministic Turing machine	Space $f(n)$
NL	Non-deterministic Turing machine	Space O($\log n$)
NPSPACE	Non-deterministic Turing machine	Space poly(n)
NEXPSPACE	Non-deterministic Turing machine	Space $2^{\text{poly}(n)}$

The logarithmic-space classes (necessarily) do not take into account the space needed to represent the problem.

It turns out that PSPACE = NPSPACE and EXPSPACE = NEXPSPACE by Savitch's theorem.

Other important complexity classes include BPP, ZPP and RP, which are defined using probabilistic Turing machines; AC and NC, which are defined using Boolean circuits; and BQP and QMA, which are defined using quantum Turing machines. #P is an important complexity class of counting problems (not decision problems). Classes like IP and AM are defined using Interactive proof systems. ALL is the class of all decision problems.

Hierarchy Theorems

For the complexity classes defined in this way, it is desirable to prove that relaxing the requirements on (say) computation time indeed defines a bigger set of problems. In particular, although DTIME(n) is contained in DTIME(n^2), it would be interesting to know if the inclusion is strict. For time and space requirements, the answer to such questions is given by the time and space hierarchy theorems respectively. They are called hierarchy theorems because they induce a proper hierarchy on the classes defined by constraining the respective resources. Thus there are pairs of complexity classes such that one is properly included in the other. Having deduced such proper set inclusions, we can proceed to make quantitative statements about how much more additional time or space is needed in order to increase the number of problems that can be solved.

More precisely, the time hierarchy theorem states that

$$\mathsf{DTIME}\big(f(n)\big) \subsetneq \mathsf{DTIME}\big(f(n) \cdot \log^2(f(n))\big)_.$$

The space hierarchy theorem states that

$$\mathsf{DSPACE}\big(f(n)\big) \subsetneq \mathsf{DSPACE}\big(f(n) \cdot \log(f(n))\big).$$

The time and space hierarchy theorems form the basis for most separation results of complexity classes. For instance, the time hierarchy theorem tells us that P is strictly contained in EXPTIME, and the space hierarchy theorem tells us that L is strictly contained in PSPACE.

Reduction

Many complexity classes are defined using the concept of a reduction. A reduction is a transformation of one problem into another problem. It captures the informal notion of a problem being at least as difficult as another problem. For instance, if a problem X can be solved using an algorithm for Y, X is no more difficult than Y, and we say that X *reduces* to Y. There are many different types of reductions, based on the method of reduction, such as Cook reductions, Karp reductions and Levin reductions, and the bound on the complexity of reductions, such as polynomial-time reductions or log-space reductions.

The most commonly used reduction is a polynomial-time reduction. This means that the reduction process takes polynomial time. For example, the problem of squaring an integer can be reduced to the problem of multiplying two integers. This means an algorithm for multiplying two integers can be used to square an integer. Indeed, this can be done by giving the same input to both inputs of the multiplication algorithm. Thus we see that squaring is not more difficult than multiplication, since squaring can be reduced to multiplication.

This motivates the concept of a problem being hard for a complexity class. A problem X is *hard* for a class of problems C if every problem in C can be reduced to X. Thus no problem in C is harder than X, since an algorithm for X allows us to solve any problem in C. Of course, the notion of hard problems depends on the type of reduction being used. For complexity classes larger than P, polynomial-time reductions are commonly used. In particular, the set of problems that are hard for NP is the set of NP-hard problems.

If a problem X is in C and hard for C, then X is said to be *complete* for C. This means that X is the hardest problem in C. (Since many problems could be equally hard, one might say that X is one of the hardest problems in C.) Thus the class of NP-complete problems contains the most difficult problems in NP, in the sense that they are the ones most likely not to be in P. Because the problem P = NP is not solved, being able to reduce a known NP-complete problem, Π_2, to another problem, Π_1, would indicate that there is no known polynomial-time solution for Π_1. This is because a polynomial-time solution to Π_1 would yield a polynomial-time solution to Π_2. Similarly, because all NP problems can be reduced to the set, finding an NP-complete problem that can be solved in polynomial time would mean that P = NP.

Important Open Problems

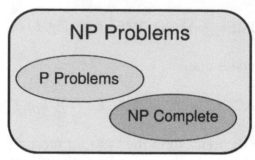

Diagram of complexity classes provided that P ≠ NP. The existence of problems in NP
outside both P and NP-complete in this case was established by Ladner.

P versus NP Problem

The complexity class P is often seen as a mathematical abstraction modeling those computational
tasks that admit an efficient algorithm. This hypothesis is called the Cobham–Edmonds thesis.
The complexity class NP, on the other hand, contains many problems that people would like to
solve efficiently, but for which no efficient algorithm is known, such as the Boolean satisfiability
problem, the Hamiltonian path problem and the vertex cover problem. Since deterministic Turing
machines are special non-deterministic Turing machines, it is easily observed that each problem
in P is also member of the class NP.

The question of whether P equals NP is one of the most important open questions in theoretical
computer science because of the wide implications of a solution. If the answer is yes, many important problems can be shown to have more efficient solutions. These include various types of integer programming problems in operations research, many problems in logistics, protein structure
prediction in biology, and the ability to find formal proofs of pure mathematics theorems. The P
versus NP problem is one of the Millennium Prize Problems proposed by the Clay Mathematics
Institute. There is a US$1,000,000 prize for resolving the problem.

Problems in NP not Known to be in P or NP-complete

It was shown by Ladner that if P ≠ NP then there exist problems in NP that are neither in P nor
NP-complete. Such problems are called NP-intermediate problems. The graph isomorphism prob-
lem, the discrete logarithm problem and the integer factorization problem are examples of problems believed to be NP-intermediate. They are some of the very few NP problems not known to be
in P or to be NP-complete.

The graph isomorphism problem is the computational problem of determining whether two finite
graphs are isomorphic. An important unsolved problem in complexity theory is whether the graph
isomorphism problem is in P, NP-complete, or NP-intermediate. The answer is not known, but it
is believed that the problem is at least not NP-complete. If graph isomorphism is NP-complete, the
polynomial time hierarchy collapses to its second level. Since it is widely believed that the polynomial hierarchy does not collapse to any finite level, it is believed that graph isomorphism is not
NP-complete. The best algorithm for this problem, due to Laszlo Babai and Eugene Luks has run
time $O(2^{\sqrt{n \log n}})$ for graphs with n vertices.

The integer factorization problem is the computational problem of determining the prime factorization of a given integer. Phrased as a decision problem, it is the problem of deciding whether the input has a prime factor less than k. No efficient integer factorization algorithm is known, and this fact forms the basis of several modern cryptographic systems, such as the RSA algorithm. The integer factorization problem is in NP and in co-NP (and even in UP and co-UP). If the problem is NP-complete, the polynomial time hierarchy will collapse to its first level (i.e., NP will equal co-NP). The best known algorithm for integer factorization is the general number field sieve, which takes time $O(e^{\left(\frac{64}{9}\right)^{1/3}(\log n)^{1/3}(\log\log n)^{2/3}})$ to factor an n-bit integer.

However, the best known quantum algorithm for this problem, Shor's algorithm, does run in polynomial time. Unfortunately, this fact doesn't say much about where the problem lies with respect to non-quantum complexity classes.

Separations Between Other Complexity Classes

Many known complexity classes are suspected to be unequal, but this has not been proved. For instance $P \subseteq NP \subseteq PP \subseteq PSPACE$, but it is possible that $P = PSPACE$. If P is not equal to NP, then P is not equal to PSPACE either. Since there are many known complexity classes between P and PSPACE, such as RP, BPP, PP, BQP, MA, PH, etc., it is possible that all these complexity classes collapse to one class. Proving that any of these classes are unequal would be a major breakthrough in complexity theory.

Along the same lines, co-NP is the class containing the complement problems (i.e. problems with the *yes/no* answers reversed) of NP problems. It is believed that NP is not equal to co-NP; however, it has not yet been proven. It is clear that if these two complexity classes are not equal then P is not equal to NP, since if P=NP we would also have P=co-NP, since problems in NP are dual to those in co-NP.

Similarly, it is not known if L (the set of all problems that can be solved in logarithmic space) is strictly contained in P or equal to P. Again, there are many complexity classes between the two, such as NL and NC, and it is not known if they are distinct or equal classes.

It is suspected that P and BPP are equal. However, it is currently open if BPP = NEXP.

Intractability

Problems that can be solved in theory (e.g. given large but finite time), but which in practice take too long for their solutions to be useful, are known as *intractable* problems. In complexity theory, problems that lack polynomial-time solutions are considered to be intractable for more than the smallest inputs. In fact, the Cobham–Edmonds thesis states that only those problems that can be solved in polynomial time can be feasibly computed on some computational device. Problems that are known to be intractable in this sense include those that are EXPTIME-hard. If NP is not the same as P, then the NP-complete problems are also intractable in this sense. To see why exponential-time algorithms might be unusable in practice, consider a program that makes 2^n operations before halting. For small n, say 100, and assuming for the sake of example that the computer does 10^{12} operations each second, the program would run for about 4×10^{10} years, which is the same order of magnitude as the age of the universe. Even with a much faster computer, the program would only be useful for very small instances and in that sense the intractability of a problem is somewhat independent of technological progress. Nevertheless, a polynomial time algorithm is not always practical. If its running time is, say, n^{15}, it is unreasonable to consider it efficient and it is still useless except on small instances.

What intractability means in practice is open to debate. Saying that a problem is not in P does not imply that all large cases of the problem are hard or even that most of them are. For example, the decision problem in Presburger arithmetic has been shown not to be in P, yet algorithms have been written that solve the problem in reasonable times in most cases. Similarly, algorithms can solve the NP-complete knapsack problem over a wide range of sizes in less than quadratic time and SAT solvers routinely handle large instances of the NP-complete Boolean satisfiability problem.

History

An early example of algorithm complexity analysis is the running time analysis of the Euclidean algorithm done by Gabriel Lamé in 1844.

Before the actual research explicitly devoted to the complexity of algorithmic problems started off, numerous foundations were laid out by various researchers. Most influential among these was the definition of Turing machines by Alan Turing in 1936, which turned out to be a very robust and flexible simplification of a computer.

The beginning of systematic studies in computational complexity is attributed to the seminal 1965 paper "On the Computational Complexity of Algorithms" by Juris Hartmanis and Richard E. Stearns, which laid out the definitions of time complexity and space complexity, and proved the hierarchy theorems. In addition, in 1965 Edmonds suggested to consider a "good" algorithm to be one with running time bounded by a polynomial of the input size.

Earlier papers studying problems solvable by Turing machines with specific bounded resources include John Myhill's definition of linear bounded automata (Myhill 1960), Raymond Smullyan's study of rudimentary sets (1961), as well as Hisao Yamada's paper on real-time computations (1962). Somewhat earlier, Boris Trakhtenbrot (1956), a pioneer in the field from the USSR, studied another specific complexity measure. As he remembers:

However, [my] initial interest [in automata theory] was increasingly set aside in favor of computational complexity, an exciting fusion of combinatorial methods, inherited from switching theory, with the conceptual arsenal of the theory of algorithms. These ideas had occurred to me earlier in 1955 when I coined the term "signalizing function", which is nowadays commonly known as "complexity measure".

In 1967, Manuel Blum developed an axiomatic complexity theory based on his axioms and proved an important result, the so-called, speed-up theorem. The field really began to flourish in 1971 when the US researcher Stephen Cook and, working independently, Leonid Levin in the USSR, proved that there exist practically relevant problems that are NP-complete. In 1972, Richard Karp took this idea a leap forward with his landmark paper, "Reducibility Among Combinatorial Problems", in which he showed that 21 diverse combinatorial and graph theoretical problems, each infamous for its computational intractability, are NP-complete.

Types of Complexities

We will restrict ourselves to two types of Complexities:

Time Complexity

Space Complexity.

By time/space complexity we mean the time/space as a function of input size required by an algorithm to solve a problem.

Problems are categorized into 2 types

(i) Decision Problem

(ii) Optimization Problem.

For the purpose of present discussion we will concentrate on decision problems. This is defined as follows.

Definition 1: Let Σ be a set of alphabets and let $L \subseteq \Sigma^*$ be a language. Given a string $x \in L$ or $x \notin L$ is decision problem.

Notation: Let p() denote a polynomial function.

We will define some complexity classes:

Definition 2: The class P comprises of all languages $L \subseteq \Sigma^*$ such that there exist a polynomial time algorithm A to decide L. In other words given a string $x \in \Sigma^*$ the algorithim A can determine in time $p(|x|)$ whether $x \in L$ or $x \notin L$.

Definition 3: The class NP comprises of all language $L \subseteq \Sigma^*$ such that given a string $x \in L$ a proof of the membership of $x \in L$ can be found and verified in time $p(|x|)$.

Definition 4: The class Co-NP comprises of all language $L \subseteq \Sigma^*$ such that $\Sigma^* - L \in NP$.

Note: We can easily verify CO-P=P and thus $P \subseteq NP \cap CO\text{-}NP$.

Definition 5: The class PSPACE comprise of all languages $L \subseteq \Sigma^*$ such that there exists an algorithm A that uses polynomial working space with respect to the input size to decide L. In other words given a string $x \in \Sigma^*$ the algorithim A can determine using space, i.e., $p(|x|)$ whether $x \in L$ or $x \notin L$.

We will state without proof the following result that follows from Savitch's theorem:

PSPACE=NSPACE

Polynomial Time reducibility:

A language $L_1 \subseteq \Sigma^*$ is said to be polynomial time reducible to $L_2 \subseteq \Sigma^*$ if there is a polynomial time computable function f ( ) such that $\forall x \in \Sigma^*$, $x \in L_1$ if and only if $f(x) \in L_2$. We denote this by $L_1 \propto_p L_2$. we can clearly observe that polynomial time reductions are transitive.

Completeness:

A language L $\subseteq \sum$* is said to be complete with respect to any complexity class C if all problems in that complexity class C can be reduced to L. Thus we formally define the notion of NP-Completeness.

Definition 6:

A language L $\subseteq \sum$ * is said to be NP-Complete if

(i) L∈NP

(ii) ∀L'∈NP, we have L' $\propto_p$ L.

The above definition is not very suitable to prove a language L to be NP-Complete since we have infinitely many language in the class NP to be reduced to L. Hence for providing NP-Completeness we resort to the following equivalent definition.

Definition 7:

A language L is said to be NP-Complete if

(i) L∈ NP

(ii) ∃ L' $\subseteq \sum$* that is NP-Complete and L' $\propto_p$ L.

The previous two definitions are equivalent since:

L' is NP-Complete ⇒ ∀ L''∈NP, L''$\propto_p$ L ' (from definition 6) ⇒ ∀ L''∈ NP, L''$\propto_p$ L' $\propto_p$ L ⇒ ∀ L''∈ NP, L'' $\propto_p$ L (from the transitivity of polynomial time reductions.) ⇒ L is NP-Complete.

Only catch in this approach is to prove the first problem to be NP-Complete for which we usually take as Satisfiability problem.

Encoding Scheme

In all the definition of computational complexity we assume the input string x is represented using some reasonable encoding scheme.

Input size will usually refer to the numbers of components of an instance. For example when we consider the problem of sorting the input size usually refers to the number of data items to be sorted ignoring the fact each item would take more than 1 bit to represent on a computer.

But when we talk about primarily testing, i.e., to test whether a given integer n is prime or composite the simple algorithm to test for all factors from $2,3,\ldots\ldots,\lfloor \sqrt{n} \rfloor$ is considered exponential since the input size I(n) is $\beta = \log_2^n$ bits and the time complexity is O($\sqrt{n}$), i.e., O($2^{\frac{1}{2}\beta}$).

Again if n is represented in unary the same algorithm would be considered polynomial. For number theoretic algorithms used for cryptography we usually deal with large precision numbers. So while analyzing the time complexity of the algorithm we will consider the size of the operands under binary encoding as the input size. We will analyze most of our programs estimating the number of arithmetic operations as function of input size β. While converting this complexity to the number of bit operations we have to consider the time complexities of addition, subtraction, multiplication & division.

Addition & subtraction:

Clearly addition and subtraction of two β bit numbers can be carried out using $O(\beta)$ bit operations.

Multiplication:

Let X and Y be two ß bit numbers

$$Let\ X = 2^{\beta/2} X_1 + X_2$$
$$Y = 2^{\beta/2} Y_1 + Y_2 ....$$

$Each\ X_1, X_2, Y_1\ Y_2$

$is\ a\ \dfrac{\beta}{2}\ bit\ long\ numbers$

Then $X \times Y = 2^{\beta} X_1 Y_1 + 2^{\beta/2} (X_1 Y_2 + X_2 Y_1) + X_2 Y_2$

$\therefore$ Thus the time complexity of the above multiplication

T (β) = 4T $(\beta/2)$ +Cβ $\rightarrow$ Time for addition

$\downarrow$

4 multiplications to Compute $X_1\ Y_1, X_1\ Y_2,$

.... $X_2\ Y_1\ \&\ X_2\ Y_2$

$\therefore$ T $(\beta) \in$ O (β^2)

The time complexity can be reduced from the following observation:

$$X_1 Y_2 + X_2 Y_1 = (X_1 + X_2).(Y_1 + Y_2) - X_1 Y_1 - X_2 Y_2$$

Thus instead of 4 we actually require 3 multiplications each of two

$\beta/2$- bit long numbers.

Thus $T(\beta) = 3T(\beta/2) + C.\beta$

$\Rightarrow T(\beta) = O(\beta^{\log_2 3})$

Fastest multiplication known to date for β bit numbers takes $O\ (\beta\log\beta\ \log\log\beta)$ time.

Division

Simple division of two β bit numbers will take $O(\beta^2)$ time through simple approach. In the numbers theoretic problems applied to cryptography over the group $Z_n{}^*$.we will consider division by a number to be equivalent to multiplication by its inverse. Thus time complexity of division is same as that of multiplication.

References

- Ladner, Richard E. (1975), "On the structure of polynomial time reducibility" (PDF), Journal of the ACM (JACM), 22 (1): 151–171, doi:10.1145/321864.321877

- "Applications of number theory to numerical analysis", Lo-keng Hua, Luogeng Hua, Yuan Wang, Springer-Verlag, 1981, ISBN 978-3-540-10382-0

- Arvind, Vikraman; Kurur, Piyush P. (2006), "Graph isomorphism is in SPP", Information and Computation, 204 (5): 835–852, doi:10.1016/j.ic.2006.02.002

- Chomsky hierarchy (1956). "Three models for the description of language". Information Theory, IRE Transactions on. IEEE. 2 (3): 113–124. doi:10.1109/TIT.1956.1056813. Retrieved 6 January 2015

- Berger, Bonnie A.; Leighton, T (1998), "Protein folding in the hydrophobic-hydrophilic (HP) model is NP-complete", Journal of Computational Biology, 5 (1): 27–40, PMID 9541869, doi:10.1089/cmb.1998.5.27

- Andrew Hodges (2012). Alan Turing: The Enigma (THE CENTENARY EDITION). Princeton University Press. ISBN 978-0-691-15564-7

- Yamada, H. (1962). "Real-Time Computation and Recursive Functions Not Real-Time Computable". IEEE Transactions on Electronic Computers. EC-11 (6): 753–760. doi:10.1109/TEC.1962.5219459

- Alan Turing (1937). "On computable numbers, with an application to the Entscheidungsproblem". Proceedings of the London Mathematical Society. IEEE. 2 (42): 230–265. doi:10.1112/plms/s2-42.1.230. Retrieved 6 January 2015

- Hopcroft, John E. and Jeffrey D. Ullman (2006). Introduction to Automata Theory, Languages, and Computation. 3rd ed. Reading, MA: Addison-Wesley. ISBN 978-0-321-45536-9

- Schöning, Uwe. "Graph isomorphism is in the low hierarchy". Proceedings of the 4th Annual Symposium on Theoretical Aspects of Computer Science. 1987: 114–124. doi:10.1007/bfb0039599. ; also: Journal of Computer and System Sciences. 37: 312–323. 1988. doi:10.1016/0022-0000(88)90010-4

- Martin Davis (2004). The undecidable: Basic papers on undecidable propositions, unsolvable problems and computable functions (Dover Ed). Dover Publications. ISBN 978-0486432281

- Jaffe, Arthur M. (2006), "The Millennium Grand Challenge in Mathematics" (PDF), Notices of the AMS, 53 (6), retrieved 2006-10-18

- Henry Gordon Rice (1953). "Classes of Recursively Enumerable Sets and Their Decision Problems". Transactions of the American Mathematical Society. American Mathematical Society. 74 (2): 358–366. JSTOR 1990888. doi:10.2307/1990888

Concepts in Computational Number Theory

Primality tests are used in various fields like mathematics and cryptography. They can be categorized into deterministic tests and probabilistic tests. Miller–Rabin primality test and Solovay–Strassen primality test are some of the significant and important topics related to computational number theory. The following section unfolds its crucial aspects in a critical yet systematic manner.

Primality Test

A primality test is an algorithm for determining whether an input number is prime. Among other fields of mathematics, it is used for cryptography. Unlike integer factorization, primality tests do not generally give prime factors, only stating whether the input number is prime or not. Factorization is thought to be a computationally difficult problem, whereas primality testing is comparatively easy (its running time is polynomial in the size of the input). Some primality tests *prove* that a number is prime, while others like Miller–Rabin prove that a number is composite. Therefore, the latter might be called *compositeness tests* instead of primality tests.

Simple Methods

The simplest primality test is *trial division*: Given an input number n, check whether any prime integer m from 2 to $\sqrt{n}$ evenly divides n (the division leaves no remainder). If n is divisible by any m then n is composite, otherwise it is prime.

For example, we can do a trial division to test the primality of 100. Let's look at all the divisors of 100:

2, 4, 5, 10, 20, 25, 50

Here we see that the largest factor is 100/2 = 50. This is true for all n: all divisors are less than or equal to $n/2$. If we take a closer look at the divisors, we will see that some of them are redundant. If we write the list differently:

$$100 = 2 \times 50 = 4 \times 25 = 5 \times 20 = 10 \times 10 = 20 \times 5 = 25 \times 4 = 50 \times 2$$

the redundancy becomes obvious. Once we reach 10, which is $\sqrt{100}$, the divisors just flip around and repeat. Therefore, we can further eliminate testing divisors greater than $\sqrt{n}$. We can also eliminate all the even numbers greater than 2, since if an even number can divide n, so can 2.

Let's look at another example, and use trial division to test the primality of 17. Since we now know we do not need to test using divisors greater than $\sqrt{n}$, we only need to use integer divisors less than or equal to $\sqrt{17} \approx 4.12$. Those would be 2, 3, and 4. As stated above, we can skip 4 because if 4 evenly divides 17, 2 must also evenly divide 17, which we already would have checked before that.

That leaves us with just 2 and 3. After dividing, we find that 17 is not divisible by 2 or 3, and we can confirm that 17 must be prime.

The algorithm can be improved further by observing that all primes are of the form $6k \pm 1$, with the exception of 2 and 3. This is because all integers can be expressed as $(6k + i)$ for some integer k and for $i = -1, 0, 1, 2, 3,$ or 4; 2 divides $(6k + 0)$, $(6k + 2)$, $(6k + 4)$; and 3 divides $(6k + 3)$. So a more efficient method is to test if n is divisible by 2 or 3, then to check through all the numbers of form $6k \pm 1 \leq \sqrt{n}$. This is 3 times as fast as testing all m.

Generalising further, it can be seen that all primes are of the form $c\#k + i$ for $i < c\#$ where i represents the numbers that are coprime to $c\#$ and where c and k are integers. For example, let $c = 6$. Then $c\# = 2 \cdot 3 \cdot 5 = 30$. All integers are of the form $30k + i$ for $i = 0, 1, 2,...,29$ and k an integer. However, 2 divides $0, 2, 4,...,28$ and 3 divides $0, 3, 6,...,27$ and 5 divides $0, 5, 10,...,25$. So all prime numbers are of the form $30k + i$ for $i = 1, 7, 11, 13, 17, 19, 23, 29$ (i.e. for $i < 30$ such that $\gcd(i,30) = 1$). Note that if i and 30 are not coprime, then $30k + i$ is divisible by a prime divisor of 30, namely 2, 3 or 5, and is therefore not prime.

As $c \to \infty$, the number of values that $c\#k + i$ can take over a certain range decreases, and so the time to test n decreases. For this method, it is also necessary to check for divisibility by all primes that are less than c. Observations analogous to the preceding can be applied recursively, giving the Sieve of Eratosthenes.

A good way to speed up these methods (and all the others mentioned below) is to pre-compute and store a list of all primes up to a certain bound, say all primes up to 200. (Such a list can be computed with the Sieve of Eratosthenes or by an algorithm that tests each incremental m against all known primes $< \sqrt{m}$). Then, before testing n for primality with a serious method, n can first be checked for divisibility by any prime from the list. If it is divisible by any of those numbers then it is composite, and any further tests can be skipped.

A simple, but very inefficient primality test uses Wilson's theorem, which states that p is prime if and only if:

$$(p-1)! \equiv -1 \pmod{p}$$

Although this method requires about p modular multiplications, rendering it impractical, theorems about primes and modular residues form the basis of many more practical methods.

Pseudocode

The following is a simple primality test in pseudocode for not very large numbers.

```
function is_prime(n)
    if n ≤ 1
        return false
    else if n ≤ 3
        return true
    else if n mod 2 = 0 or n mod 3 = 0
```

```
        return false
    let i ← 5
    while i * i ≤ n
        if n mod i = 0 or n mod (i + 2) = 0
            return false
        i ← i + 6
    return true
```

Heuristic Tests

These are tests that seem to work well in practice, but are unproven and therefore are not, technically speaking, algorithms at all. The Fermat test and the Fibonacci test are simple examples, and they are *very* effective when combined. John Selfridge has conjectured that if p is an odd number, and $p \equiv \pm 2 \pmod 5$, then p will be prime if both of the following hold:

- $2^{p-1} \equiv 1 \pmod p$,

- $f_{p+1} \equiv 0 \pmod p$,

where f_k is the k-th Fibonacci number. The first condition is the Fermat primality test using base 2.

Selfridge, Carl Pomerance, and Samuel Wagstaff together offer \$620 for a counterexample. The problem is still open as of September 11, 2015. Pomerance thinks that Selfridge's estate would probably pay his share of the reward.

The Baillie-PSW primality test is another excellent heuristic, using the Lucas sequence in place of the Fibonacci sequence. It has no known counterexamples.

Probabilistic Tests

Probabilistic tests are more rigorous than heuristics in that they provide provable bounds on the probability of being fooled by a composite number. Many popular primality tests are probabilistic tests. These tests use, apart from the tested number n, some other numbers a which are chosen at random from some sample space; the usual randomized primality tests never report a prime number as composite, but it is possible for a composite number to be reported as prime. The probability of error can be reduced by repeating the test with several independently chosen values of a; for two commonly used tests, for *any* composite n at least half the a's detect n's compositeness, so k repetitions reduce the error probability to at most 2^{-k}, which can be made arbitrarily small by increasing k.

The basic structure of randomized primality tests is as follows:

1. Randomly pick a number a.

2. Check some equality (corresponding to the chosen test) involving a and the given number n. If the equality fails to hold true, then n is a composite number, a is known as a *witness* for the compositeness, and the test stops.

3. Repeat from step 1 until the required accuracy is achieved.

After one or more iterations, if n is not found to be a composite number, then it can be declared probably prime.

Fermat Primality Test

The simplest probabilistic primality test is the Fermat primality test (actually a compositeness test). It works as follows:

> Given an integer n, choose some integer a coprime to n and calculate a^{n-1} modulo n. If the result is different from 1, then n is composite. If it is 1, then n may or may not be prime.

If a^{n-1} (modulo n) is 1 but n is not prime, then n is called a pseudoprime to base a. In practice, we observe that, if a^{n-1} (modulo n) is 1, then n is usually prime. But here is a counterexample: if $n = 341$ and $a = 2$, then

$$2^{340} \equiv 1 \pmod{341}$$

even though $341 = 11 \cdot 31$ is composite. In fact, 341 is the smallest pseudoprime base 2.

There are only 21853 pseudoprimes base 2 that are less than 2.5×10^{10}. This means that, for n up to 2.5×10^{10}, if 2^{n-1} (modulo n) equals 1, then n is prime, unless n is one of these 21853 pseudoprimes.

Some composite numbers (Carmichael numbers) have the property that a^{n-1} is 1 (modulo n) for every a that is coprime to n. The smallest example is $n = 561 = 3 \cdot 11 \cdot 17$, for which a^{560} is 1 (modulo 561) for all a coprime to 561. Nevertheless, the Fermat test is often used if a rapid screening of numbers is needed, for instance in the key generation phase of the RSA public key cryptographic algorithm.

Miller–Rabin and Solovay–Strassen Primality Test

The Miller–Rabin primality test and Solovay–Strassen primality test are more sophisticated variants, which detect all composites (once again, this means: for *every* composite number n, at least 3/4 (Miller–Rabin) or 1/2 (Solovay–Strassen) of numbers a are witnesses of compositeness of n). These are also compositeness tests.

The Miller–Rabin primality test works as follows: Given an integer n, choose some positive integer $a < n$. Let $2^s d = n - 1$, where d is odd. If

$$a^d \not\equiv 1 \pmod{n}$$

and

$$a^{2^r d} \not\equiv -1 \pmod{n} \text{ for all } 0 \le r \le s-1,$$

then n is composite and a is a witness for the compositeness. Otherwise, n may or may not be prime. The Miller–Rabin test is a strong pseudoprime test.

The Solovay–Strassen primality test uses another equality: Given an odd number n, choose some integer $a < n$, if

$$a^{(n-1)/2} \not\equiv \left(\frac{a}{n}\right) \pmod{n}, \text{ where } \left(\frac{a}{n}\right) \text{ is the Jacobi symbol,}$$

then n is composite and a is a witness for the compositeness. Otherwise, n may or may not be prime. The Solovay–Strassen test is an Euler pseudoprime test.

For each individual value of a, the Solovay–Strassen test is weaker than the Miller–Rabin test. For example, if $n = 1905$ and $a = 2$, then the Miller-Rabin test shows that n is composite, but the Solovay–Strassen test does not. This is because 1905 is an Euler pseudoprime base 2 but not a strong pseudoprime base 2.

Frobenius Primality Test

The Miller–Rabin and the Solovay–Strassen primality tests are simple and are much faster than other general primality tests. One method of improving efficiency further in some cases is the Frobenius pseudoprimality test; a round of this test takes about three times as long as a round of Miller–Rabin, but achieves a probability bound comparable to seven rounds of Miller–Rabin.

The Frobenius test is a generalization of the Lucas pseudoprime test. One can also combine a Miller–Rabin type test with a Lucas pseudoprime test to get a primality test that has no known counterexamples. That is, this combined test has no known composite n for which the test reports that n is probably prime. One such test is the Baillie–PSW primality test, several variations of which exist.

Other Tests

Leonard Adleman and Ming-Deh Huang presented an errorless (but expected polynomial-time) variant of the elliptic curve primality test. Unlike the other probabilistic tests, this algorithm produces a primality certificate, and thus can be used to prove that a number is prime. The algorithm is prohibitively slow in practice.

If quantum computers were available, primality could be tested asymptotically faster than by using classical computers. A combination of Shor's algorithm, an integer factorization method, with the Pocklington primality test could solve the problem in $O(\log^3 n \log\log n \log\log\log n)$.

Fast Deterministic Tests

Near the beginning of the 20th century, it was shown that a corollary of Fermat's little theorem could be used to test for primality. This resulted in the Pocklington primality test. However, as this test requires a partial factorization of $n - 1$ the running time was still quite slow in the worst case. The first deterministic primality test significantly faster than the naive methods was the cyclotomy test; its runtime can be proven to be $O((\log n)^{c \log\log\log n})$, where n is the number to test for primality and c is a constant independent of n. Many further improvements were made, but none could be proven to have polynomial running time. (Note that running time is measured in terms of the size of the input, which in this case is $\sim \log n$, that being the number of bits needed to represent the number n.) The elliptic curve primality test can be proven to run in $O((\log n)^6)$, if some conjectures on analytic number theory are true. Similarly, under the generalized Riemann hypothesis, the deterministic Miller's test, which forms the basis of the probabilistic Miller–Rabin test, can be proved to run in $\tilde{O}((\log n)^4)$. In practice, this algorithm is slower than the other two for sizes of numbers that can be dealt with at all. Because the implementation of these two methods is rather difficult and creates a risk of programming errors, slower but simpler tests are often preferred.

In 2002, the first provably unconditional deterministic polynomial time test for primality was invented by Manindra Agrawal, Neeraj Kayal, and Nitin Saxena. The AKS primality test runs in $\tilde{O}((\log n)^{12})$ (improved to $\tilde{O}((\log n)^{7.5})$ in the published revision of their paper), which can be further reduced to $\tilde{O}((\log n)^6)$ if the Sophie Germain conjecture is true. Subsequently, Lenstra and Pomerance presented a version of the test which runs in time $\tilde{O}((\log n)^6)$ unconditionally.

Agrawal, Kayal and Saxena suggest a variant of their algorithm which would run in $\tilde{O}((\log n)^3)$ if Agrawal's conjecture is true; however, a heuristic argument by Hendrik Lenstra and Carl Pomerance suggests that it is probably false. A modified version of the Agrawal's conjecture, the Agrawal–Popovych conjecture, may still be true.

Complexity

In computational complexity theory, the formal language corresponding to the prime numbers is denoted as PRIMES. It is easy to show that PRIMES is in Co-NP: its complement COMPOSITES is in NP because one can decide compositeness by nondeterministically guessing a factor.

In 1975, Vaughan Pratt showed that there existed a certificate for primality that was checkable in polynomial time, and thus that PRIMES was in NP, and therefore in NP ∩ coNP.

The subsequent discovery of the Solovay–Strassen and Miller–Rabin algorithms put PRIMES in coRP. In 1992, the Adleman–Huang algorithm reduced the complexity to ZPP = RP ∩ coRP, which superseded Pratt's result.

The Adleman–Pomerance–Rumely primality test from 1983 put PRIMES in QP (quasi-polynomial time), which is not known to be comparable with the classes mentioned above.

Because of its tractability in practice, polynomial-time algorithms assuming the Riemann hypothesis, and other similar evidence, it was long suspected but not proven that primality could be solved in polynomial time. The existence of the AKS primality test finally settled this long-standing question and placed PRIMES in P. However, PRIMES is not known to be P-complete, and it is not known whether it lies in classes lying inside P such as NC or L. It is known that PRIMES is not in AC^0.

Number-theoretic Methods

Certain number-theoretic methods exist for testing whether a number is prime, such as the Lucas test and Proth's test. These tests typically require factorization of $n + 1$, $n - 1$, or a similar quantity, which means that they are not useful for general-purpose primality testing, but they are often quite powerful when the tested number n is known to have a special form.

The Lucas test relies on the fact that the multiplicative order of a number a modulo n is $n-1$ for a prime n when a is a primitive root modulo n. If we can show a is primitive for n, we can show n is prime.

Jacobi Symbol

n \ m	0	1	2	3	4	5	6	7	8	9	10	11	12	13	14	15	16
1	1																
3	0	1	−1														
5	0	1	−1	−1	1												
7	0	1	1	−1	1	−1	−1										
9	0	1	1	0	1	1	0	1	1								
11	0	1	−1	1	1	1	−1	−1	−1	1	−1						
13	0	1	−1	1	1	−1	−1	−1	−1	1	1	−1	1				
15	0	1	1	0	1	0	0	−1	1	0	0	−1	0	−1	−1		
17	−0	−1	1	−1	−1	−1	−1	−1	1	−1	−1	−1	−1	1	−1	1	1

Jacobi symbol $\left(\dfrac{m}{n}\right)$ for various m (along top) and n (along left side). Only $0 \le m < n$ are shown, since due to rule (2) below any other m can be reduced modulo n. Quadratic residues are highlighted in yellow — note that no entry with a Jacobi symbol of −1 is a quadratic residue, and if m is a quadratic residue modulo a coprime n, then $\left(\dfrac{m}{n}\right)=1$, but not all entries with a Jacobi symbol of 1 are quadratic residues. Notice also that when either n or m is a square, all values are nonnegative.

The Jacobi symbol is a generalization of the Legendre symbol. Introduced by Jacobi in 1837, it is of theoretical interest in modular arithmetic and other branches of number theory, but its main use is in computational number theory, especially primality testing and integer factorization; these in turn are important in cryptography.

Definition

For any integer a and any positive odd integer n, the Jacobi symbol $\left(\dfrac{a}{n}\right)$ is defined as the product of the Legendre symbols corresponding to the prime factors of n:

$$\left(\frac{a}{n}\right)=\left(\frac{a}{p_1}\right)^{\alpha_1}\left(\frac{a}{p_2}\right)^{\alpha_2}\cdots\left(\frac{a}{p_k}\right)^{\alpha_k},$$

where

$$n = p_1^{\alpha_1} p_2^{\alpha_2} \cdots p_k^{\alpha_k}$$

is the prime factorization of n.

The Legendre symbol $(\dfrac{a}{p})$ is defined for all integers a and all odd primes p by

$$\left(\frac{a}{p}\right)=\begin{cases}0 & \text{if } a \equiv 0 \pmod{p}, \\ 1 & \text{if } a \not\equiv 0 \pmod{p} \text{ and for some integer } x: a \equiv x^2 \pmod{p}, \\ -1 & \text{if } a \not\equiv 0 \pmod{p} \text{ and there is no such } x.\end{cases}$$

Following the normal convention for the empty product, $(\dfrac{a}{1})=1$.

The Legendre and Jacobi symbols are indistinguishable exactly when the lower argument is an odd prime, in which case they have the same value.

Table of Values

The following is a table of values of Jacobi symbol $(\dfrac{k}{n})$ with $n \le 59$, $k \le 30$, n odd.

k / n	1	2	3	4	5	6	7	8	9	10	11	12	13	14	15	16	17	18	19	20	21	22	23	24	25	26	27	28	29	30
1	-1	1	1	-1	1	1	1	1	-1	1	1	1	1	1	1	-1	1	1	1	1	1	1	1	1	-1	1	1	1	1	1
3	1	-1	0	1	-1	0	1	-1	0	1	-1	0	1	-1	0	1	-1	0	1	-1	0	1	-1	0	1	-1	0	1	-1	0
5	1	-1	-1	1	0	1	-1	-1	1	0	1	-1	-1	1	0	1	-1	-1	1	0	1	-1	-1	1	0	1	-1	-1	1	0
7	1	1	-1	1	-1	-1	0	1	1	-1	1	-1	-1	0	1	1	-1	1	-1	-1	0	1	1	-1	1	-1	-1	0	1	1
9	1	1	0	1	1	0	1	1	0	1	1	0	1	1	0	1	1	0	1	1	0	1	1	0	1	1	0	1	1	0
11	1	-1	1	1	1	-1	-1	-1	1	-1	0	1	-1	1	1	1	-1	-1	-1	1	-1	0	1	-1	1	1	1	-1	-1	-1
13	1	-1	1	1	-1	-1	-1	-1	1	1	-1	1	0	1	-1	1	1	-1	-1	-1	-1	1	1	-1	1	0	1	-1	1	1
15	1	1	0	1	0	0	-1	1	0	0	-1	0	-1	-1	0	1	1	0	1	0	0	-1	1	0	0	-1	0	-1	-1	0
17	1	1	-1	1	-1	-1	-1	1	1	-1	-1	-1	1	-1	1	1	0	1	1	-1	1	-1	-1	-1	1	1	-1	-1	-1	1

	1	3	5	7	9	11	13	15	17	19	21	23	25	27	29	31	33	35	37	39	41	43	45	47	49	51	53	55	57	59
19	1	-1	-1	1	1	1	1	-1	1	-1	1	-1	-1	-1	-1	1	1	-1	0	1	-1	-1	1	1	1	1	-1	1	-1	1
21	1	-1	0	1	1	0	0	-1	0	-1	-1	0	-1	0	0	1	1	0	-1	1	0	1	-1	0	1	1	0	0	-1	0
23	1	1	1	1	-1	1	-1	1	1	-1	-1	1	1	-1	-1	1	-1	1	-1	-1	-1	-1	0	1	1	1	1	-1	1	-1
25	1	1	1	1	0	1	1	1	1	0	1	1	1	1	0	1	1	1	1	0	1	1	1	1	0	1	1	1	1	0
27	1	-1	0	1	-1	0	1	-1	0	1	-1	0	1	-1	0	1	-1	0	1	-1	0	1	-1	0	1	-1	0	1	-1	0
29	1	-1	-1	1	1	1	1	-1	1	-1	-1	-1	1	-1	-1	1	-1	-1	-1	1	-1	1	1	1	1	-1	-1	1	0	1
31	1	1	-1	1	1	-1	1	1	1	1	-1	-1	-1	1	-1	1	-1	1	1	1	-1	-1	-1	-1	1	-1	-1	1	-1	-1
33	1	1	0	1	-1	0	-1	1	0	-1	0	0	-1	-1	0	1	1	0	-1	-1	0	0	-1	0	1	-1	0	-1	1	0
35	1	-1	1	1	0	-1	0	-1	1	0	1	1	1	0	0	1	1	-1	-1	0	0	-1	-1	-1	0	-1	1	0	1	0
37	1	-1	1	1	-1	-1	1	-1	1	1	1	1	-1	-1	-1	1	-1	-1	-1	-1	1	-1	-1	-1	1	1	1	1	-1	1
39	1	1	0	1	1	0	-1	1	0	1	1	0	0	-1	0	1	-1	0	-1	1	0	1	-1	0	1	0	0	-1	-1	0
41	1	1	-1	1	1	-1	-1	1	1	1	-1	-1	-1	-1	-1	1	-1	1	-1	1	1	-1	1	-1	1	-1	-1	-1	-1	-1
43	1	-1	-1	1	-1	1	-1	-1	1	1	1	-1	1	1	1	1	1	-1	-1	-1	1	-1	1	1	1	-1	-1	-1	-1	-1
45	1	-1	0	1	0	0	-1	-1	0	0	1	0	-1	1	0	1	-1	0	1	0	0	-1	-1	0	0	1	0	-1	1	0
47	1	1	1	1	-1	1	1	1	1	-1	-1	1	-1	1	-1	1	1	1	-1	-1	1	-1	-1	1	1	-1	1	1	-1	-1
49	1	1	1	1	1	1	0	1	1	1	1	1	1	0	1	1	1	1	1	0	1	1	1	1	1	1	0	1	1	1
51	1	-1	0	1	1	0	-1	-1	0	-1	1	0	1	1	0	1	0	0	1	1	0	-1	1	0	1	-1	0	-1	1	0
53	1	-1	-1	1	-1	1	1	-1	1	1	1	-1	1	-1	1	1	1	-1	-1	-1	-1	-1	-1	1	1	-1	-1	1	1	-1
55	1	1	-1	1	0	-1	1	1	1	0	0	-1	1	1	0	1	1	1	-1	0	-1	0	-1	-1	0	1	-1	1	-1	0
57	1	1	0	1	-1	0	1	1	0	-1	-1	0	-1	1	0	1	-1	0	0	-1	0	-1	-1	0	1	-1	0	1	1	0
59	1	-1	1	1	1	-1	1	-1	1	-1	-1	1	-1	-1	1	1	1	-1	1	1	1	1	-1	-1	1	1	1	1	1	-1

Properties

The following facts, even the reciprocity laws, are straightforward deductions from the definition of the Jacobi symbol and the corresponding properties of the Legendre symbol.

The Jacobi symbol is defined only when the upper argument ("numerator") is an integer and the lower argument ("denominator") is a positive odd integer.

1. If n is (an odd) prime, then the Jacobi symbol $\left(\dfrac{a}{n}\right)$ is equal to (and written the same as) the corresponding Legendre symbol.

2. If $a \equiv b \pmod{n}$, then $\left(\dfrac{a}{n}\right) = \left(\dfrac{b}{n}\right)$.

3. $\left(\dfrac{a}{n}\right) = \begin{cases} 0 & \text{if } \gcd(a,n) \neq 1, \\ \pm 1 & \text{if } \gcd(a,n) = 1. \end{cases}$

If either the top or bottom argument is fixed, the Jacobi symbol is a completely multiplicative function in the remaining argument:

4. $\left(\dfrac{ab}{n}\right) = \left(\dfrac{a}{n}\right)\left(\dfrac{b}{n}\right)$, so $\left(\dfrac{a^2}{n}\right) = 1 \text{ or } 0.$

5. $\left(\dfrac{a}{mn}\right) = \left(\dfrac{a}{m}\right)\left(\dfrac{a}{n}\right)$, so $\left(\dfrac{a}{n^2}\right) = 1 \text{ or } 0.$

The law of quadratic reciprocity: if m and n are odd positive coprime integers, then

6. $\left(\dfrac{m}{n}\right)\left(\dfrac{n}{m}\right) = (-1)^{\frac{m-1}{2} \cdot \frac{n-1}{2}} = \begin{cases} 1 & \text{if } n \equiv 1 \pmod 4 \text{ or } m \equiv 1 \pmod 4, \\ -1 & \text{if } n \equiv m \equiv 3 \pmod 4 \end{cases}$

and its supplements

7. $\left(\dfrac{-1}{n}\right) = (-1)^{\frac{n-1}{2}} = \begin{cases} 1 & \text{if } n \equiv 1 \pmod 4, \\ -1 & \text{if } n \equiv 3 \pmod 4, \end{cases}$

8. $\left(\dfrac{2}{n}\right) = (-1)^{\frac{n^2-1}{8}} = \begin{cases} 1 & \text{if } n \equiv 1,7 \pmod 8, \\ -1 & \text{if } n \equiv 3,5 \pmod 8. \end{cases}$

Like the Legendre symbol:

- If $\left(\dfrac{a}{n}\right) = -1$ then a is a quadratic nonresidue modulo n'.
- If a is a quadratic residue modulo n and $\gcd(a,n) = 1$, then $\left(\dfrac{a}{n}\right) = 1$.

But, unlike the Legendre symbol:

If $\left(\dfrac{a}{n}\right) = 1$ then a may or may not be a quadratic residue modulo n.

This is because for a to be a quadratic residue modulo n, it has to be a quadratic residue modulo *every* prime factor of n. However, the Jacobi symbol equals one if, for example, a is a non-residue modulo exactly two of the prime factors of n.

Although the Jacobi symbol cannot be uniformly interpreted in terms of squares and non-squares, it can be uniformly interpreted as the sign of a permutation by Zolotarev's lemma.

The Jacobi symbol $\left(\dfrac{a}{n}\right)$ is a Dirichlet character to the modulus n.

Calculating the Jacobi Symbol

The above formulas lead to an efficient $O(\log a \log b)$ algorithm for calculating the Jacobi symbol, analogous to the Euclidean algorithm for finding the gcd of two numbers. (This should not be surprising in light of rule 2).

1. Reduce the "numerator" modulo the "denominator" using rule 2.

2. Extract any factors of 2 from the "numerator" using rule 4 and evaluate them using rule 8.

3. If the "numerator" is 1, rules 3 and 4 give a result of 1. If the "numerator" and "denominator" are not coprime, rule 3 gives a result of 0.

4. Otherwise, the "numerator" and "denominator" are now odd positive coprime integers, so we can flip the symbol using rule 6, then return to step 1.

Example of Calculations

The Legendre symbol $\left(\dfrac{a}{p}\right)$ is only defined for odd primes p. It obeys the same rules as the Jacobi symbol (i.e., reciprocity and the supplementary formulas for $\left(\dfrac{-1}{p}\right)$ and $\left(\dfrac{2}{p}\right)$ and multiplicativity of the

"numerator".)

Problem: Given that 9907 is prime, calculate $\left(\dfrac{1001}{9907}\right)$.

Using the Legendre Symbol

$$\left(\frac{1001}{9907}\right)=\left(\frac{7}{9907}\right)\left(\frac{11}{9907}\right)\left(\frac{13}{9907}\right).$$

$$\left(\frac{7}{9907}\right)=-\left(\frac{9907}{7}\right)=-\left(\frac{2}{7}\right)=-1.$$

$$\left(\frac{11}{9907}\right)=-\left(\frac{9907}{11}\right)=-\left(\frac{7}{11}\right)=\left(\frac{11}{7}\right)=\left(\frac{4}{7}\right)=1.$$

$$\left(\frac{13}{9907}\right)=\left(\frac{9907}{13}\right)=\left(\frac{1}{13}\right)=1.$$

$$\left(\frac{1001}{9907}\right)=-1.$$

Using the Jacobi Symbol

$$\left(\frac{1001}{9907}\right)=\left(\frac{9907}{1001}\right)=\left(\frac{898}{1001}\right)=\left(\frac{2}{1001}\right)\left(\frac{449}{1001}\right)$$

$$=\left(\frac{449}{1001}\right)=\left(\frac{1001}{449}\right)=\left(\frac{103}{449}\right)=\left(\frac{449}{103}\right)=\left(\frac{37}{103}\right)=\left(\frac{103}{37}\right)$$

$$=\left(\frac{29}{37}\right)=\left(\frac{37}{29}\right)=\left(\frac{8}{29}\right)=\left(\frac{2}{29}\right)^{3}=-1.$$

The difference between the two calculations is that when the Legendre symbol is used the "numerator" has to be factored into prime powers before the symbol is flipped. This makes the calculation using the Legendre symbol significantly slower than the one using the Jacobi symbol, as there is no known polynomial-time algorithm for factoring integers. In fact, this is why Jacobi introduced the symbol.

Primality Testing

There is another way the Jacobi and Legendre symbols differ. If the Euler criterion formula is used modulo a composite number, the result may or may not be the value of the Jacobi symbol, and in fact may not even be −1 or 1. For example,

$$\left(\frac{19}{45}\right)=1 \qquad \text{and} \qquad 19^{\frac{45-1}{2}}\equiv1 \;\;(\mathrm{mod}\,45).$$

$$\left(\frac{8}{21}\right)=-1 \qquad \text{but} \qquad 8^{\frac{21-1}{2}}\equiv1 \;\;(\mathrm{mod}\,21).$$

$$\left(\frac{5}{21}\right)=1 \qquad \text{but} \qquad 5^{\frac{21-1}{2}}\equiv16 \;\;(\mathrm{mod}\,21).$$

So if it is unknown whether a number n is prime or composite, we can pick a random number a, calculate the Jacobi symbol $\left(\frac{a}{n}\right)$ and compare it with Euler's formula; if they differ modulo n, then n is composite; if they have the same residue modulo n for many different values of a, then n is "probably prime".

This is the basis for the probabilistic Solovay–Strassen primality test and refinements such as the Baillie-PSW primality test and the Miller–Rabin primality test.

Suppose we want to determine whether or not $x^2\equiv a$ (mod p) has a solution, where p is prime, If p is small, we could square all of the numbers mod p and see if a is on the list. When p is large, this is impractical. If $p\equiv3$ mod 4 we can find out the by using a technique in which we compute $s\equiv a^{(p+1)/4}$ (mod p). If a has a square root, then s is one of them, so we simply have to square s and see if we get a. If not, then a has no square root mod p. The following proposition gives a method for deciding whether a is a square mod p that works for arbitrary odd p.

Proposition: let p be a odd prime and let a be an integer with a $\not\equiv$ 0 (mod p). Then a$^{(p-1)/2}\equiv \pm 1$ (mod p). The congruence x$^2\equiv$ a (mod p) has a solution if and only if a$^{(p-1)/2}\equiv 1$ (mod p).

Proof: Let y $\equiv$ a$^{(p-1)/2}$ (mod p). Then y$^2\equiv$ a$^{p-1} \equiv$ 1 (mod p), by Fermat's theorem. Therefore, y $\equiv\pm 1$ (mod p).

If a$\equiv$x^2, then a$^{(p-1)/2} \equiv$ x$^{p-1} \equiv$ 1 (mod p). The hard part is showing the converse. Let g be a primitive root mod p. Then a $\equiv$ g^j for some j. If a$^{(p-1)/2} \equiv$1 (mod p), then

$$g^{\,j(p-1)/2} \equiv a^{(p-1)/2} \equiv 1 \text{ (mod p)}.$$

Which implies j.(p-1)/2 $\equiv$0 (mod p-1). This implies that j must be even: j=2k. Therefore, a $\equiv$ g$^j \equiv$ g$^{(k)2}$ (mod p), so a is a square mod p.

Although the above proposition is easy to implement by a computer , it is rather difficult to use by hand. In the following we introduce the Legendre and Jacobi symbols, which gave us an easy way to determine whether or not a number is a square mod p. they are also very useful in Primality testing.

Let p be an odd prime and let a (not) $\equiv$0 (mod p). Define the Legendre symbol

$$\left(\frac{a}{p}\right) = \begin{cases} 1 \text{ if } x^2 \equiv a \ (mod \ p) \text{ has a solution.} \\ -1 \text{ if } x^2 \equiv a \ (mod \ p) \text{ has a solution.} \end{cases}$$

Some important properties of the Legendre symbol are given in the following.

Properties: Let p be an odd prime.

1. If $a \equiv b \not\equiv 0 \,(\text{mod } p), then$

$$\left(\frac{a}{p}\right) = \left(\frac{b}{p}\right)$$

2. If $a \not\equiv 0 \,(\text{mod } p), then$

$$\left(\frac{a}{p}\right) = a^{(p-1)/2} \,(\text{mod } p)$$

3. If $ab \not\equiv 0 \,(\text{mod } p), then$

$$\left(\frac{ab}{p}\right) = \left(\frac{a}{p}\right)\left(\frac{b}{p}\right), \left(\frac{a}{pq}\right) = \left(\frac{a}{p}\right)\left(\frac{a}{q}\right)$$

4. $\left(\dfrac{-1}{p}\right) = (-1)^{(p-1)/2}$

5. $\left(\dfrac{a}{p}\right) = \left(\dfrac{a \bmod p}{p}\right)$

6. if m, n are both odd positive numbers then

$$\left(\frac{m}{n}\right) = (-1)^{(m-1)(n-1)/4}\left(\frac{n}{m}\right)$$

7. $\left(\dfrac{2}{n}\right) = (-1)^{(n^2-1)/8}, \left(\dfrac{1}{n}\right) = 1, \left(\dfrac{0}{n}\right) = 0$

The properties above can be used to build a recursive algorithm to compute the Jacobi symbol efficiently. In fact, the algorithm is strongly reminiscent of Euclid's algorithm for the gcd. Here is how the algorithm applies to compute $\left(\dfrac{m}{n}\right)$:

If m > n then use the invariance property: return $\left(\dfrac{m \bmod n}{n}\right)$. If m=0 or m=1, then use(7) : return 0 or 1 Factor m as $2^k l$, where l is odd. If k >0 use formulas (7) and (3) : return $.\left(\dfrac{2}{n}\right)^{k \bmod 2}\left(\dfrac{1}{n}\right)$ Use reciprocity : if m=n=3 mod 4 then return $-\left(\dfrac{n}{m}\right)$; otherwise return $\left(\dfrac{n}{m}\right)$.

As this method is similar to Euclidean GCD algorithm, its complexity too is $O\left(\log^2(n)\right)$.

The Jacobi symbol extends the Legendre symbol from primes p to composite odd integers n. One might define the symbol to be +1 if a is a square mod n and -1 if not. However, this would cause the property (3) to fail.

In order to preserve property (3), we define the Jacobi symbol as follows. Let n be an odd positive integer and let a be a nonzero integer with gcd (a, n) =1. Let

$$n = p_1^a p_2^b p_3^c \ldots\ldots p_r^q$$

be prime factorization of n. Then

$$\left(\frac{a}{n}\right)=\left(\frac{a}{p1}\right)^a\left(\frac{a}{p2}\right)^b\left(\frac{a}{p3}\right)^c \ldots\ldots\left(\frac{a}{pr}\right)^q$$

The symbols on the right side are Legendre symbols introduced earlier. Note that if n=p, the right side is simply one Legendre symbol, so the Jacobi symbol reduces to the Legendre symbol.

Properties:

1. *If $a \equiv b \pmod n$ and $\gcd(a,n)=1, then$*

$$\left(\frac{a}{n}\right)=\left(\frac{b}{n}\right)$$

2. *if $\gcd(ab,n)=1 then$*

$$\left(\frac{ab}{n}\right)=\left(\frac{a}{n}\right)\left(\frac{b}{n}\right).$$

3. $\left(\dfrac{-1}{n}\right)=(-1)^{(n-1)/2}$.

4. $\left(\dfrac{2}{n}\right)=\begin{cases} +1 if\ n \equiv 1\, or\, 7\, (\bmod 8). \\ -1 if\ n \equiv 3\, or\, 5\, (\bmod 8). \end{cases}$

8. *Let m be odd* $\gcd(m,n)=1. Then$

$$\left(\frac{m}{n}\right)=\begin{cases} -\left(\dfrac{n}{m}\right) if\ m = n\,(\bmod 4). \\ \\ +\left(\dfrac{n}{m}\right) otherwise. \end{cases}$$

Before going into any of the primality tests we give a basic principle on which the tests depend upon.

Basic principle: let n be an integer and suppose there exist integers x and y with $x^2 \equiv y^2$ (mod n), but $x \not\equiv \pm y$ (mod n). Then n is composite. Morover, gcd(x-y,n) gives a nontrivial factor of n.

Proof: Let d = gcd(x-y, n). if d= n then $x \equiv y$ (mod n), which is assumed not to happen. Suppose d=1. A basic result on divisibility is that if a| bc and gcd(a,b) =1, then a |c.In our case, since n divides $x^2 - y^2 = (x-y)(x+y)$ and d=1, we must have that n divides x+y, which contradicts the assumption that $x \not\equiv -y$ (mod n). Therefore d ≠ 1, n so d is nontrivial factor of n.

Fermat Primality Test

The Fermat primality test is a probabilistic test to determine whether a number is a probable prime.

Concept

Fermat's little theorem states that if p is prime and a is not divisible by p, then

$$a^{p-1} \equiv 1 \pmod{p}.$$

If we want to test whether p is prime, then we can pick random a's not divisible by p and see whether the equality holds. If the equality does not hold for a value of a, then p is composite. This congruence is unlikely to hold for a random a if p is composite. Therefore, if the equality does hold for one or more values of a, then we say that p is probably prime.

However, note that for $a \equiv 1 \pmod{p}$, the above congruence holds trivially. It also holds trivially if p is odd and $a \equiv -1 \pmod{p}$. For this reason, one usually chooses a number a in the interval $1 < a < p-1$.

Any a such that

$$a^{n-1} \equiv 1 \pmod{n}$$

when n is composite is known as a *Fermat liar*. In this case n is called Fermat pseudoprime to base a.

If we do pick an a such that

$$a^{n-1} \not\equiv 1 \pmod{n}$$

then a is known as a *Fermat witness* for the compositeness of n.

Example

Suppose we wish to determine whether $n = 221$ is prime. Randomly pick $1 < a < 221$, say $a = 38$. We check the above equality and find that it holds:

$$a^{n-1} = 38^{220} \equiv 1 \pmod{221}.$$

Either 221 is prime, or 38 is a Fermat liar, so we take another a, say 24:

$$a^{n-1} = 24^{220} \equiv 81 \neq 1 \quad (\bmod\, 221).$$

So 221 is composite and 38 was indeed a Fermat liar. Furthermore, 24 is a Fermat witness for the compositeness of 221.

Algorithm and Running Time

The algorithm can be written as follows:

> Inputs: n: a value to test for primality, $n>3$; k: a parameter that determines the number of times to test for primality
>
> Output: *composite* if n is composite, otherwise *probably prime*
>
> Repeat k times:
>
> Pick a randomly in the range $[2, n-2]$
>
> If $a^{n-1} \neq 1 \quad (\bmod\, n)$, then return *composite*
>
> If composite is never returned: return *probably prime*

The a values 1 and n-1 are not used as the equality holds for all n and all odd n respectively, hence testing them adds no value.

Using fast algorithms for modular exponentiation and multiprecision multiplication, the running time of this algorithm is $O(k \times \log^2 n \times \log \log n \times \log \log \log n)$, where k is the number of times we test a random a, and n is the value we want to test for primality.

Flaw

First, there are infinitely many Fermat pseudoprimes.

A more serious flaw is that there are infinitely many Carmichael numbers. These are numbers n for which all values of a with $gcd(a,n) = 1$ are Fermat liars. For these numbers, repeated application of the Fermat primality test performs the same as a simple random search for factors. While Carmichael numbers are substantially rarer than prime numbers (Erdös' upper bound for the number of Carmichael numbers is lower than the prime number function n/log(n)) there are enough of them that Fermat's primality test is not often used in the above form. Instead, other more powerful extensions of the Fermat test, such as Baillie-PSW, Miller-Rabin, and Solovay-Strassen are more commonly used.

In general, if n is a composite number that is not a Carmichael number, then at least half of all

$$a \in (\mathbb{Z}\,/\,n\mathbb{Z})^*$$

are Fermat witnesses. For proof of this, let a be a Fermat witness and $a_1, a_2, ..., a_s$ be Fermat liars.

Then

$$(a \cdot a_i)^{n-1} \equiv a^{n-1} \cdot a_i^{n-1} \equiv a^{n-1} \not\equiv 1 \pmod{n}$$

and so all $a \times a_i$ for $i = 1, 2, \ldots, s$ are Fermat witnesses.

Applications

As mentioned above, most applications use a Miller-Rabin or Baillie-PSW test for primality. Sometimes a Fermat test (along with some trial division by small primes) is performed first to improve performance. GMP since version 3.0 uses a base-210 Fermat test after trial division and before running Miller-Rabin tests. Libgcrypt uses a similar process with base 2 for the Fermat test, but OpenSSL does not.

In practice with most big number libraries such as GMP, the Fermat test is not noticeably faster than a Miller-Rabin test, and can be slower for many inputs.

As an exception, OpenPFGW uses only the Fermat test for probable prime testing. The program is typically used with multi-thousand digit inputs with a goal of maximum speed with very large inputs. Another well known program that relies only on the Fermat test is PGP where it is only used for testing of self-generated large random values (an open source counterpart, GNU Privacy Guard, uses a Fermat pretest followed by Miller-Rabin tests).

Fermat Primality Test:

Let n >1 be an integer. Choose a random integer a with 1 < a < n-1.

If $a^{n-1} \not\equiv 1 \pmod{n}$ then n is composite. If $a^{n-1} \equiv 1 \pmod{n}$, then n is probably prime.

If we are careful about how we do this successive squaring, the Fermat test can be combined with the basic principle to yield the following stronger result.

Miller- Rabin Primality test:

Let n >1 be an odd integer. Write a-1 $= 2^k m$ with m odd. Choose a random integer a with 1< a< n-1. Compute $b_0 \equiv a^m \pmod{n}$. If $b_0 \equiv \pm 1 \pmod{n}$, then stop and declare that n is probably prime. Otherwise, let $b_1 \equiv b_0^2 \pmod{n}$. If $b_1 \equiv 1 \pmod{n}$, then n is composite (and gcd (b_0 -1, n) gives a nontrivial factor of n). If $b_1 \equiv -1 \pmod{n}$, then stop and declare that n is probably prime. Otherwise, let $b_2 \equiv b_1^2 \pmod{n}$. If $b_2 \equiv 1 \pmod{n}$, then n is composite. If $b_2 \equiv -1 \pmod{n}$, then stop and declare that n is probably prime. Continue in this way until stopping and reaching b_{k-1}. If $b_{k-1} \not\equiv -1 \pmod{n}$, then n is composite.

The reason why the test works is- suppose, for example that $b_3 \equiv 1 \pmod{n}$. This means that $b_2^2 \equiv 1 \pmod{n}$. This means that $b_2^2 \equiv 12 \pmod{n}$. Apply the basic principle from before. Either $b_2 \equiv \pm 1 \pmod{n}$, or $b_2 \not\equiv \pm 1 \pmod{n}$ and n is composite. In the latter case, gcd (b_2-1, n) give a nontrivial factor of n. In the former case, the algorithm would have stopped by the previous step.

MILLER-RABIN (n, s)

For j← 1 to s

    do a ← RANDOM(1,n-1)

If WITNESS (a,n)

   then return COMPOSITE

return PRIME

WITNESS (a, n)

Let $<b_k, b_{k-1}...b_0>$ be the binary representation of n-1.

d←1

   for I ← k down to 0

      do x ← d

         d←(d. d) mod n

         if d=1 and x≠1 and x≠n-1

            then return TRUE

         if(b_i=1) then

            d← (d. a) mod n

      end for

      if d≠1

         then return TRUE

      return FALSE

If we reach b_{k-1}, we computed $b_{k-1} \equiv a^{(n-1)/2}$ (mod n). The square of this is a^{n-1}, which must be 1 (mod n) if n is prime, by Fermat's Theorem. Therefore, if n is prime, $b_{k-1} \equiv \pm 1$ (mod n). All other choices mean that n is composite. Moreover, if $b_{k-1} \equiv 1$ then, if we didn't stop at an earlier step, $b_{k-2}^2 \equiv 1^2$ (mod n) with $b_{k-2} \not\equiv \pm 1$ (mod n). This means that n is composite (and we can factor n).

Although all prime numbers will be detected through this test, however the converse is not true. There are numbers which pass this test but are composite, i.e n is composite and $a^{n-1} \equiv 1$ (mod n) for all possible bases a. Such numbers are called Carmichael numbers. For example 561 is a Carmichael number. Carmichael numbers are usually of the form $(p_1.p_2.p_3)$ where the number is product of primes.

An alternative and equivalent definition of Carmichael numbers is given by Korselt's criterion.

Theorem : A positive composite integer n is a Carmichael number if and only if n is square-free, and for all prime divisors p of n, it is true that $p - 1 \mid n - 1$.

For example:

561= 3.11.17 is square-free and 2 |560, 10|560, 16 |560.

1105= 5.13.17 is square-free and 4 |1104, 12|1104, 16 |1104.

Solovay-Strassen Primality test: let n be an odd integer. Choose several random integers a with 1<a<n-1. if

$$\left(\frac{a}{n}\right) \not\equiv a^{(n-1)/2}(\bmod\, n)$$

For some a, then n is composite. If

$$\left(\frac{a}{n}\right) \equiv a^{(n-1)/2}(\bmod\, n)$$

For all a, then n is probably prime.

Running time: $O((\log n)^3)$. This follows from running times of separate parts of the algorithm: finding gcd, computing of Jacobi symbol, and finally computing powers of a.

Respectively, $O((\log n)^2) + O((\log n)^2) + O((\log n)^3)$.

Definition 1. For odd n > 3, we define $E(n) = \left\{a \in Z_n^* \mid \left(\dfrac{a}{n}\right) = a^{\frac{(n-1)}{2}} \bmod n\right\}$

We will use the following lemma.

Lemma 2.1. For odd n > 3, n is prime if and only if $E(n) = Z_n^*$

Theorem 2.2. If n is an odd prime, and a $\in$ {1, . . . , n – 1}, the probability that the algorithm returns "prime" is $Pr_{a\in\{1,2,...n-1\}}$ [Solovay – Strassen(n) = "prime"] = 1.

If n is an odd composite, the probability that algorithm returns "composite" is $Pr_{a\in\{1,2,...n-1\}}$ [Solovay – Strassen(n) = "composite"] $\geq 1/2$

Proof: If n is an odd prime, then the algorithm will obviously always output "prime". Let us now prove the second part of the theorem. Assume that n is an odd composite. We will show that the probability of the algorithm returning "prime" is $\leq 1/2$

$Pr_{a\in\{1,2,...n-1\}}$ [Solovay – Strassen(n) = "prime"] =

$Pr_{a\in\{1,2,...n-1\}}$ $[\{gcd\left(a,\, n\right)\, =\, 1\} \in \{=a^{(n-1)/2}\, mod\, n\}] = \dfrac{E(n)}{n-1}$

From Lemma 2.1 it follows that $E(n) \neq Z_n^*$

Now it is easy to show that E(n) is a subgroup of the multiplicative group Z_n^*

a, b $\in$ E(n) $\in$ (ab mod n) $\in$ E(n)

a $\in$ E(n) $\Rightarrow$ a^{-1} $\in$ E(n).

E(n) is thus a proper subgroup of Z_n^*

and, from elementary group theory, we conclude that

$$| E(n) | \leq \frac{|Z_n^*|}{2} \leq \frac{(n-1)}{2.}$$

Thus $Pr_{a \in \{1,2,\ldots n-1\}}$ [Solovay – Strassen(n) = "prime"] $\leq \frac{1}{2}$

Miller–Rabin Primality Test

The Miller–Rabin primality test or Rabin–Miller primality test is a primality test: an algorithm which determines whether a given number is prime, similar to the Fermat primality test and the Solovay–Strassen primality test. Its original version, due to Gary L. Miller, is deterministic, but the determinism relies on the unproven Extended Riemann hypothesis; Michael O. Rabin modified it to obtain an unconditional probabilistic algorithm.

Concepts

Just like the Fermat and Solovay–Strassen tests, the Miller–Rabin test relies on an equality or set of equalities that hold true for prime values, then checks whether or not they hold for a number that we want to test for primality.

First, a lemma about square roots of unity in the finite field Z/pZ, where p is prime and $p > 2$. Certainly 1 and −1 always yield 1 when squared modulo p; call these trivial square roots of 1. There are no *nontrivial* square roots of 1 modulo p (a special case of the result that, in a field, a polynomial has no more zeroes than its degree). To show this, suppose that x is a square root of 1 modulo p. Then:

$$x^2 \equiv 1 \pmod{p}$$

$$(x-1)(x+1) \equiv 0 \pmod{p}.$$

In other words, prime p divides the product $(x - 1)(x + 1)$. By Euclid's lemma it divides one of the factors $x - 1$ or $x + 1$, implying that x is congruent to either 1 or −1 modulo p.

Now, let n be prime, and odd, with $n > 2$. It follows that $n - 1$ is even and we can write it as $2^s \cdot d$, where s and d are positive integers and d is odd. For each a in $(Z/nZ)^*$, either

$$a^d \equiv 1 \pmod{n}$$

or

$$a^{2^r \cdot d} \equiv -1 \pmod{n}$$

for some $0 \leq r \leq s - 1$.

To show that one of these must be true, recall Fermat's little theorem, that for a prime number n:

$$a^{n-1} \equiv 1 \pmod{n}.$$

By the lemma above, if we keep taking square roots of a^{n-1}, we will get either 1 or −1. If we get −1 then the second equality holds and it is done. If we never get −1, then when we have taken out every power of 2, we are left with the first equality.

The Miller–Rabin primality test is based on the contrapositive of the above claim. That is, if we can find an a such that

$$a^d \not\equiv 1 \pmod{n}$$

and

$$a^{2^r d} \not\equiv -1 \pmod{n}$$

for all $0 \le r \le s - 1$, then n is not prime. We call a a witness for the compositeness of n (sometimes misleadingly called a *strong witness*, although it is a certain proof of this fact). Otherwise a is called a *strong liar*, and n is a strong probable prime to base a. The term "strong liar" refers to the case where n is composite but nevertheless the equations hold as they would for a prime.

Every odd composite n has many witnesses a, however, no simple way of generating such an a is known. The solution is to make the test probabilistic: we choose a non-zero a in $\mathbb{Z}/n\mathbb{Z}$ randomly, and check whether or not it is a witness for the compositeness of n. If n is composite, most of the choices for a will be witnesses, and the test will detect n as composite with high probability. There is, nevertheless, a small chance that we are unlucky and hit an a which is a strong liar for n. We may reduce the probability of such error by repeating the test for several independently chosen a.

For testing large numbers, it is common to choose random bases a, as, a priori, we don't know the distribution of witnesses and liars among the numbers 1, 2, ..., $n − 1$. In particular, Arnault gave a 397-digit composite number for which all bases a less than 307 are strong liars. As expected this number was reported to be prime by the Maple isprime() function, which implemented the Miller–Rabin test by checking the specific bases 2,3,5,7, and 11. However, selection of a few specific small bases can guarantee identification of composites for n less than some maximum determined by said bases. This maximum is generally quite large compared to the bases. As random bases lack such determinism for small n, specific bases are better in some circumstances.

Example

Suppose we wish to determine if $n = 221$ is prime. We write $n − 1 = 220$ as $2^2 \cdot 55$, so that we have $s = 2$ and $d = 55$. We randomly select a number a such that $1 < a < n - 1$, say $a = 174$. We proceed to compute:

- $a^{2^0 \cdot d} \bmod n = 174^{55} \bmod 221 = 47 \neq 1, n − 1$

- $a^{2^1 \cdot d} \bmod n = 174^{110} \bmod 221 = 220 = n − 1.$

Since $220 \equiv −1 \bmod n$, either 221 is prime, or 174 is a strong liar for 221. We try another random a, this time choosing $a = 137$:

- $a^{2^0 \cdot d} \bmod n = 137^{55} \bmod 221 = 188 \neq 1, n − 1$

- $a^{2^1 \cdot d} \bmod n = 137^{110} \bmod 221 = 205 \neq n − 1.$

Hence 137 is a witness for the compositeness of 221, and 174 was in fact a strong liar. Note that this tells us nothing about the factors of 221 (which are 13 and 17).

Computational Complexity

The algorithm can be written in pseudocode as follows:

```
Input #1: n > 3, an odd integer to be tested for primality;

Input #2: k, a parameter that determines the accuracy of the test

Output: composite if n is composite, otherwise probably prime

write n - 1 as 2ʳ·d with d odd by factoring powers of 2 from n - 1

WitnessLoop: repeat k times:

    pick a random integer a in the range [2, n - 2]

    x ← aᵈ mod n

    if x = 1 or x = n - 1 then

        continue WitnessLoop

    repeat r - 1 times:

        x ← x² mod n

        if x = 1 then

            return composite

        if x = n - 1 then

            continue WitnessLoop

    return composite

return probably prime
```

Using modular exponentiation by repeated squaring, the running time of this algorithm is $O(k \log^3 n)$, where k is the number of different values of a that we test; thus this is an efficient, polynomial-time algorithm. FFT-based multiplication can push the running time down to $O(k \log^2 n \log \log n \log \log \log n) = \tilde{O}(k \log^2 n)$.

If we insert Greatest common divisor calculations into the above algorithm, we can sometimes obtain a factor of n instead of merely determining that n is composite. In particular, if n is a probable prime base a but not a strong probable prime base a, then either $GCD((a^d \bmod n) - 1, n)$ or (for some r in the above range) $GCD((a^{2^r \cdot d} \bmod n) - 1, n)$ will produce a (not necessarily prime) factor of n. If factoring is a goal, these GCDs can be inserted into the above algorithm at little additional computational cost.

For example, consider $n = 341$. We have $n - 1 = 85 \cdot 4$. Then $2^{85} \bmod 341 = 32$. This tells us that n is not a strong probable prime base 2, so we know n is composite. If we take a GCD at this stage, we can get a factor of 341: $GCD((2^{85} \bmod 341) - 1, 341) = 31$. This works because 341 is a pseudoprime base 2, but is not a strong pseudoprime base 2.

In the case that the algorithm returns "composite" because $x = 1$, it has also discovered that $d2^r$ is (an odd multiple of) the order of a—a fact which can (as in Shor's algorithm) be used to factorize n, since n then divides

$$a^{d2^r} - 1 = (a^{d2^{r-1}} - 1)(a^{d2^{r-1}} + 1)$$

but not either factor by itself. The reason Miller–Rabin does *not* yield a probabilistic factorization algorithm is that if

$$a^{n-1} \not\equiv 1 \pmod{n}$$

(i.e., n is not a pseudoprime to base a) then no such information is obtained about the period of a, and the second "return composite" is taken.

Accuracy

The more bases a we test, the better the accuracy of the test. It can be shown that for any odd composite n, at least $3/4$ of the bases a are witnesses for the compositeness of n. The Miller–Rabin test is strictly stronger than the Solovay–Strassen primality test in the sense that for every composite n, the set of strong liars for n is a subset of the set of Euler liars for n, and for many n, the subset is proper. If n is composite then the Miller–Rabin primality test declares n probably prime with a probability at most 4^{-k}. On the other hand, the Solovay–Strassen primality test declares n probably prime with a probability at most 2^{-k}.

It is important to note that in many common applications of this algorithm, we are not interested in the error bound described above. The above error bound is the probability of a composite number being declared as a probable prime after k rounds of testing. We are often instead interested in the probability that, after passing k rounds of testing, the number being tested is actually a composite number. Formally, if we call the event of declaring n a probable prime after k rounds of Miller–Rabin Y_k, and we call the event that n is composite X (and denote the event that n is prime $\bar{X}$), then the above bound gives us $P(Y_k \mid X)$, whereas we are interested in $P(X \mid Y_k)$. Bayes' theorem gives us a way to relate these two conditional probabilities, namely

$$P(X \mid Y_k) = \frac{P(Y_k \mid X)P(X)}{P(Y_k \mid X)P(X) + P(Y_k \mid \bar{X})P(\bar{X})}$$

This tells us that the probability that we are often interested in is related not just to the 4^{-k} bound above, but also probabilities related to the density of prime numbers in the region near n.

In addition, for large values of n, on average the probability that a composite number is declared *probably prime* is significantly smaller than 4^{-k}. Damgård, Landrock and Pomerance compute some explicit bounds and provide a method to make a reasonable selection for k for a desired error bound. Such bounds can, for example, be used to *generate* probable primes; however, they should not be used to *verify* primes with unknown origin, since in cryptographic applications an adversary might try to send you a pseudoprime in a place where a prime number is required. In such cases, only the error bound of 4^{-k} can be relied upon.

Deterministic Variants

The Miller–Rabin algorithm can be made deterministic by trying all possible a below a certain limit. The problem in general is to set the limit so that the test is still reliable.

If the tested number n is composite, the strong liars a coprime to n are contained in a proper subgroup of the group $(Z/nZ)^*$, which means that if we test all a from a set which generates $(Z/nZ)^*$, one of them must be a witness for the compositeness of n. Assuming the truth of the generalized Riemann hypothesis (GRH), it is known that the group is generated by its elements smaller than $O((\log n)^2)$, which was already noted by Miller. The constant involved in the Big O notation was reduced to 2 by Eric Bach. This leads to the following conditional primality testing algorithm:

```
Input: n > 1, an odd integer to test for primality.

Output: composite if n is composite, otherwise prime

write n-1 as 2ˢ·d by factoring powers of 2 from n-1
```

repeat for all $a \in [2, \min(n-1, \lfloor 2(\ln n)^2 \rfloor)]$:

    if $a^d \neq 1 \pmod{n}$ and $a^{2^r \cdot d} \neq -1 \pmod{n}$ for all $r \in [0, s-1]$ then

```
        return composite

return prime
```

The running time of the algorithm is, in the soft-O notation, $\tilde{O}((\log n)^4)$ (with FFT-based multiplication). The full power of the generalized Riemann hypothesis is not needed to ensure the correctness of the test: as we deal with subgroups of even index, it suffices to assume the validity of GRH for quadratic Dirichlet characters.

The Miller test (the algorithm above) is not used in practice. For most purposes, proper use of the probabilistic Miller-Rabin test or the Baillie-PSW primality test gives sufficient confidence while running much faster. It is also slower in practice than commonly used proof methods such as APR-CL and ECPP which give results that do not rely on unproven assumptions. For theoretical purposes requiring a deterministic polynomial time algorithm, it was superseded by the AKS primality test, which also does not rely on unproven assumptions.

Note that Miller-Rabin pseudoprimes are called strong pseudoprimes.

When the number n to be tested is small, trying all $a < 2(\ln n)^2$ is not necessary, as much smaller sets of potential witnesses are known to suffice. For example, Pomerance, Selfridge and Wagstaff and Jaeschke have verified that

- if $n < 2{,}047$, it is enough to test $a = 2$;
- if $n < 1{,}373{,}653$, it is enough to test $a = 2$ and 3;
- if $n < 9{,}080{,}191$, it is enough to test $a = 31$ and 73;
- if $n < 25{,}326{,}001$, it is enough to test $a = 2$, 3, and 5;
- if $n < 3{,}215{,}031{,}751$, it is enough to test $a = 2$, 3, 5, and 7;

- if $n < 4{,}759{,}123{,}141$, it is enough to test $a = 2, 7,$ and 61;

- if $n < 1{,}122{,}004{,}669{,}633$, it is enough to test $a = 2, 13, 23,$ and 1662803;

- if $n < 2{,}152{,}302{,}898{,}747$, it is enough to test $a = 2, 3, 5, 7,$ and 11;

- if $n < 3{,}474{,}749{,}660{,}383$, it is enough to test $a = 2, 3, 5, 7, 11,$ and 13;

- if $n < 341{,}550{,}071{,}728{,}321$, it is enough to test $a = 2, 3, 5, 7, 11, 13,$ and 17.

Using the work of Feitsma and Galway enumerating all base 2 pseudoprimes in 2010, this was extended, with the first result later shown using different methods in Jiang and Deng:

- if $n < 3{,}825{,}123{,}056{,}546{,}413{,}051$, it is enough to test $a = 2, 3, 5, 7, 11, 13, 17, 19,$ and 23.

- if $n < 18{,}446{,}744{,}073{,}709{,}551{,}616 = 2^{64}$, it is enough to test $a = 2, 3, 5, 7, 11, 13, 17, 19, 23, 29, 31,$ and 37.

Sorenson and Webster verify the above and calculate precise results for these larger than 64-bit results:

- if $n < 318{,}665{,}857{,}834{,}031{,}151{,}167{,}461$, it is enough to test $a = 2, 3, 5, 7, 11, 13, 17, 19, 23, 29, 31,$ and 37.

- if $n < 3{,}317{,}044{,}064{,}679{,}887{,}385{,}961{,}981$, it is enough to test $a = 2, 3, 5, 7, 11, 13, 17, 19, 23, 29, 31, 37,$ and 41.

Other criteria of this sort, often more efficient (fewer bases required) than those shown above, exist and these results give very fast deterministic primality tests for numbers in the appropriate range without any assumptions.

There is a small list of potential witnesses for every possible input size (at most n values for n-bit numbers). However, no finite set of bases is sufficient for all composite numbers. Alford, Granville, and Pomerance have shown that there exist infinitely many composite numbers n whose smallest compositeness witness is at least $(\ln n)^{1/(3 \ln \ln \ln n)}$. They also argue heuristically that the smallest number w such that every composite number below n has a compositeness witness less than w should be of order $\Theta(\log n \log \log n)$.

Solovay–Strassen Primality Test

The Solovay–Strassen primality test, developed by Robert M. Solovay and Volker Strassen, is a probabilistic test to determine if a number is composite or probably prime. It has been largely superseded by the Baillie-PSW primality test and the Miller–Rabin primality test, but has great historical importance in showing the practical feasibility of the RSA cryptosystem. The Solovay–Strassen test is essentially a Euler-Jacobi pseudoprime test.

Concepts

Euler proved that for any prime number p and any integer a,

$$a^{(p-1)/2} \equiv \left(\frac{a}{p} \right) \pmod{p}$$

where $\left(\frac{a}{p}\right)$ is the Legendre symbol. The Jacobi symbol is a generalisation of the Legendre symbol to $\left(\frac{a}{n}\right)$, where n can be any odd integer. The Jacobi symbol can be computed in time $O((\log n)^2)$ using Jacobi's generalization of law of quadratic reciprocity.

Given an odd number n we can contemplate whether or not the congruence

$$a^{(n-1)/2} \equiv \left(\frac{a}{n}\right) \pmod{n}$$

holds for various values of the "base" a, given that a is relatively prime to n. If n is prime then this congruence is true for all a. So if we pick values of a at random and test the congruence, then as soon as we find an a which doesn't fit the congruence we know that n is not prime (but this does not tell us a nontrivial factorization of n). This base a is called an *Euler witness* for n; it is a witness for the compositeness of n. The base a is called an *Euler liar* for n if the congruence is true while n is composite.

For every composite odd n at least half of all bases

$$a \in (\mathbb{Z}/n\mathbb{Z})^*$$

are (Euler) witnesses: this contrasts with the Fermat primality test, for which the proportion of witnesses may be much smaller. Therefore, there are no (odd) composite n without many witnesses, unlike the case of Carmichael numbers for Fermat's test.

Example

Suppose we wish to determine if $n = 221$ is prime. We write $(n-1)/2 = 110$.

We randomly select an a (smaller than n): 47. Using an efficient method for raising a number to a power (mod n) such as binary exponentiation, we compute:

- $a^{(n-1)/2} \bmod n = 47^{110} \bmod 221 = -1 \bmod 221$

- $\left(\frac{a}{n}\right) \bmod n = \left(\frac{47}{221}\right) \bmod 221 = -1 \bmod 221$.

This gives that, either 221 is prime, or 47 is an Euler liar for 221. We try another random a, this time choosing $a = 2$:

- $a^{(n-1)/2} \bmod n = 2^{110} \bmod 221 = 30 \bmod 221$

- $\left(\frac{a}{n}\right) \bmod n = \left(\frac{2}{221}\right) \bmod 221 = -1 \bmod 221$.

Hence 2 is an Euler witness for the compositeness of 221, and 47 was in fact an Euler liar. Note that this tells us nothing about the prime factors of 221, which are actually 13 and 17.

Algorithm and Running Time

The algorithm can be written in pseudocode as follows:

```
Inputs: n, a value to test for primality; k, a parameter that determines the
accuracy of the test
```

```
Output: composite if n is composite, otherwise probably prime

repeat k times:

    choose a randomly in the range [2,n - 1]
```

$$x \leftarrow \left(\frac{a}{n}\right)$$

```
    if x = 0 or
```
$a^{(n-1)/2} \not\equiv x \pmod{n}$ `then`

```
        return composite

return probably prime
```

Using fast algorithms for modular exponentiation, the running time of this algorithm is O($k \cdot \log^3$ n), where k is the number of different values of a we test.

Accuracy of the Test

It is possible for the algorithm to return an incorrect answer. If the input n is indeed prime, then the output will always correctly be *probably prime*. However, if the input n is composite then it is possible for the output to be incorrectly *probably prime*. The number n is then called a Euler-Jacobi pseudoprime.

When n is odd and composite, at least half of all a with gcd(a,n) = 1 are Euler witnesses. We can prove this as follows: let $\{a_1, a_2, ..., a_m\}$ be the Euler liars and a an Euler witness. Then, for $i = 1,2,...,m$:

$$(a \cdot a_i)^{(n-1)/2} = a^{(n-1)/2} \cdot a_i^{(n-1)/2} = a^{(n-1)/2} \cdot \left(\frac{a_i}{n}\right) \not\equiv \left(\frac{a}{n}\right)\left(\frac{a_i}{n}\right) \pmod{n}.$$

Because the following holds:

$$\left(\frac{a}{n}\right)\left(\frac{a_i}{n}\right) = \left(\frac{a \cdot a_i}{n}\right),$$

now we know that

$$(a \cdot a_i)^{(n-1)/2} \not\equiv \left(\frac{a \cdot a_i}{n}\right) \pmod{n}.$$

This gives that each a_i gives a number $a \cdot a_i$, which is also an Euler witness. So each Euler liar gives an Euler witness and so the number of Euler witnesses is larger or equal to the number of Euler liars. Therefore, when n is composite, at least half of all a with gcd(a,n) = 1 is an Euler witness.

Hence, the probability of failure is at most 2^{-k} (compare this with the probability of failure for the Miller-Rabin primality test, which is at most 4^{-k}).

For purposes of cryptography the more bases a we test, i.e. if we pick a sufficiently large value of k, the better the accuracy of test. Hence the chance of the algorithm failing in this way is so small that the (pseudo) prime is used in practice in cryptographic applications, but for applications for which it is important to have a prime, a test like ECPP or Pocklington should be used which *proves* primality.

Average-case Behaviour

The bound 1/2 on the error probability of a single round of the Solovay–Strassen test holds for any input n, but those numbers n for which the bound is (approximately) attained are extremely rare. On the average, the error probability of the algorithm is significantly smaller: it is less than

$$2^{-k} \exp\left(-(1+o(1)) \frac{\log x \log \log \log x}{\log \log x} \right)$$

for k rounds of the test, applied to uniformly random $n \le x$. The same bound also applies to the related problem of what is the conditional probability of n being composite for a random number $n \le x$ which has been declared prime in k rounds of the test.

Complexity

The Solovay–Strassen algorithm shows that the decision problem COMPOSITE is in the complexity class RP.

AKS PRIMALITY TEST:

First we describe a characterization of prime numbers that will provide the conceptual mathematical foundation for our polynomial time algorithm.

Lemma 3.1: Let $a \in Z$, $n \in N$, such that $(a, n) = 1$. Then n is prime iff $(x+a)^n \equiv x^n + a \pmod{n}$.

Proof:

By the Binomial theorem we have:

$$(x+a)^n = \sum_{k=0}^{n} \binom{n}{k} x^k a^{n-k}$$

If n is prime then $\binom{n}{k}$ is divisible by n according to the binomial theorem. By Fermat's little theorem, we have $a^n \equiv a \pmod{n}$ and hence the equivalence in the above equation holds.

If n is composite, then let q be a prime divisor of n with $q^s \mid n$. The coefficient of x^{n-q} in the binomial

expansion of $(x + a)^n$ is $\dfrac{n(n-1)...(n-q+1)}{q!} . a^q$. The numerator is divisible by q^s but not by

q^{s+1}. The denominator is divisible by q. Hence $\dfrac{n(n-1)...(n-q+1)}{q!} . a^q \not\equiv 0 \pmod{n}$. Since $(a,n) = 1$,

implies $(a, q^s) = 1$, implies $(a^q, q^s) = 1$, implies $\dfrac{n(n-1)...(n-q+1)}{q!} . a^q \not\equiv 0 \pmod{n}$.

Therefore $(x+a)^n \neq x^n + a \pmod{n}$

The above identity suggests a simple method for testing the primality of an integer n. We can choose an integer a such that $(a, n) = 1$ and calculate $f(x) = (x + a)^n - (x^n + a)$. If this function is equal to 0 (mod n) then n is prime, else n is composite. Although this is certainly a valid primality test, it is horribly inefficient as it involves the computation of n coefficients. The trick however is in choosing a suitable integer a. The simplest method for reducing the number of coefficients that need to be computed is to evaluate f(x) modulo n and modulo some polynomial of small degree, say $(x^r - 1)$.

Although it is clear that all primes p satisfy $(x + a)^p - (x^p + a) \equiv 0 \bmod (p, x^r - 1)$, some composite numbers may satisfy this equation for all values of a and r. It turns out that for a judiciously chosen r, if the above identity is satisfied for several values of a, then n can be shown to be a prime power. The number of a's and the appropriate value of r are bounded by log(n). Therefore we have just described a deterministic polynomial time primality testing algorithm.

Algorithm:

INPUT: $n \geq 1$

STEP 1: If $\exists\, a, b > 1 \in N$ such that $n = a^b$, then output COMPOSITE.

STEP2: Find the minimal $r \in N$ such that $o_r(n) > \log^2(n)$

STEP3 : For a=1 to r do

If $1 < (a,n) < n$, then output COMPOSITE

STEP4: if $r \geq n$, then output PRIME

STEP5: For a=1 to $\left\lfloor \sqrt{\varphi(r)} . \log n \right\rfloor$ do

If $(x+a)^n - (x^n +a) \neq 0 \bmod (n, x^r -1)$, then output COMPOSITE.

STEP 6: output PRIME.

Proof: If n is prime, STEP 1 cannot return COMPOSITE. Similarly, STEP 3 cannot return COMPOSITE. Hence, the AKS algorithm will always return PRIME if n is prime.

Conversely, if the AKS algorithm returns PRIME, we will prove that n is indeed prime. If the algorithm returns PRIME in STEP 4, n must be prime because otherwise a non trivial factor a would have been found in STEP 3. The only case which remains is that if the algorithm returns PRIME in STEP 6.

Lemma: There exists an integer $r \in N$ with the following properties:

$$1. r \leq \max\left\{3, \left\lceil \log^5(n) \right\rceil\right\}$$
$$2. O_r(n) > \log^2(n)$$
$$3. (r,n) = 1$$

Proof:

For n=2, r=3 satisfies all the conditions.

For $n > 2, \lceil \log^5(n) \rceil > 10$.

We know that for n ≥ 7, lcm(n) ≥ 2ⁿ where lcm(m) denote the LCM of first m numbers.

So we get the following:

$$lcm\left(\left\lceil \log^5(n) \right\rceil\right) \geq 2^{\left\lceil \log^5(n) \right\rceil}$$

$$Now\,consider : N = n.\prod_{i=1}^{\left\lfloor \log\left(\frac{2}{n}\right) \right\rfloor} (n^i - 1).$$

Let r be the smallest integer not dividing N. then condition (2) is obviously satisfies as r is not divisor ($n^i - 1$) $for\,i \leq \left\lfloor \log^2(n) \right\rfloor$ Condition (1) is also satisfies because

$$N \leq n^{1+2\ldots\log^2(n)} = n^{\frac{1(\log^4(n)+\log^2(n))}{2}} < n^{\log^4(n)} < 2^{\log^5(n)}$$

Thus $N < lcm\left(\left\lceil \log^5(n) \right\rceil\right)$ and hence $r < \left\lceil \log^5(n) \right\rceil$

Now we prove (3). It is clear that (r,n) <r,as otherwise r would divide n and hence N. Thus $\dfrac{r}{(r,n)}$ is an integer less than max $\left\{3, \left\lceil \log^5(n) \right\rceil\right\}$ not dividing N. Because r was chosen to be minimal, it must be case that $\left\{3, \left\lceil \log^5(n) \right\rceil\right\}$ .hence we have found the r.

Because $O_r(n) > 1$, n must have some prime divisor p such that $O_r(p) > 1$. STEP 3 did not output COMPOSITE, so we know that (n, r)=(p, r) =1. Additionally, we know that p > r as otherwise STEP 3 or STEP 4 would have returned a decision regarding the primality n.

Hypothesis:

1. *Natural number n has p prime divisor.*

2. $r < \left\lceil \log^5(n) \right\rceil and\, O_r(n) > \log^2(n)$

3. $(r,n) = 1$

4. $l := \left\lfloor \sqrt{\varphi(r)}.\log n \right\rfloor$

We now focus our attention on STEP 5 of the algorithm. Let us define an introspective. For polynomial f(X) and number m ∈ N, we say that m is introspective for f(X) if

f(X)ᵐ = f(Xᵐ) (mod Xʳ-1, p).

Lemma: let n ∈ N have prime divisor p and let a ∈ N with $0 \leq a \leq l$. If n,p are introspective for (x+a), then $\dfrac{n}{p}$ is introspective for (x+a) as well.

Proof: As p and n are both introspective for (x+a), we have

$$(x^{\frac{n}{p}} + a)^p \equiv (x^n + a) \equiv (x+a)^n \equiv (x+a)^{p.\frac{n}{p}} \pmod{x^r - 1, p}$$

$$(x^{\frac{n}{p}} + a)^p \equiv ((x+a)^{\frac{n}{p}})^p \ implies \ (x^{\frac{n}{p}} + a)^p + (-((x+a)^{\frac{n}{p}})^p) \equiv 0 \pmod{p}$$

$$Therefore, ((x^{\frac{n}{p}} + a) - (x+a)^{\frac{n}{p}})^p \equiv 0 \pmod{p}$$

$$Let \ ((x^{\frac{n}{p}} + a) - (x+a)^{\frac{n}{p}}) = h$$

We must show $h \equiv 0 \pmod{x^r - 1}$. Because $(r, p) = 1$, $x^r - 1$ factors into distinct irreducible $h_i(x)$ over Z_p. Using the Chinese Remainder theorem, we get

$$h^p \in \prod_i \frac{z(x)_p}{h(x)_i}$$

As $x^r - 1$ divides h^p, each of the irreducible factors $h_i(x)$ divide h. Hence $x^r - 1$ divides h. Hence the proof.

It is easy to see the introspective numbers are closed under multiplication and that the set of functions for which a given integer is introspective is closed under multiplication.

We can now state a fact as a consequence of the above results.

Every element if the set $I = \{(\frac{n}{p})^i . p^j : i, j \geq 0\}$ is introspective for every polynomial in the set $\{\prod_{a=0}^{l}(x+a)^{e_a} \mid e_a \geq 0\}$. We now define two groups based on these sets that will play a crucial role in the proof.

1. $l_r = \{i \pmod r : i \in l\}$ This is a subgroup of Z_r^* since $(n,r) = (p,r) = 1$. Let G be this group and $|G| = t$. G is generated by n and p modulo r and since $O_r(n) > \log^2(n)$, $t > \log^2(n)$.

2. $G = \{f \pmod{h(x), p} : f \in P\}$ Let $Q_r(X)$ be r^{th} cyclotomic polynomial over F_p. Polynomial $Q_r(X)$ divides $X^r - 1$ and factors into irreducible factors of degree $o_r(p)$. Let $h(X)$ be one such irreducible factor. Since $o_r(p) > 1$, the degree of $h(X)$ is greater than one. The second group is the set of all residues of polynomials in P modulo $h(X)$ and p. Let G be this group. This group is generated by elements $X, X+1, X+2, ..., X+l$ in the field $F = F_p X / (h(X))$ and is a subgroup of the multiplicative group of F.

Lemma : $|G| \geq \binom{t+1}{t-1}$

Proof: Note that because h(x) is a factor of $Q_r(X)$, x is a primitive r^{th} root of unity in F. We now show that if $f, g \in P$ are distinct polynomials with degrees less than t, then they map to distinct elements in G.

Suppose, that f(x) = g(x) in F. Let $m \in I$. Then m is introspective for f and g, so $f(x^m) = g(x^m)$ within F. Then x^m is a root of j(z) = f(z) - g(z) for every $m \in I_r$. We know, $(m,r) = 1$, so each such x^m is a primitive r^{th} root of unity. Hence there are $|I_r| = t$ distinct roots of j(z) in F. But the degree j(z) < t by the choice of f and g. This contradiction (a polynomial cannot have more roots in a field than its degree) implies that f(x)≠ g(x) in F.

Notice that i≠ j in F_p whenever 1≤ i, j≤ l since $l = \lfloor \sqrt{\varphi(r)}.\log n \rfloor < \sqrt{r}.\log n < r < p$ Then by above ,x,x+1,x+2,x+3...x+l are a. Since the degree of h(x) is greater than 1, all of these linear polynomials are nonzero in F. therefore there are atleast, l+1 distinct polynomials of degree 1 in G. hence there atleast $\binom{l+s}{s}$ polynomials of degree s in G. Then the order of G is atleast $\binom{t+1}{t-1}$. hence the proof.

Lemma : If n is not a power of p then $|G| \leq n^{\sqrt{t}}$. .

Proof: Consider the following subset of I:

$$I = \left\{ \left(\frac{n}{p} \right)^i .p^j \mid o \leq i, j \leq \lfloor \sqrt{t} \rfloor \right\}$$

If n is not a power of p, then $|I'| \geq (1+\lfloor \sqrt{t} \rfloor)^2 > t$ Since $|I_r| = t$ there are at least two elements of I' that are equivalent modulo r. Label these elements m_1, m_2 where $m_1 > m_2$.

Then $x^{m_1} \equiv x^{m_2} \pmod{x^r - 1}$

Let f(x)∈P Then because m_1, m_2 are introspective $f(x)^{m_1} = f(x^{m_1}) = f(x^{m_2}) = f(x)^{m_2} \pmod{x^r - 1, p}$.

Thus $f(x)^{m_1} = f(x)^{m_2}$ in the field F. Therefore the polynomial $Q(y) = y^{m_1} - y^{m_2}$ has atleast |G| roots in F (since f(x) ∈ P was arbitrary). Then because $fracnp)^{\lfloor \sqrt{t} \rfloor}.p^{\lfloor \sqrt{t} \rfloor}$ is the largest element of I'.

$$\deg(Q(y)) = m_1 \leq fracnp.p)^{\lfloor \sqrt{t} \rfloor} = n^{\lfloor \sqrt{t} \rfloor}$$

It follows that $|G| \leq n^{\sqrt{t}}$. Hence the proof.

Lemma: If AKS algorithm return PRIME then n is prime.

Proof: Assume that the algorithm return prime. Recall that $|I_r| = t$ and is generated by n and p, therefore t≥ Or(n) > log² (n) or t> $\lfloor \sqrt{t}.\log(n) \rfloor$.
We know that $\lfloor \sqrt{\varphi(r)}.\log(n) \rfloor and |G| \geq \binom{t+1}{t-1}$

$$|G| \geq \binom{l+1+\lfloor \sqrt{t}\log(n) \rfloor}{\lfloor \sqrt{t}.\log(n) \rfloor}$$

$$|G| \geq \binom{2.\lfloor \sqrt{t}\log(n) \rfloor}{\lfloor \sqrt{t}.\log(n) \rfloor}$$

$$|G| \geq 2^{\lfloor \sqrt{t}\log(n) \rfloor + 1}$$

$$|G| \geq 2^{\lfloor \sqrt{t}\log(n) \rfloor}$$

$$|G| \geq n^{\sqrt{t}}$$

Also by lemma, $|G| \leq n^{\sqrt{t}}$ if p is not a power of p. Therefore it must be the case that n= p^k for some k>0 . But STEP 1 did not output COMPOSIT, so k=1, proving that n is indeed prime. This completes our proof of theorem.

Time Complexity:

The overall complexity of AKS algorithm is O ($\log^{10.5}(n)$).

Integer Factorization

In number theory, integer factorization is the decomposition of a composite number into a product of smaller integers. If these integers are further restricted to prime numbers, the process is called prime factorization.

When the numbers are very large, no efficient, non-quantum integer factorization algorithm is known. An effort by several researchers, concluded in 2009, to factor a 232-digit number (RSA-768) utilizing hundreds of machines took two years and the researchers estimated that a 1024-bit RSA modulus would take about a thousand times as long. However, it has not been proven that no efficient algorithm exists. The presumed difficulty of this problem is at the heart of widely used algorithms in cryptography such as RSA. Many areas of mathematics and computer science have been brought to bear on the problem, including elliptic curves, algebraic number theory, and quantum computing.

Not all numbers of a given length are equally hard to factor. The hardest instances of these problems (for currently known techniques) are semiprimes, the product of two prime numbers. When they are both large, for instance more than two thousand bits long, randomly chosen, and about the same size (but not too close, e.g., to avoid efficient factorization by Fermat's factorization method), even the fastest prime factorization algorithms on the fastest computers can take enough time to make the search impractical; that is, as the number of digits of the primes being factored increases, the number of operations required to perform the factorization on any computer increases drastically.

Many cryptographic protocols are based on the difficulty of factoring large composite integers or a related problem—for example, the RSA problem. An algorithm that efficiently factors an arbitrary integer would render RSA-based public-key cryptography insecure.

Prime Decomposition

By the fundamental theorem of arithmetic, every positive integer has a unique prime factorization. (By convention 1 is the empty product.) If the integer is prime then it can be recognized as such in polynomial time. If composite however, the theorem gives no insight into how to obtain the factors.

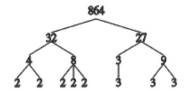

This image demonstrates the prime decomposition of 864. A shorthand
way of writing the resulting prime factors is $2^5 \times 3^3$

Given a general algorithm for integer factorization, any integer can be factored down to its constituent prime factors simply by repeated application of this algorithm. The situation is more complicated with special-purpose factorization algorithms, whose benefits may not be realized as well or even at all with the factors produced during decomposition. For example, if $N = 10 \times p \times q$ where $p < q$ are very large primes, trial division will quickly produce the factors 2 and 5 but will take p divisions to find the next factor. As a contrasting example, if N is the product of the primes 13729, 1372933, and 18848997161, where $13729 \times 1372933 = 18848997157$, Fermat's factorization method will start out with $a = \lceil \sqrt{N} \rceil = 18848997159$ which immediately yields $b = \sqrt{a^2 - N} = \sqrt{4} = 2$ and hence the factors $a - b = 18848997157$ and $a + b = 18848997161$. While these are easily recognized as respectively composite and prime, Fermat's method will take much longer to factorize the composite one because the starting value of $\lceil \sqrt{18848997157} \rceil = 137292$ for a is nowhere near 1372933.

Current State of the Art

Among the b-bit numbers, the most difficult to factor in practice using existing algorithms are those that are products of two primes of similar size. For this reason, these are the integers used in cryptographic applications. The largest such semiprime yet factored was RSA-768, a 768-bit number with 232 decimal digits, on December 12, 2009. This factorization was a collaboration of several research institutions, spanning two years and taking the equivalent of almost 2000 years of computing on a single-core 2.2 GHz AMD Opteron. Like all recent factorization records, this factorization was completed with a highly optimized implementation of the general number field sieve run on hundreds of machines.

Difficulty and Complexity

No algorithm has been published that can factor all integers in polynomial time, i.e., that can factor b-bit numbers in time $O(b^k)$ for some constant k. Neither the existence nor non-existence of such algorithms has been proved, but it is generally suspected that they do not exist and hence that the problem is not in class P. The problem is clearly in class NP but has not been proved to be or not be NP-complete. It is generally suspected not to be NP-complete.

There are published algorithms that are faster than $O((1+\varepsilon)^b)$ for all positive ε, i.e., sub-exponential. The best published asymptotic running time is for the general number field sieve (GNFS) algorithm, which, for a b-bit number n, is:

$$O\left(\exp \sqrt[3]{\frac{64}{9} b (\log b)^2} \right).$$

For current computers, GNFS is the best published algorithm for large n (more than about 100 digits). For a quantum computer, however, Peter Shor discovered an algorithm in 1994 that solves it in polynomial time. This will have significant implications for cryptography if quantum computation is possible. Shor's algorithm takes only $O(b^3)$ time and $O(b)$ space on b-bit number inputs. In 2001, the first seven-qubit quantum computer became the first to run Shor's algorithm. It factored the number 15.

When discussing what complexity classes the integer factorization problem falls into, it is necessary to distinguish two slightly different versions of the problem:

- The function problem version: given an integer N, find an integer d with $1 < d < N$ that divides N (or conclude that N is prime). This problem is trivially in FNP and it's not known whether it lies in FP or not. This is the version solved by practical implementations.

- The decision problem version: given an integer N and an integer M with $1 < M < N$, does N have a factor d with $1 < d \le M$? This version is useful because most well studied complexity classes are defined as classes of decision problems, not function problems.

For $\sqrt{N} \le M < N$, the decision problem is equivalent to asking if N is not prime.

An algorithm for either version provides one for the other. Repeated application of the function problem (applied to d and N/d, and their factors, if needed) will eventually provide either a factor of N no larger than M or a factorization into primes all greater than M. All known algorithms for the decision problem work in this way. Hence it is only of theoretical interest that, with at most $\log N$ queries using an algorithm for the decision problem, one would isolate a factor of N (or prove it prime) by binary search.

It is not known exactly which complexity classes contain the decision version of the integer factorization problem. It is known to be in both NP and co-NP. This is because both YES and NO answers can be verified in polynomial time. An answer of YES can be certified by exhibiting a factorization $N = d(N/d)$ with $d \le M$. An answer of NO can be certified by exhibiting the factorization of N into distinct primes, all larger than M. We can verify their primality using the AKS primality test and that their product is N by multiplication. The fundamental theorem of arithmetic guarantees that there is only one possible string that will be accepted (providing the factors are required to be listed in order), which shows that the problem is in both UP and co-UP. It is known to be in BQP because of Shor's algorithm. It is suspected to be outside of all three of the complexity classes P, NP-complete, and co-NP-complete. It is therefore a candidate for the NP-intermediate complexity class. If it could be proved that it is in either NP-Complete or co-NP-Complete, that would imply NP = co-NP. That would be a very surprising result, and therefore integer factorization is widely suspected to be outside both of those classes. Many people have tried to find classical polynomial-time algorithms for it and failed, and therefore it is widely suspected to be outside P.

In contrast, the decision problem "is N a composite number?" (or equivalently: "is N a prime number?") appears to be much easier than the problem of actually finding the factors of N. Specifically, the former can be solved in polynomial time (in the number n of digits of N) with the AKS primality test. In addition, there are a number of probabilistic algorithms that can test primality very quickly in practice if one is willing to accept the vanishingly small possibility of error. The ease of primality testing is a crucial part of the RSA algorithm, as it is necessary to find large prime numbers to start with.

Factoring Algorithms

Special-purpose

A special-purpose factoring algorithm's running time depends on the properties of the number to be factored or on one of its unknown factors: size, special form, etc. Exactly what the running time depends on varies between algorithms.

An important subclass of special-purpose factoring algorithms is the *Category 1* or *First Category* algorithms, whose running time depends on the size of smallest prime factor. Given an integer of unknown form, these methods are usually applied before general-purpose methods to remove small factors. For example, trial division is a Category 1 algorithm.

- Trial division

- Wheel factorization

- Pollard's rho algorithm

- Algebraic-group factorisation algorithms, among which are Pollard's $p - 1$ algorithm, Williams' $p + 1$ algorithm, and Lenstra elliptic curve factorization

- Fermat's factorization method

- Euler's factorization method

- Special number field sieve

General-purpose

A general-purpose factoring algorithm, also known as a *Category 2*, *Second Category*, or *Kraitchik family* algorithm (after Maurice Kraitchik), has a running time which depends solely on the size of the integer to be factored. This is the type of algorithm used to factor RSA numbers. Most general-purpose factoring algorithms are based on the congruence of squares method.

- Dixon's algorithm

- Continued fraction factorization (CFRAC)

- Quadratic sieve

- Rational sieve

- General number field sieve

- Shanks' square forms factorization (SQUFOF)

Other Notable Algorithms

- Shor's algorithm, for quantum computers

Heuristic Running Time

In number theory, there are many integer factoring algorithms that heuristically have expected running time

$$L_n\left[\tfrac{1}{2},1+o(1)\right]=e^{(1+o(1))\sqrt{(\log n)(\log\log n)}}$$

in big O and L-notation. Some examples of those algorithms are the elliptic curve method and the quadratic sieve. Another such algorithm is the class group relations method proposed by Schnorr, Seysen, and Lenstra, that is proved under the assumption of the Generalized Riemann Hypothesis (GRH).

Rigorous Running Time

The Schnorr-Seysen-Lenstra probabilistic algorithm has been rigorously proven by Lenstra and Pomerance to have expected running time $L_n\left[\tfrac{1}{2},1+o(1)\right]$ by replacing the GRH assumption with the use of multipliers. The algorithm uses the class group of positive binary quadratic forms of discriminant Δ denoted by G_Δ. G_Δ is the set of triples of integers (a, b, c) in which those integers are relative prime.

Schnorr-Seysen-Lenstra Algorithm

Given is an integer n that will be factored, where n is an odd positive integer greater than a certain constant. In this factoring algorithm the discriminant Δ is chosen as a multiple of n, $\Delta = -dn$, where d is some positive multiplier. The algorithm expects that for one d there exist enough smooth forms in G_Δ. Lenstra and Pomerance show that the choice of d can be restricted to a small set to guarantee the smoothness result.

Denote by P_Δ the set of all primes q with Kronecker symbol $\left(\tfrac{\Delta}{q}\right)=1$. By constructing a set of generators of G_Δ and prime forms f_q of G_Δ with q in P_Δ a sequence of relations between the set of generators and f_q are produced. The size of q can be bounded by $c_0(\log|\Delta|)^2$ for some constant c_0.

The relation that will be used is a relation between the product of powers that is equal to the neutral element of G_Δ. These relations will be used to construct a so-called ambiguous form of G_Δ, which is an element of G_Δ of order dividing 2. By calculating the corresponding factorization of Δ and by taking a gcd, this ambiguous form provides the complete prime factorization of n. This algorithm has these main steps:

Let n be the number to be factored.

1. Let Δ be a negative integer with $\Delta = -dn$, where d is a multiplier and Δ is the negative discriminant of some quadratic form.

2. Take the t first primes $p_1 = 2, p_2 = 3, p_3 = 5, \ldots, p_t$, for some $t \in \mathbb{N}$.

3. Let be f_q a random prime form of G_Δ with $\left(\tfrac{\Delta}{q}\right)=1$.

4. Find a generating set X of G_Δ

5. Collect a sequence of relations between set X and $\{f_q : q \in P_\Delta\}$ satisfying:

$$\left(\prod_{x\in X} x^{r(x)}\right)\cdot\left(\prod_{q\in P_\Delta} f_q^{t(q)}\right)=1$$

6. Construct an ambiguous form (a,b,c) that is an element $f \in G_\Delta$ of order dividing 2 to obtain a coprime factorization of the largest odd divisor of Δ in which

$$\Delta = -4ac \text{ or } a(a-4c) \text{ or } (b-2a)(b+2a)$$

7. If the ambiguous form provides a factorization of n then stop, otherwise find another ambiguous form until the factorization of n is found. In order to prevent useless ambiguous forms from generating, build up the 2-Sylow group $Sll_2(\Delta)$ of $G(\Delta)$.

To obtain an algorithm for factoring any positive integer, it is necessary to add a few steps to this algorithm such as trial division, and the Jacobi sum test.

Expected Running Time

The algorithm as stated is a probabilistic algorithm as it makes random choices. Its expected running time is at most $L_n\left[\frac{1}{2}, 1 + o(1)\right]$.

Integer Factorization Algorithms

Trial division is the simplest and easiest to understand of the integer factorization algorithms.

Given an odd composite integer n there must be a prime factor less than $\sqrt{n}$. Thus we need to test for all primes $p \le \lfloor \sqrt{n} \rfloor$ that divides n. Let π(n) denote the number of primes less than n. From the prime number theorem we have the following:

$$Limit_{n \to \infty} \pi(n) = \frac{n}{\ln n}$$

Thus we have to test for all $\pi\lfloor \sqrt{n} \rfloor$ prime factors of n. From the previous theorem we have:

$$\pi(\sqrt{n}) \approx \frac{2\sqrt{n}}{\ln n}$$

If a variant is used without primality testing, but simply dividing by every odd number less than the square root of n, prime or not, it can take up to about $\frac{\sqrt{n}}{2}$ trial divisions which for large n is worse.

If n has small prime factors then this algorithm performs quite well. This means that for n with large prime factors of similar size (like those used in public key cryptography), trial division is computation ally infeasible. For most significant factoring concerns, however, other algorithms are more efficient and therefore feasible.

Given a composite integer n, trial division consists of trial-dividing n by every prime number less than or equal to $\sqrt{n}$. If a number is found which divides evenly into n, that number is a factor of n.

A definite bound on the prime factors is possible. Suppose P(i) is the i'th prime, so that P(1) = 2, P(2) = 3, etc. Then the last prime number worth testing as a possible factor o n is P(i) where

P(i + 1)² > n; equality here would mean that P(i + 1) was a factor. This is all very well, but usually inconvenient to apply for the inspection of a single n since determining the correct value for i is more effort than simply trying the one unneeded candidate P(i + 1) that would be involved in testing with all P(i) such that $P(i <= \sqrt{n})$. Should the square root of n be integral, then it is a factor and n is a Perfect square, not that this is a good way of finding them.

Trial division is guaranteed to find a factor of n, since it checks all possible prime factors of n. Thus, if the algorithm finds no factor, it is proof that n is prime.

In the worst case, trial division is a laborious algorithm. If it starts from 2 and works up to the square root of n, the algorithm requires trial divisions, where π(x) denotes the prime counting function, the number of primes less than x. This does not take into account the overhead of primality testing to obtain the prime numbers as candidate factors. If a variant is used without primality testing, but simply dividing by every odd number less than the square root of n, prime or not, it can take up to about $\frac{\sqrt{n}}{2}$ trial divisions which for large n is worse.

This means that for n with large prime factors of similar size (like those used in public key cryptography), trial division is computationally infeasible.

However, for n with at least one small factor, trial division can be a quick way to find that small factor. It is worthwhile to note that for random n, there is a 50% chance that 2 is a factor of n, and a 33% chance that 3 is a factor, and so on. It can be shown that 88% of all positive integers have a factor under 100, and that 91% have a factor under 1000.

For most significant factoring concerns, however, other algorithms are more efficient and therefore feasible.

Pollard's p-1 Algorithm

Pollard's p − 1 algorithm is a number theoretic integer factorization algorithm, invented by John Pollard in 1974. It is a special-purpose algorithm, meaning that it is only suitable for integers with specific types of factors.

The algorithm is based on the insight that numbers of the form $a^b − 1$ tend to be highly composite when b is itself composite. Since it is computationally simple to evaluate numbers of this form in modular arithmetic, the algorithm allows one to quickly check many potential factors with great efficiency. In particular, the method will find a factor p if b is divisible by p − 1, hence the name. When p − 1 is smooth (the product of only small integers) then this algorithm is well-suited to discovering the factor p.

Base Concepts

Let *n* be a composite integer with prime factor *p*. By Fermat's little theorem, we know that $a^{p-1} \equiv 1 \pmod{p}$ for a coprime to *p*

Let us assume that p − 1 is B-powersmooth for some reasonably sized B (more on the selection of this value later). Recall that a positive integer m is called B-smooth if all prime factors p_i of m are such that $p_i \le B$. m is called B-powersmooth if all prime powers i dividing m are such that $p_{i\,i} \le B$.

Let $p_1, ..., p_L$ be the primes less than B and let $e_1, ..., e_L$ be the exponents such that

$$p_i^{e_i} \leq B < p_i^{e_i+1}$$

Let

$$M = \prod_{i=1}^{L} p_i^{e_i}$$

As a shortcut, M = lcm{1, ..., B}. As a consequence of this, (p – 1) divides M, and also if p^e divides M this implies that $p^e \leq B$. Since (p – 1) divides M we know that $a^M \equiv 1 \pmod{p}$, and because p divides n this means $\gcd(a^M - 1, n) > 1$.

Therefore if $\gcd(a^M - 1, n) \neq n$, then the gcd is a non-trivial factor of n.

If p – 1 is not B-power-smooth, then $a^M \not\equiv 1 \pmod{p}$ for at least half of all a.

Pollard Concepts

Let n = pqr, where p and q are distinct primes and r is an integer, such that p – 1 is B- powersmooth and q – 1 is not B-powersmooth. Now, $\gcd(a^M - 1, n)$ yields a proper factor of n.

In the case where q – 1 is B-powersmooth, the gcd may yield a trivial factor because q divides a $^M - 1$. This is what makes the algorithm specialized. For example, 172189 = 421× 409. 421 – 1 = $2^2 \times 3 \times 5 \times 7$ and 409 – 1 = $2^3 \times 3 \times 17$. So, an appropriate value of B would be from 7 to 16. If B was selected less than 7 the gcd would have been 1 and if B was selected higher than 16 the gcd would have been n. Of course, we do not know what value of B is appropriate in advance, so this will factor into the algorithm.

To speed up calculations, we also know that when taking the gcd we can reduce one part modulo the other, so $\gcd(a^M - 1, n) = \gcd(a^M - 1 \bmod n, n)$. This can be efficiently calculated using modular exponentiation and the Euclidean algorithm.

Algorithm and Running Time

The basic algorithm can be written as follows:

Inputs: n: a composite integer

Output: a non-trivial factor of n or failure

1. select a smoothness bound B

2. randomly pick a coprime to n (note: we can actually fix a, random selection here is not imperative)

3. for each prime q ≤ B

$$e \leftarrow \left\lfloor \frac{\log B}{\log q} \right\rfloor$$

$a \leftarrow a^{q^e}$ mode n (note: this is a^M)

4. $g \leftarrow \gcd(a - 1, n)$

5. f 1 < g < n then return g

6. if g = 1 then select a higher B and go to step 2 or return failure

7. if g = n then go to step 2 or return failure

If g = 1 in step 6, this indicates that for all p − 1 that none were B-powersmooth. If g = n in step 7, this usually indicates that all factors were B-powersmooth, but in rare cases it could indicate that a had a small order modulo p.

The running time of this algorithm is $O(B \times \log B \times \log^2 n)$, so it is advantageous to pick a small value of B.

Large Prime Variant

A variant of the basic algorithm is sometimes used. Statistically, there is often a factor p of n such that p − 1 = fq such that f is B-powersmooth and B < q ≤ B', where q is a prime and B' is called a semi-smoothness bound.

As a starting point, this would work into the basic algorithm at step 6 if we encountered gcd = 1 but didn't want to increase B. For all primes $B < q_1, ..., q_L \le B'$, we check if

$$\gcd(a^{q_i m} - 1, n) \neq 1$$

to obtain a non-trivial factor of n. This is quickly accomplished, because if we let $c = a^M$, and $d_1 = q_1$ and $d_i = q_i - q_i - 1$, then we can compute

$$a^{q_1 m} = c^{d_1}, a^{q_2 m} = c^{d_1} c^{d_2} = a^{q_1 m} c^{d_2}, ...$$

The running time of the algorithm with this variant then becomes $O(B' \times \log B' \times \log^2 n)$.

Additional Information

Because of this algorithm's effectiveness on certain types of numbers the RSA specifications require that the primes, p and q, be such that p-1 and q-1 are non-B- power-smooth for small values of B.

Williams' p Plus 1 Algorithm

In computational number theory, Williams' p + 1 algorithm is an integer factorization algorithm invented by H. C. Williams.

It works well if the number N to be factored contains one or more prime factors p such that p + 1 is smooth, i.e. p + 1 contains only small factors. It uses Lucas sequences. It is analogous to Pollard's p-1 algorithm.

Algorithm

Choose some integer A greater than 2 which characterizes the sequence:

$$V_0 = 2, V_1 = A, V_j = AV_{j-1} - V_{j-2}$$

where all operations are performed modulo N.

Then any odd prime p divides $gcd(N, V_M - 2)$ whenever M is a multiple of $p - (D / p)$, where $D = A^2 - 4$ and (D / p) is the Jacobi symbol.

We require that $(D / p) = -1$, that is, D should be a quadratic non-residue modulo p. But as we don't know p beforehand, more than one value of A may be required before finding a solution. If $(D / p) = +1$, this algorithm degenerates into a slow version of Pollard's p-1 algorithm.

So, for different values of M we calculate $gcd(N, V_M - 2)$, and when the result is not equal to 1 or to N, we have found a non-trivial factor of N. The values of M used are successive factorials, and V_M is the M-th value of the sequence characterized by V_{M-1}.

To find the M-th element V of the sequence characterized by B, we proceed in a manner similar to left-to-right exponentiation:

x=B

y=(B^2-2) mod N

for each bit of M to the right of the most significant bit if the bit is 1

    x=(x*y-B) mod N

    y=(y^2-2) mod N

else

    y=(x*y-B) mod N

    x=(x^2-2) mod N

V=x

Example

With N=112729 and A=5, successive values of V_M are:

V_1 of seq(5) = V_1! of seq(5) = 5

V_2 of seq(5) = V_2! of seq(5) = 23

V_3 of seq(23) = V_3! of seq(5) = 12098

V_4 of seq(12098) = V_4! of seq(5) = 87680

V_5 of seq(87680) = V_5! of seq(5) = 53242

V_6 of seq(53242) = V_6! of seq(5) = 27666

V_7 of seq(27666) = V_7! of seq(5) = 110229

At this point, gcd(110229-2,112729) = 139, so 139 is a non-trivial factor of 112729. Notice that p+1 = 140 = 2 × 5 × 7. The number 7! is the lowest factorial which is multiple of 140, so the proper factor 139 is found in this step.

Lenstra Elliptic Curve Factorization

The Lenstra elliptic curve factorization or the elliptic curve factorization method (ECM) is a fast, sub-exponential running time algorithm for integer factorization which employs elliptic curves. For general purpose factoring, ECM is the third-fastest known factoring method. The second fastest is the multiple polynomial quadratic sieve and the fastest is the general number field sieve. The Lenstra elliptic curve factorization is named after Hendrik Lenstra.

Practically speaking, ECM is considered a special purpose factoring algorithm as it is most suitable for finding small factors. Currently, it is still the best algorithm for divisors not greatly exceeding 20 to 25 digits (64 to 83 bits or so), as its running time is dominated by the size of the smallest factor p rather than by the size of the number n to be factored. Frequently, ECM is used to remove small factors from a very large integer with many factors; if the remaining integer is still composite, then it has only large factors and is factored using general purpose techniques. The largest factor found using ECM so far has 83 digits and was discovered on 7 September 2013 by R. Propper. Increasing the number of curves tested improves the chances of finding a factor, but they are not linear with the increase in the number of digits.

Lenstra's Elliptic Curve Factorization

The Lenstra elliptic curve factorization method to find a factor of the given natural number n works as follows:

1. Pick a random elliptic curve over $\mathbb{Z}/n\mathbb{Z}$, with equation of the form $y^2 = x^3 + ax + b \pmod{n}$ together with a non-trivial point $P(x_0, y_0)$ on it.

   This can be done by first picking random $x_0, y_0, a \in \mathbb{Z}/n\mathbb{Z}$, and then calculating $b = y_0^2 - x_0^3 - ax_0 \pmod{n}$.

2. 'Addition' of P and Q as points in general defines a group operation $P \oplus Q$ on the curve whose product can be computed from formulas given in elliptic curves.

   Using this assumption, we can form repeated multiples of a point P: $kP = P \oplus ... \oplus P$ (k times). The addition formulas involve the taking the modular slope of a chord joining P and Q, and thus division between residue classes modulo n, performed using the extended Euclidean algorithm. In particular, division by some $v \pmod{n}$ includes calculation of the gcd(v, n).

   If the slope is of the form u/v with gcd(u, n) = 1, then $v = 0 \pmod{n}$ means that the result of the $\oplus$-addition will be ∞, the point 'at infinity' corresponding to the intersection of the 'vertical' line joining P (x, y), $P'(x, -y)$ and the curve. However, if gcd(v, n) is neither 1 nor n, then the $\oplus$-addition will not produce a meaningful point on the curve, which shows that our elliptic curve is not a group (mod n), but, more importantly for now, gcd(v, n) is a non-trivial factor of n.

3. Compute eP on the elliptic curve (mod n), where e is product of many small numbers: say, a product of small primes raised to small powers, as in the $p - 1$ algorithm, or the factorial B ! $B!$ for some not too large B. This can be done efficiently, one small factor at a time. Say, to get $B!P$, first compute $2P$, then $3(2P)$, then $4(3!P)$, and so on. Of course, B should be small enough so that B-wise $\oplus$-addition can be performed in reasonable time.

    o   If we were able to finish all the calculations above without encountering non-invertible elements (mod n), then we need to try again with some other curve and starting point.

    o   If at some stage we found $kP = \infty$ (*infinity* on the elliptic curve), we should start over with a new curve and starting point, since this point ∞ is the group identity element, so is unchanged under any further addition operations.

    o   If we encountered a $\gcd(v, n)$ at some stage that was neither 1 nor n, then we are done: it is a non-trivial factor of n.

The time complexity depends on the size of the factor and can be represented by $exp((\sqrt{2} + o(1))\sqrt{ln\, p\, ln\, ln\, p})$, where p is the smallest factor of n, or $L_p\left[\frac{1}{2}, \sqrt{2}\right]$, in L-notation.

Why Does the Algorithm Work?

If p and q are two prime divisors of n, then $y^2 = x^3 + ax + b$ (mod n) implies the same equation also modulo p and modulo q. These two smaller elliptic curves with the $\boxplus$-addition are now genuine groups. If these groups have N_p and N_q elements, respectively, then for any point P on the original curve, by Lagrange's theorem, $k > 0$ is minimal such that $kP = \infty$ on the curve modulo p implies that k divides N_p; moreover, $N_p P = \infty$. The analogous statement holds for the curve modulo q. When the elliptic curve is chosen randomly, then N_p and N_q are random numbers close to $p + 1$ and $q + 1$, respectively. Hence it is unlikely that most of the prime factors of N_p and N_q are the same, and it is quite likely that while computing eP, we will encounter some kP that is ∞ modulo p but not modulo q, or vice versa. When this is the case, kP does not exist on the original curve, and in the computations we found some v with either $\gcd(v,p) = p$ or $\gcd(v, q) = q$, but not both. That is, $\gcd(v, n)$ gave a non-trivial factor of n.

ECM is at its core an improvement of the older $p - 1$ algorithm. The $p - 1$ algorithm finds prime factors p such that $p - 1$ is b-powersmooth for small values of b. For any e, a multiple of $p - 1$, and any a relatively prime to p, by Fermat's little theorem we have $a^e \equiv 1$ (mod p). Then $\gcd(a^e - 1, n)$ is likely to produce a factor of n. However, the algorithm fails when $p - 1$ has large prime factors, as is the case for numbers containing strong primes, for example.

ECM gets around this obstacle by considering the group of a random elliptic curve over the finite field Z_p, rather than considering the multiplicative group of Z_p which always has order $p - 1$.

The order of the group of an elliptic curve over Z_p varies (quite randomly) between $p+1-2\sqrt{p}$ and $p+1+2\sqrt{p}$ by Hasse's theorem, and is likely to be smooth for some elliptic curves. Although there is no proof that a smooth group order will be found in the Hasse-interval, by using heuristic probabilistic methods, the Canfield–Erdős–Pomerance theorem with suitably optimized parameter choices, and the L-notation, we can expect to try $L[\sqrt{2}/2, \sqrt{2}]$ curves before getting a smooth group order. This heuristic estimate is very reliable in practice.

An Example

The following example is from Trappe & Washington (2006), with some details added.

We want to factor $n = 455839$. Let's choose the elliptic curve $y^2 = x^3 + 5x - 5$, with the point $P = (1, 1)$ on it, and let's try to compute $(10!)P$.

The slope of the tangent line at some point $A=(x, y)$ is $s = (3x^2 + 5)/(2y)$ (mod n). Using s we can compute $2A$. If the value of s is of the form a/b where $b > 1$ and $\gcd(a,b) = 1$, we have to find the modular inverse of b. If it does not exist, $\gcd(n,b)$ is a non-trivial factor of n.

First we compute $2P$. We have $s(P) = s(1,1) = 4$, so the coordinates of $2P = (x', y')$ are $x' = s^2 - 2x = 14$ and $y' = s(x - x') - y = 4(1 - 14) - 1 = -53$, all numbers understood (mod n). Just to check that this $2P$ is indeed on the curve: $(-53)^2 = 2809 = 14^3 + 5 \cdot 14 - 5$.

Then we compute $3(2P)$. We have $s(2P) = s(14,-53) = -593/106$ (mod n). Using the Euclidean algorithm: $455839 = 4300 \cdot 106 + 39$, then $106 = 2 \cdot 39 + 28$, then $39 = 28 + 11$, then $28 = 2 \cdot 11 + 6$, then $11 = 6 + 5$, then $6 = 5 + 1$. Hence $\gcd(455839, 106) = 1$, and working backwards (a version of the extended Euclidean algorithm): $1 = 6 - 5 = 2 \cdot 6 - 11 = 2 \cdot 28 - 5 \cdot 11 = 7 \cdot 28 - 5 \cdot 39 = 7 \cdot 106 - 19 \cdot 39 = 817$ $07 \cdot 106 - 19 \cdot 455839$. Hence $106^{-1} = 81707$ (mod 455839), and $-593/106 = -133317$ (mod 455839). Given this s, we can compute the coordinates of $2(2P)$, just as we did above: $4P = (259851, 116255)$. Just to check that this is indeed a point on the curve: $y^2 = 54514 = x^3 + 5x - 5$ (mod 455839). After this, we can compute $3(2P) = 4P \boxplus 2P$.

We can similarly compute $4!P$, and so on, but $8!P$ requires inverting 599 (mod 455839). The Euclidean algorithm gives that 455839 is divisible by 599, and we have found a factorization $455839 = 599 \cdot 761$.

The reason that this worked is that the curve (mod 599) has $640 = 2^7 \cdot 5$ points, while (mod 761) it has $777 = 3 \cdot 7 \cdot 37$ points. Moreover, 640 and 777 are the smallest positive integers k such that $kP = \infty$ on the curve (mod 599) and (mod 761), respectively. Since $8!$ is a multiple of 640 but not a multiple of 777, we have $8!P = \infty$ on the curve (mod 599), but not on the curve (mod 761), hence the repeated addition broke down here, yielding the factorization.

The Algorithm with Projective Coordinates

Before considering the projective plane over $(\mathbb{Z}/n\mathbb{Z})/\sim$, first consider a 'normal' projective space over $\mathbb{R}$: Instead of points, lines through the origin are studied. A line may be represented as a non-zero point (x, y, z), under an equivalence relation $\sim$ given by: $(x, y, z) \sim (x', y', z') \Leftrightarrow \exists\ c \neq 0$ such that $x' = cx$, $y' = cy$ and $z' = cz$. Under this equivalence relation, the space is called the projective plane (P^2); points, denoted by $(x : y : z)$, correspond to lines in a three-dimensional space that pass through the origin. Note that the point $(0 : 0 : 0)$ does not exist in this space since to draw a line in any possible direction requires at least one of x',y' or z' $\neq$ 0. Now observe that almost all lines go through any given reference plane - such as the $(X,Y,1)$-plane, whilst the lines precisely parallel to this plane, having coordinates $(X, Y, 0)$, specify directions uniquely, as 'points at infinity' that are used in the affine (X, Y)-plane it lies above.

In the algorithm, only the group structure of an elliptic curve over the field $\mathbb{R}$ is used. Since we do not necessarily need the field $\mathbb{R}$, a finite field will also provide a group structure on an elliptic curve. However, considering the same curve and operation over $(\mathbb{Z}/n\mathbb{Z})/\sim$ with n not a prime does not give a group. The Elliptic Curve Method makes use of the failure cases of the addition law.

We now state the algorithm in projective coordinates. The neutral element is then given by the point at infinity $(0:1:0)$. Let n be a (positive) integer and consider the elliptic curve (a set of points with some structure on it) $E(Z/nZ) = \{(x:y:z) \in P^2 \mid y^2 z = x^3 + axz^2 + bz^3\}$.

1. Pick x_P, y_P, a in $\mathbb{Z}/n\mathbb{Z}$ $(a \neq 0)$.

2. Calculate $b = y_P^2 - x_P^3 - ax_P$. The elliptic curve E is then in Weierstrass form given by $y^2 = x^3 + ax + b$ and by using projective coordinates the elliptic curve is given by the homogeneous equation $ZY^2 = X^3 + aZ^2X + bZ^3$. It has the point $P = (x_P : y_P : 1)$.

3. Choose an upperbound $B \in \mathbb{Z}$ for this elliptic curve. Remark: You will only find factors p if the group order of the elliptic curve E over $\mathbb{Z}/p\mathbb{Z}$ (denoted by $\# E(\mathbb{Z}/p\mathbb{Z})$) is B-smooth, which means that all prime factors of $\# E(\mathbb{Z}/p\mathbb{Z})$ have to be less or equal to B.

4. Calculate $k = \mathrm{lcm}(1, \ldots, B)$.

5. Calculate $kP := P + P + \cdots + P$ (k times) in the ring $E(\mathbb{Z}/n\mathbb{Z})$. Note that if $\# E(\mathbb{Z}/n\mathbb{Z})$ is B-smooth and n is prime (and therefore $\mathbb{Z}/n\mathbb{Z}$ is a field) that $kP = (0:1:0)$. However, if only $E(\mathbb{Z}/p\mathbb{Z})$ is B-smooth for some divisor p of n, the product might not be $(0:1:0)$ because addition and multiplication are not well-defined if n is not prime. In this case, a non-trivial divisor can be found.

6. If not, then go back to step 2. If this does occur, then you will notice this when simplifying the product kP.

In point 5 it is said that under the right circumstances a non-trivial divisor can be found. As pointed out in Lenstra's article (Factoring Integers with Elliptic Curves) the addition needs the assumption $\gcd(x_1 - x_2, n) = 1$. If P, Q are not $(0:1:0)$ and distinct (otherwise addition works similarly, but is a little different), then addition works as follows:

-   To calculate: $R = P + Q$; $P = (x_1 : y_1 : 1)$, $Q = (x_2 : y_2 : 1)$,

-   $\lambda = (y_1 - y_2)(x_1 - x_2)^{-1}$,

-   $x_3 = \lambda^2 - x_1 - x_2$,

-   $y_3 = \lambda(x_1 - x_3) - y_1$,

-   $R = P + Q = (x_3 : y_3 : 1)$.

If addition fails, this will be due to a failure calculating λ. In particular, because $(x_1 - x_2)^{-1}$ can not always be calculated if n is not prime (and therefore $\mathbb{Z}/n\mathbb{Z}$ is not a field). Without making use of $\mathbb{Z}/n\mathbb{Z}$ being a field, one could calculate:

- $\lambda' = y_1 - y_2$,

- $x_3' = \lambda'^2 - x_1(x_1 - x_2)^2 - x_2(x_1 - x_2)^2$,

- $y_3' = \lambda'(x_1(x_1 - x_2)^2 - x_3') - y_1(x_1 - x_2)^3$,

- $R = P + Q = (x_{3'}(x_1 - x_2) : y_{3'} : (x_1 - x_2)^3)$, and simplify if possible.

This calculation is always legal and if the gcd of the Z-coordinate with $n \neq$ (1 or n), so when simplifying fails, a non-trivial divisor of n is found.

Twisted Edwards Curves

The use of Edwards curves needs fewer modular multiplications and less time than the use of Montgomery curves or Weierstrass curves (other used methods). Using Edwards curves you can also find more primes.

Definition: Let k be a field in which $2 \neq 0$, and let $a, d \in k \setminus \{0\}$ with $a \neq d$. Then the twisted Edwards curve $E_{E,a,d}$ is given by $ax^2 + y^2 = 1 + dx^2y^2$. An Edwards curve is a twisted Edwards curve in which $a = 1$.

There are five known ways to build a set of point on an Edwards curve: the set of affine points, the set of projective points, the set of inverted points, the set of extended points and the set of completed points.

The set of affine points is given by: $\{(x, y) \in A^2 : ax^2 + y^2 = 1 + dx^2y^2\}$.

The addition law is given by $(e, f), (g, h) \mapsto \left(\dfrac{eh + fg}{1 + degfh}, \dfrac{fh - aeg}{1 - degfh} \right)$. The point (0,1) is its neutral element and the negative of (e, f) is $(-e, f)$. The other representations are defined similar to how the projective Weierstrass curve follows from the affine.

Any elliptic curve in Edwards form has a point of order 4. So the torsion group of an Edwards curve over $\mathbb{Q}$ is isomorphic to either $\mathbb{Z}/4\mathbb{Z}, \mathbb{Z}/8\mathbb{Z}, \mathbb{Z}/12\mathbb{Z}, \mathbb{Z}/2\mathbb{Z} \times \mathbb{Z}/4\mathbb{Z}$ or $\mathbb{Z}/2\mathbb{Z} \times \mathbb{Z}/8\mathbb{Z}$.

The most interesting cases for ECM are $\mathbb{Z}/12\mathbb{Z}$ and $\mathbb{Z}/2\mathbb{Z} \times \mathbb{Z}/8\mathbb{Z}$, since they force the group orders of the curve modulo primes to be divisible by 12 and 16 respectively. The following curves have a torsion group isomorphic to $\mathbb{Z}/12\mathbb{Z}$:

- $x^2 + y^2 = 1 + dx^2y^2$ with point (a, b) where $b \notin \{-2, -1/2, 0, \pm 1\}, a^2 = -(b^2 + 2b)$ and $d = -(2b + 1)/(a^2b^2)$

- $x^2 + y^2 = 1 + dx^2y^2$ with (a, b) where $a = \dfrac{u^2 - 1}{u^2 + 1}, b = -\dfrac{(u-1)^2}{u^2 + 1}$

$$d = \dfrac{(u^2 + 1)^3(u^2 - 4u + 1)}{(u-1)^6(u+1)^2}, u \notin \{0, \pm 1\}.$$

Every Edwards curve with a point of order 3 can be written in the ways shown above.

Stage 2

The above text is about the first stage of elliptic curve factorisation. There one hopes to find a prime divisor p such that sP is the neutral element of $E(\mathbb{Z}/p\mathbb{Z})$. In the second stage one hopes to have found a prime divisor q such that sP has small prime order in $E(\mathbb{Z}/q\mathbb{Z})$.

We hope the order to be between B_1 and B_2, B_1 is determined in stage 1 and B_2 is new stage 2 parameter. Checking for a small order of sP, can be done by computing $(ls)P$ modulo n for each prime l.

Hyperelliptic Curve Method (HECM)

There are recent developments in using hyperelliptic curves to factor integers. Cosset shows in his article that one can build a hyperelliptic curve with genus two (so a curve $y^2 = f(x)$ with f of degree 5) which gives the same result as using two 'normal' elliptic curves at the same time. By making use of the Kummer Surface calculation is more efficient. The disadvantages of the hyperelliptic curve (versus an elliptic curve) are compensated by this alternative way of calculating. Therefore, Cosset roughly claims that using hyperelliptic curves for factorization is no worse than using elliptic curves.

Discrete Logarithm

In mathematics, a discrete logarithm is an integer k exponent solving the equation $b^k = g$, where b and g are elements of a finite group. Discrete logarithms are thus the finite group-theoretic analogue of ordinary logarithms, which solve the same equation for real numbers b and g, where b is the base of the logarithm and g is the value whose logarithm is being taken.

No efficient general method for computing discrete logarithms on conventional computers is known. Several important algorithms in public-key cryptography base their security on the assumption that the discrete logarithm problem over carefully chosen groups has no efficient solution.

Examples

Powers of 10

The powers of 10 form an infinite subset $G = \{..., 0.001, 0.01, 0.1, 1, 10, 100, 1000, ...\}$ of the rational numbers. This set G is a cyclic group under multiplication, and 10 is a generator. For any element g of the group, one can compute $\log_{10} g$. For example, $\log_{10} 10000 = 4$, and $\log_{10} 0.001 = -3$. These are instances of the discrete logarithm problem.

Other base-10 logarithms in the real numbers are not instances of the discrete logarithm problem, because they involve non-integer exponents. For example, the equation $\log_{10} 53 = 1.724276...$ means that $10^{1.724276...} = 53$. While integer exponents can be defined in any group using products and inverses, non-integer exponents in the real numbers arise through quite a different mechanism — the exponential function.

Modular Arithmetic

One of the simplest settings for discrete logarithms is the group $(Z_p)^\times$. This is the group of multiplication modulo the prime p. Its elements are congruence classes modulo p, and the group product of two elements may be obtained by ordinary integer multiplication of the elements followed by reduction modulo p.

The kth power of one of the numbers in this group may be computed by finding its kth power as an integer and then finding the remainder after division by p. When the numbers involved are large, it is more efficient to reduce modulo p multiple times during the computation. Regardless of the specific algorithm used, this operation is called modular exponentiation. For example, consider $(Z_{17})^\times$. To compute 3^4 in this group, compute $3^4 = 81$, and then divide 81 by 17, obtaining a remainder of 13. Thus $3^4 = 13$ in the group $(Z_{17})^\times$.

The discrete logarithm is just the inverse operation. For example, consider the equation $3^k \equiv 13$ (mod 17) for k. From the example above, one solution is $k = 4$, but it is not the only solution. Since $3^{16} \equiv 1$ (mod 17)—as follows from Fermat's little theorem—it also follows that if n is an integer then $3^{4+16n} \equiv 3^4 \times (3^{16})^n \equiv 13 \times 1^n \equiv 13$ (mod 17). Hence the equation has infinitely many solutions of the form $4 + 16n$. Moreover, since 16 is the smallest positive integer m satisfying $3^m \equiv 1$ (mod 17), i.e. 16 is the order of 3 in $(Z_{17})^\times$, these are the only solutions. Equivalently, the set of all possible solutions can be expressed by the constraint that $k \equiv 4$ (mod 16).

Definition

In general, let G be any group, with its group operation denoted by multiplication. Let b and g be any elements of G. Then any integer k that solves $b^k = g$ is termed a discrete logarithm (or simply logarithm, in this context) of g to the base b. We write $k = \log_b g$. Depending on b and g, it is possible that no discrete logarithm exists, or that more than one discrete logarithm exists. Let H be the subgroup of G generated by b. Then H is a cyclic group, and integral $\log_b g$ exists for all g in H. If H is infinite, then $\log_b g$ is also unique, and the discrete logarithm amounts to a group isomorphism

$$\log_b : H \to \mathbf{Z}.$$

On the other hand, if H is finite of size n, then $\log_b g$ is unique only up to congruence modulo n, and the discrete logarithm amounts to a group isomorphism

$$\log_b : H \to \mathbf{Z}_n,$$

where Z_n denotes the ring of integers modulo n. The familiar base change formula for ordinary logarithms remains valid: If c is another generator of H, then

$$\log_c(g) = \log_c(b) \cdot \log_b(g).$$

Algorithms

The discrete logarithm problem is considered to be computationally intractable. That is, no efficient classical algorithm is known for computing discrete logarithms in general.

A general algorithm for computing $\log_b g$ is to raise b to higher and higher powers k until the desired g is found. This algorithm is sometimes called *trial multiplication*. It requires running time linear in the size of the group G and thus exponential in the number of digits in the size of the group. Therefore it is an exponential-time algorithm, practical only for small groups G.

More sophisticated algorithms exist, usually inspired by similar algorithms for integer factorization. These algorithms run faster than the naïve algorithm, some of them linear in the *square root* of the size of the group, and thus exponential in half the number of digits in the size of the group. However none of them run in polynomial time (in the number of digits in the size of the group).

- Baby-step giant-step

- Function field sieve

- Index calculus algorithm

- Number field sieve

- Pohlig–Hellman algorithm

- Pollard's rho algorithm for logarithms

- Pollard's kangaroo algorithm (aka Pollard's lambda algorithm)

There is an efficient quantum algorithm due to Peter Shor.

Efficient classical algorithms also exist in certain special cases. For example, in the group of the integers modulo p under addition, the power b^k becomes a product bk, and equality means congruence modulo p in the integers. The extended Euclidean algorithm finds k quickly.

Comparison with Integer Factorization

While computing discrete logarithms and factoring integers are distinct problems, they share some properties:

- both problems are difficult (no efficient algorithms are known for non-quantum computers),

- for both problems efficient algorithms on quantum computers are known,

- algorithms from one problem are often adapted to the other, and

- the difficulty of both problems has been used to construct various cryptographic systems.

Cryptography

There exist groups for which computing discrete logarithms is apparently difficult. In some cases (e.g. large prime order subgroups of groups $(Z_p)^{\times}$) there is not only no efficient algorithm known for the worst case, but the average-case complexity can be shown to be about as hard as the worst case using random self-reducibility.

At the same time, the inverse problem of discrete exponentiation is not difficult (it can be computed efficiently using exponentiation by squaring, for example). This asymmetry is analogous to the one between integer factorization and integer multiplication. Both asymmetries (and other possibly one-way functions) have been exploited in the construction of cryptographic systems.

Popular choices for the group G in discrete logarithm cryptography are the cyclic groups $(Z_p)^{\times}$ (e.g. ElGamal encryption, Diffie–Hellman key exchange, and the Digital Signature Algorithm) and cyclic subgroups of elliptic curves over finite fields.

While there is no publicly known algorithm for solving the discrete logarithm problem in general, the first three steps of the number field sieve algorithm only depend on the group G, not on the specific elements of G whose finite log is desired. By precomputing these three steps for a specific group, one need only carry out the last step, which is much less computationally expensive than the first three, to obtain a specific logarithm in that group.

It turns out that much Internet traffic uses one of a handful of groups that are of order 1024-bits or less, e.g. cyclic groups with order of the Oakley primes specified in RFC 2409. The Logjam attack used this vulnerability to compromise a variety of Internet services that allowed the use of groups whose order was a 512-bit prime number, so called export grade.

The authors of the Logjam attack estimate that the much more difficult precomputation needed to solve the discrete log problem for a 1024-bit prime would be within the budget of a large national intelligence agency such as the U.S. National Security Agency (NSA). The Logjam authors speculate that precomputation against widely reused 1024 DH primes is behind claims in leaked NSA documents that NSA is able to break much of current cryptography.

Theorem 1: If g is a generator of Z_n^{*} then the equation $g^x \equiv g^y \pmod{n}$ holds if and only if the equation $x \equiv y \pmod{\Phi(n)}$ holds

Proof : To prove the if part we assume $x \equiv y \pmod{\Phi(n)}$. Thus $x = y + k\Phi(n)$ for some integer k.

Therefore $g^x = g^{y+k\Phi(n)}$

$$= g^y \, (g^{\Phi(n)k}) \pmod{n}$$

$$= g^y \, (1)^k \pmod{n}$$

$$= g^y \pmod{n}$$

To prove the only if part we assume that $g^x \equiv g^y \pmod{n}$. The sequence of powers of y generates every element of $<g>$ and $|<g>| = \Phi(n)$. Thus the sequence of powers of g is periodic with period $\Phi(n)$. Therefore if $g^x \equiv g^y \pmod{n}$, then we must have $x \equiv y \pmod{\Phi(n)}$.

Discrete Logarithm: Let g be the generator of the group Z_n^{*}. Given an element $y = g^x \pmod{n}$ the discrete logarithm is defined as $dlog_{n,g}(y) = x$.

Let us consider and the group (Z_7^*, x_n). Clearly the group is cyclic since $n = 7$ is a prime number. We can see that 3 is a generator of the group. Thus discrete logarithm according to the previous definition is defined by the following table:

x	1	2	3	4	5	6
$dlog_{7,3}(x)$	0	2	1	4	5	1

Table

Given g, x and n it is easy to determine y. By the word easy we mean it is polynomial time computable. This clearly follows from the fact that we can perform modular exponentiation in polynomial time. But given g, y and n it is difficult to compute x. This problem is known as the discrete logarithm problem. Till to-date we are not aware of any polynomial time algorithm for this problem. Many cryptographic algorithms utilize the difficulty of solving the discrete logarithm problem.

Now we can clearly see that given n if we pre-compute the entire Table by computing sequentially the indices $g^0 \mod n$, $g^1 \mod n$,...so on and storing the corresponding exponent of g in the indexed array location. Once we are done with this preprocessing given an arbitrary x we can compute $dlog_{n,g}(x)$ in polynomial time. But there comes the trade off between time and memory .

Note: Discrete Logarithm Problem $\in$ NP. This follows from the fact that given a guess of x clearly the verification whether $y = g^x \pmod{n}$ can be carried out in polynomial time using modular exponentiation algorithm.

Properties of Logarithms:

$log_a 1 = 0$

$log_a a = 1$

$log_a xy = log_a x + log_a y$

$log_a x^n = n log_a x$

Properties of Discrete Logarithms:

$dlog_{n,g}(1) = 0 \qquad g^0 = 1 \pmod{n}$

$dlog_{n,g}(g) = 1 \qquad g^1 = g \pmod{n}$

$dlog_{n,g}(xy) = (dlog_{n,g}(x) + dlog_{n,g}(y)) \ (mod(\Phi(n)))$

[Proof is provided in the Explanation]

$dlog_{n,g} x^r = r \ dlog_{n,g}(x) \ (mod \ \Phi(n))$

[Using repeated application of the earlier property]

Explanation :

$x = g^{dlogn}n,g^{(x)}$

$y = g^{dlogn}n, g^{(y)}$

$(xy) \bmod n = g^{(dlog_{n,g}(x)+dlog_{n,g}(y))} \bmod n$

$xy = g^{dlogn}n, g^{x,y} (\bmod n)$

$g^{dlog}n, g^{(xy)} \equiv (g^{(dlog}n, g^{(x)+dlog}n, g^{(y)}) \bmod n$

Applying Theorem 1 we have:

$dlog_{n,g}(xy) = (dlog_{n,g}(x)+dlog_{n,g}(y)) \bmod(\Phi(n)))$

Index Calculus Algorithm

In computational number theory, the index calculus algorithm is a probabilisticalgorithm for computing discrete logarithms. Dedicated to the discrete logarithm in $(\mathbb{Z}/q\mathbb{Z})^*$ where q is a prime, index calculus lead to a family of algorithms adapted to finite fields and to some families of elliptic curves. The algorithm collects relations among the discrete logarithms of small primes, computes them by a linear algebra procedure and finally expresses the desired discrete logarithm with respect to the discrete logarithms of small primes.

Description

Roughly speaking, the discrete log problem asks us to find an x such that $g^x \equiv h \pmod{n}$, where g, h, and the modulus n are given.

The algorithm (described in detail below) applies to the group $(\mathbb{Z}/q\mathbb{Z})^*$ where q is prime. It requires a *factor base* as input. This *factor base* is usually chosen to be the number −1 and the first r primes starting with 2. From the point of view of efficiency, we want this factor base to be small, but in order to solve the discrete log for a large group we require the *factor base* to be (relatively) large. In practical implementations of the algorithm, those conflicting objectives are compromised one way or another.

The algorithm is performed in three stages. The first two stages depend only on the generator g and prime modulus q, and find the discrete logarithms of a *factor base* of r small primes. The third stage finds the discrete log of the desired number h in terms of the discrete logs of the factor base.

The first stage consists of searching for a set of $r$linearly independent *relations* between the factor base and power of the generator$g$. Each relation contributes one equation to a system of linear equations in r unknowns, namely the discrete logarithms of the r primes in the factor base. This stage is embarrassingly parallel and easy to divide among many computers.

The second stage solves the system of linear equations to compute the discrete logs of the factor base. Although a minor computation compared to the other stages, a system of hundreds of thousands or millions of equations is a significant computation requiring large amounts of memory, and it is *not* embarrassingly parallel, so a supercomputer is typically used.

The third stage searches for a power s of the generator g which, when multiplied by the argument h, may be factored in terms of the factor base $g^s h = (-1)^{f_0} 2^{f_1} 3^{f_2} \cdots p_r^{f_r}$.

Finally, in an operation too simple to really be called a fourth stage, the results of the second and third stages can be rearranged by simple algebraic manipulation to work out the desired discrete logarithm $x = f_0 \log_g(-1) + f_1 \log_g 2 + f_2 \log_g 3 + \cdots + f_r \log_g p_r - s$.

The first and third stages are both embarrassingly parallel, and in fact the third stage does not depend on the results of the first two stages, so it may be done in parallel with them.

The choice of the factor base size r is critical, and the details are too intricate to explain here. The larger the factor base, the easier it is to find relations in stage 1, and the easier it is to complete stage 3, but the more relations you need before you can proceed to stage 2, and the more difficult stage 2 is. The relative availability of computers suitable for the different types of computation required for stages 1 and 2 is also important.

Applications in Other Groups

It is noteworthy that the lack of the notion of *prime elements* in the group of points on elliptic curves, makes it impossible to find an efficient *factor base* to run index calculus method as presented here in these groups. Therefore this algorithm is incapable of solving discrete logarithms efficiently in elliptic curve groups. However: For special kinds of curves (so called supersingular elliptic curves) there are specialized algorithms for solving the problem faster than with generic methods. While the use of these special curves can easily be avoided, in 2009 it has been proven that for certain fields the discrete logarithm problem in the group of points on *general* elliptic curves over these fields can be solved faster than with generic methods. The algorithms are indeed adaptations of the index calculus method.

The Algorithm

Input: Discrete logarithm generator g, modulus q and argument h. Factor base $\{-1,2,3,5,7,11,\ldots,p_r\}$, of length $r+1$.

Output: x such that $g^x \equiv h \pmod{q}$.

- relations $\leftarrow$ empty_list

- for k = 1, 2, ...

    o   Using an integer factorization algorithm optimized for smooth numbers, try to factor $g^k \mod q$ (Euclidean residue) using the factor base, i.e. find e_i's such that $g^k \mod q = (-1)^{e_0} 2^{e_1} 3^{e_2} \cdots p_r^{e_r}$

    o   Each time a factorization is found:

        ▪   Store k and the computed e_i's as a vector $(e_0, e_1, e_2, \ldots, e_r, k)$ (this is a called a relation)

        ▪   If this relation is linearly independent to the other relations:

            ◇   Add it to the list of relations

        ◇   If there are at least $r+1$ relations, exit loop

- Form a matrix whose rows are the relations

- Obtain the reduced echelon form of the matrix

    o   The first element in the last column is the discrete log of -1 and the second element is the discrete log of 2 and so on

- for $s = 0, 1, 2, \ldots$

    o   Try to factor $g^s h \mod q = (-1)^{f_0} 2^{f_1} 3^{f_2} \cdots p_r^{f_r}$ over the factor base

    o   When a factorization is found:

        ▪   Output $x = f_0 \log_g(-1) + f_1 \log_g 2 + \cdots + f_r \log_g p_r - s$.

Complexity

Assuming an optimal selection of the factor base, the expected running time (using L-notation) of the index-calculus algorithm can be stated as $L_n[1/2, \sqrt{2} + o(1)]$.

History

The first to discover the idea was Kraitchik in 1922. After DLP became important in 1976 with the creation of the Diffie-Hellman cryptosystem, R. Merkle from Stanford University rediscovered the idea in 1977. Finally, Adleman optimized the algorithm and presented it in the form we know it today.

The Index Calculus family

Index Calculus inspired a large family of algorithms. In finite fields $\mathbb{F}_q$ with $q = p^n$ for some prime p, the state-of-art algorithms are the Number Field Sieve for Discrete Logarithms, $L_q\left[1/3, \sqrt[3]{64/9}\right]$ when p is large compared to q, the function field sieve, $L_q\left[1/3, \sqrt[3]{32/9}\right]$, and Joux, $L_q[1/4 + \epsilon, c]$ for $c > 0$, when p is small compared to q and the Number Field Sieve in High Degree, $L_q[1/3, c]$ for $c > 0$ when p is middle-sided. Discrete logarithm in some families of elliptic curves can be solved in time $L_q[1/3,c]$ for $c > 0$, but the general case remains exponential.

Baby-step Giant-step

In group theory, a branch of mathematics, the baby-step giant-step is a meet-in-the-middle algorithm for computing the discrete logarithm. The discrete log problem is of fundamental importance to the area of public key cryptography. Many of the most commonly used cryptography systems are based on the assumption that the discrete log is extremely difficult to compute; the more difficult it is, the more security it provides a data transfer. One way to increase the difficulty of the discrete log problem is to base the cryptosystem on a larger group.

Theory

The algorithm is based on a space-time tradeoff. It is a fairly simple modification of trial multiplication, the naive method of finding discrete logarithms.

Given a cyclic group G of order n, a generator α of the group and a group element β, the problem is to find an integer x such that

$$\alpha^x = \beta.$$

The baby-step giant-step algorithm is based on rewriting x as $x = im + j$, with $m = \lceil \sqrt{n} \rceil$ and $0 \le i < m$ and $0 \le j < m$. Therefore, we have:

$$\beta(\alpha^{-m})^i = \alpha^j.$$

The algorithm precomputes α^j for several values of j. Then it fixes an m and tries values of i in the left-hand side of the congruence above, in the manner of trial multiplication. It tests to see if the congruence is satisfied for any value of j, using the precomputed values of α^j.

The Algorithm

Input: A cyclic group G of order n, having a generator α and an element β.

Output: A value x satisfying $\alpha^x = \beta$.

1. $m \leftarrow$ Ceiling($\sqrt{n}$)

2.   For all j where $0 \le j < m$:

     1.   Compute α^j and store the pair (j, α^j) in a table.

3.   Compute α^{-m}.

4. $\gamma \leftarrow \beta$. (set $\gamma = \beta$)

5.   For all i where $0 \le i < m$:

     1.   Check to see if γ is the second component (α^j) of any pair in the table.

     2.   If so, return $im + j$.

     3.   If not, $\gamma \leftarrow \gamma \cdot \alpha^{-m}$.

C Algorithm with the GNU MP Lib

Contrary to the recommendation below to use a hash table, this implementation uses binary search in a sorted array as table; this incurs an extra $O(\log m)$ factor in the lookup complexity. Indeed, since the bit-size of the group elements involved is also $O(\log m)$, this is arguably enough to make the table lookups dominate the total time complexity.

```
void baby_step_giant_step (mpz_t g, mpz_t h, mpz_t p, mpz_t n, mpz_t x ){
    unsigned long int i;
    long int j = 0;
    mpz_t N;
```

```
mpz_t* gr ; /* list g^r */
unsigned long int* indices; /* indices[ i ] = k <=> gr[ i ] = g^k */
mpz_t hgNq ; /* hg^(Nq) */
mpz_t inv ; /* inverse of g^(N) */
mpz_init (N) ;
mpz_sqrt (N, n ) ;
mpz_add ui (N, N, 1 ) ;


gr = malloc (mpz_get_ui (N) * sizeof (mpz_t) ) ;
indices = malloc ( mpz_get_ui (N) * sizeof (long int ) ) ;
mpz_init_set_ui (gr[ 0 ], 1);


/* find the sequence {g^r} r = 1 ,.. ,N (Baby step ) */
for ( i = 1 ; i <= mpz_get_ui (N) ; i++) {
   indices[i - 1] = i - 1 ;
   mpz_init (gr[ i ]) ;
   mpz_mul (gr[ i ], gr[ i - 1 ], g ); /* multiply gr[i - 1] for g */
   mpz_mod (gr[ i ], gr[ i ], p );
}
/* sort the values (k , g^k) with respect to g^k */
qsort ( gr, indices, mpz_get_ui (N), mpz_cmp ) ;
/* compute g^(-Nq)    (Giant step) */
mpz_init_set (inv, g);
mpz_powm (inv, inv, N, p);  /* inv <- inv ^ N (mod p)   */
mpz_invert (inv, p, inv) ;


mpz_init_set (hgNq, h);


/* find the elements in the two sequences */
for ( i = 0 ; i <= mpz_get_ui (N) ; i++){
   /* find hgNq in the sequence gr ) */
   j = bsearch (gr, hgNq, 0, mpz_get_ui (N), mpz_cmp ) ;
   if ( j >= 0 ){
```

```
        mpz_mul_ui (N, N, i);

        mpz_add_ui (N, N, indices [j]);

        mpz_set (x, N) ;

        break;

    }

    /* if j < 0, find the next value of g^(Nq) */

    mpz_mul (hgNq, hgNq, inv);

    mpz_mod (hgNq, hgNq, p);

  }

}
```

In Practice

The best way to speed up the baby-step giant-step algorithm is to use an efficient table lookup scheme. The best in this case is a hash table. The hashing is done on the second component, and to perform the check in step 1 of the main loop, γ is hashed and the resulting memory address checked. Since hash tables can retrieve and add elements in $O(1)$ time (constant time), this does not slow down the overall baby-step giant-step algorithm.

The running time of the algorithm and the space complexity is $O(\sqrt{n})$, much better than the $O(n)$ running time of the naive brute force calculation.

The Baby-step giant-step algorithm is often used to solve for the shared key in the Diffie Hellman key exchange, when the modulus is a prime number. If the modulus is not prime, the Pohlig–Hellman algorithm has a smaller algorithmic complexity, and solves the same problem.

References

- Adleman, Leonard M.; Huang, Ming-Deh (1992). Primality testing and Abelian varieties over finite field. Lecture notes in mathematics. 1512. Springer-Verlag. ISBN 3-540-55308-8

- Bernstein, Daniel J.; Birkner, Peter; Lange, Tanja; Peters, Christiane (2013). "ECM using Edwards curves". Mathematics of Computation. 82 (282): 1139–1179. MR 3008853. doi:10.1090/S0025-5718-2012-02633-0

- Ireland, Kenneth; Rosen, Michael (1990). A Classical Introduction to Modern Number Theory (Second edition). New York: Springer. ISBN 0-387-97329-X

- Gary L. Miller (1976). "Riemann's Hypothesis and Tests for Primality". Journal of Computer and System Sciences. 13 (3): 300–317. doi:10.1016/S0022-0000(76)80043-8

- Thomas H. Cormen, Charles E. Leiserson, Ronald L. Rivest, Clifford Stein (2001). "Section 31.8: Primality testing". Introduction to Algorithms (Second ed.). MIT Press; McGraw-Hill. p. 889–890. ISBN 0-262-03293-7

- Brent, Richard P. (1999). "Factorization of the tenth Fermat number". Mathematics of Computation. 68 (225): 429–451. MR 1489968. doi:10.1090/S0025-5718-99-00992-8

3

Basics of Cryptography

Cryptography helps in securing communication from third parties. Topics like data integrity, authentication and data confidentiality are central in cryptography. Public-key cryptography is especially used in the creation of cryptosystems. The topics discussed in the section are of great importance to broaden the existing knowledge on public key cryptography.

Cryptography

Cryptography or cryptology is the practice and study of techniques for secure communication in the presence of third parties called adversaries. More generally, cryptography is about constructing and analyzing protocols that prevent third parties or the public from reading private messages; various aspects in information security such as data confidentiality, data integrity, authentication, and non-repudiation are central to modern cryptography. Modern cryptography exists at the intersection of the disciplines of mathematics, computer science, and electrical engineering. Applications of cryptography include military communications, electronic commerce, ATM cards, and computer passwords.

German Lorenz cipher machine, used in World War II to encrypt very-high-level general staff messages

Cryptography prior to the modern age was effectively synonymous with *encryption*, the conversion of information from a readable state to apparent nonsense. The originator of an encrypted message (Alice) shared the decoding technique needed to recover the original information only with intended recipients (Bob), thereby precluding unwanted persons (Eve) from doing the same. The cryptography literature often uses Alice ("A") for the sender, Bob ("B") for the intended recipient, and Eve ("eavesdropper") for the adversary. Since the development of rotor cipher machines in World War I and the advent of computers in World War II, the methods used to carry out cryptology have become increasingly complex and its application more widespread.

Modern cryptography is heavily based on mathematical theory and computer science practice; cryptographic algorithms are designed around computational hardness assumptions, making such algorithms hard to break in practice by any adversary. It is theoretically possible to break such a system, but it is infeasible to do so by any known practical means. These schemes are therefore termed computationally secure; theoretical advances, e.g., improvements in integer factorization algorithms, and faster computing technology require these solutions to be continually adapted. There exist information-theoretically secure schemes that provably cannot be broken even with unlimited computing power—an example is the one-time pad—but these schemes are more difficult to implement than the best theoretically breakable but computationally secure mechanisms.

The growth of cryptographic technology has raised a number of legal issues in the information age. Cryptography's potential for use as a tool for espionage and sedition has led many governments to classify it as a weapon and to limit or even prohibit its use and export. In some jurisdictions where the use of cryptography is legal, laws permit investigators to compel the disclosure of encryption keys for documents relevant to an investigation. Cryptography also plays a major role in digital rights management and copyright infringement of digital media.

Terminology

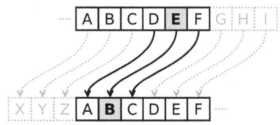

Alphabet shift ciphers are believed to have been used by Julius Caesar over 2,000 years ago. This is an example with k=3. In other words, the letters in the alphabet are shifted three in one direction to encrypt and three in the other direction to decrypt.

Until modern times, cryptography referred almost exclusively to *encryption*, which is the process of converting ordinary information (called plaintext) into unintelligible text (called ciphertext). Decryption is the reverse, in other words, moving from the unintelligible ciphertext back to plaintext. A *cipher* (or *cypher*) is a pair of algorithms that create the encryption and the reversing decryption. The detailed operation of a cipher is controlled both by the algorithm and in each instance by a "key". The key is a secret (ideally known only to the communicants), usually a short string of characters, which is needed to decrypt the ciphertext. Formally, a "cryptosystem" is the ordered list of elements of finite possible plaintexts, finite possible cyphertexts, finite possible keys, and the encryption and decryption algorithms which correspond to each key. Keys are important both formally and in actual practice, as ciphers without variable keys can be trivially broken with only the knowledge of the cipher used and are therefore useless (or even counter-productive) for most purposes. Historically, ciphers were often used directly for encryption or decryption without additional procedures such as authentication or integrity checks. There are two kinds of cryptosystems: symmetric and asymmetric. In symmetric systems the same key (the secret key) is used to encrypt and decrypt a message. Data manipulation in symmetric systems is faster than asymmetric systems as they generally use shorter key lengths. Asymmetric systems use a public key to encrypt a message and a private key to decrypt it. Use of asymmetric systems enhances the security of communication. Examples of asymmetric systems include RSA (Rivest-Shamir-Adleman), and ECC

(Elliptic Curve Cryptography). Symmetric models include the commonly used AES (Advanced Encryption Standard) which replaced the older DES (Data Encryption Standard).

In colloquial use, the term "code" is often used to mean any method of encryption or concealment of meaning. However, in cryptography, *code* has a more specific meaning. It means the replacement of a unit of plaintext (i.e., a meaningful word or phrase) with a code word (for example, "wallaby" replaces "attack at dawn").

Cryptanalysis is the term used for the study of methods for obtaining the meaning of encrypted information without access to the key normally required to do so; i.e., it is the study of how to crack encryption algorithms or their implementations.

Some use the terms *cryptography* and *cryptology* interchangeably in English, while others (including US military practice generally) use *cryptography* to refer specifically to the use and practice of cryptographic techniques and *cryptology* to refer to the combined study of cryptography and cryptanalysis. English is more flexible than several other languages in which *cryptology* (done by cryptologists) is always used in the second sense above. RFC 2828 advises that steganography is sometimes included in cryptology.

The study of characteristics of languages that have some application in cryptography or cryptology (e.g. frequency data, letter combinations, universal patterns, etc.) is called cryptolinguistics.

History of Cryptography and Cryptanalysis

Before the modern era, cryptography focused on message confidentiality (i.e., encryption)—conversion of messages from a comprehensible form into an incomprehensible one and back again at the other end, rendering it unreadable by interceptors or eavesdroppers without secret knowledge (namely the key needed for decryption of that message). Encryption attempted to ensure secrecy in communications, such as those of spies, military leaders, and diplomats. In recent decades, the field has expanded beyond confidentiality concerns to include techniques for message integrity checking, sender/receiver identity authentication, digital signatures, interactive proofs and secure computation, among others.

Classic Cryptography

Reconstructed ancient Greek *scytale*, an early cipher device

The main classical cipher types are transposition ciphers, which rearrange the order of letters in a message (e.g., 'hello world' becomes 'ehlol owrdl' in a trivially simple rearrangement scheme), and substitution ciphers, which systematically replace letters or groups of letters with other letters or groups of letters (e.g., 'fly at once' becomes 'gmz bu podf' by replacing each letter with the one following it in the Latin alphabet). Simple versions of either have never offered much confidentiality from enterprising opponents. An early substitution cipher was the Caesar cipher, in which each letter in the plaintext was replaced by a letter some fixed number of positions further down the alphabet. Suetonius reports that Julius Caesar used it with a shift of three to communicate with his generals. Atbash is an example of an early Hebrew cipher. The earliest known use of cryptography is some carved ciphertext on stone in Egypt (ca 1900 BCE), but this may have been done for the amusement of literate observers rather than as a way of concealing information.

The Greeks of Classical times are said to have known of ciphers (e.g., the scytale transposition cipher claimed to have been used by the Spartan military). Steganography (i.e., hiding even the existence of a message so as to keep it confidential) was also first developed in ancient times. An early example, from Herodotus, was a message tattooed on a slave's shaved head and concealed under the regrown hair. More modern examples of steganography include the use of invisible ink, microdots, and digital watermarks to conceal information.

In India, the 2000-year-old Kamasutra of Vātsyāyana speaks of two different kinds of ciphers called Kautiliyam and Mulavediya. In the Kautiliyam, the cipher letter substitutions are based on phonetic relations, such as vowels becoming consonants. In the Mulavediya, the cipher alphabet consists of pairing letters and using the reciprocal ones.

In Sassanid Persia, there were two secret scripts, according to the Muslim author Ibn al-Nadim: the *šāh-dabīrīya* (literally "King's script") which was used for official correspondence, and the *rāz-saharīya* which was used to communicate secret messages with other countries.

First page of a book by Al-Kindi which discusses encryption of messages

Ciphertexts produced by a classical cipher (and some modern ciphers) will reveal statistical information about the plaintext, and that information can often be used to break the cipher. After the discovery of frequency analysis, perhaps by the Arab mathematician and polymath Al-Kindi (also known as *Alkindus*) in the 9th century, nearly all such ciphers could be broken by an informed attacker. Such classical ciphers still enjoy popularity today, though mostly as puzzles. Al-Kindi wrote a book on cryptography entitled *Risalah fi Istikhraj al-Mu'amma* (*Manuscript for the De-*

ciphering Cryptographic Messages), which described the first known use of frequency analysis cryptanalysis techniques.

16th-century book-shaped French cipher machine, with arms of Henri II of France

Enciphered letter from Gabriel de Luetz d'Aramon, French Ambassador to the Ottoman Empire, after 1546, with partial decipherment

Language letter frequencies may offer little help for some extended historical encryption techniques such as homophonic cipher that tend to flatten the frequency distribution. For those ciphers, language letter group (or n-gram) frequencies may provide an attack.

Essentially all ciphers remained vulnerable to cryptanalysis using the frequency analysis technique until the development of the polyalphabetic cipher, most clearly by Leon Battista Alberti around the year 1467, though there is some indication that it was already known to Al-Kindi. Alberti's innovation was to use different ciphers (i.e., substitution alphabets) for various parts of a message (perhaps for each successive plaintext letter at the limit). He also invented what was probably the first automatic cipher device, a wheel which implemented a partial realization of his invention. In the polyalphabetic Vigenère cipher, encryption uses a *key word*, which controls letter substitution depending on which letter of the key word is used. In the mid-19th century Charles Babbage showed that the Vigenère cipher was vulnerable to Kasiski examination, but this was first published about ten years later by Friedrich Kasiski.

Although frequency analysis can be a powerful and general technique against many ciphers, encryption has still often been effective in practice, as many a would-be cryptanalyst was unaware of the technique. Breaking a message without using frequency analysis essentially required knowledge of the cipher used and perhaps of the key involved, thus making espionage, bribery, burglary, defection, etc., more attractive approaches to the cryptanalytically uninformed. It was finally explicitly recognized in the 19th century that secrecy of a cipher's algorithm is not a sensible nor practical safeguard of message security; in fact, it was further realized that any adequate cryptographic scheme (including ciphers) should remain secure even if the adversary fully understands the cipher algorithm itself. Security of the key used should alone be sufficient for a good cipher to maintain confidentiality under an attack. This fundamental principle was first explicitly stated in 1883 by Auguste Kerckhoffs and is generally called Kerckhoffs's Principle; alternatively and more bluntly, it was restated by Claude Shannon, the inventor of information theory and the fundamentals of theoretical cryptography, as *Shannon's Maxim*—'the enemy knows the system'.

Different physical devices and aids have been used to assist with ciphers. One of the earliest may have been the scytale of ancient Greece, a rod supposedly used by the Spartans as an aid for a transposition cipher. In medieval times, other aids were invented such as the cipher grille, which was also used for a kind of steganography. With the invention of polyalphabetic ciphers came more sophisticated aids such as Alberti's own cipher disk, Johannes Trithemius' tabula recta scheme, and Thomas Jefferson's wheel cypher (not publicly known, and reinvented independently by Bazeries around 1900). Many mechanical encryption/decryption devices were invented early in the 20th century, and several patented, among them rotor machines—famously including the Enigma machine used by the German government and military from the late 1920s and during World War II. The ciphers implemented by better quality examples of these machine designs brought about a substantial increase in cryptanalytic difficulty after WWI.

Computer Era

Cryptanalysis of the new mechanical devices proved to be both difficult and laborious. In the United Kingdom, cryptanalytic efforts at Bletchley Park during WWII spurred the development of more efficient means for carrying out repetitious tasks. This culminated in the development of the Colossus, the world's first fully electronic, digital, programmable computer, which assisted in the decryption of ciphers generated by the German Army's Lorenz SZ40/42 machine.

Just as the development of digital computers and electronics helped in cryptanalysis, it made possible much more complex ciphers. Furthermore, computers allowed for the encryption of any kind of data representable in any binary format, unlike classical ciphers which only encrypted written language texts; this was new and significant. Computer use has thus supplanted linguistic cryptography, both for cipher design and cryptanalysis. Many computer ciphers can be characterized by their operation on binary bit sequences (sometimes in groups or blocks), unlike classical and mechanical schemes, which generally manipulate traditional characters (i.e., letters and digits) directly. However, computers have also assisted cryptanalysis, which has compensated to some extent for increased cipher complexity. Nonetheless, good modern ciphers have stayed ahead of cryptanalysis; it is typically the case that use of a quality cipher is very efficient (i.e., fast and requiring few resources, such as memory or CPU capability), while breaking it requires an effort many orders of magnitude larger, and vastly larger than that required for any classical cipher, making cryptanalysis so inefficient and impractical as to be effectively impossible.

Extensive open academic research into cryptography is relatively recent; it began only in the mid-1970s. In recent times, IBM personnel designed the algorithm that became the Federal (i.e., US) Data Encryption Standard; Whitfield Diffie and Martin Hellman published their key agreement algorithm; and the RSA algorithm was published in Martin Gardner's *Scientific American* column. Since then, cryptography has become a widely used tool in communications, computer networks, and computer security generally. Some modern cryptographic techniques can only keep their keys secret if certain mathematical problems are intractable, such as the integer factorization or the discrete logarithm problems, so there are deep connections with abstract mathematics. There are very few cryptosystems that are proven to be unconditionally secure. The one-time pad is one. There are a few important ones that are proven secure under certain unproven assumptions. For example, the infeasibility of factoring extremely large integers is the basis for believing that RSA is secure, and some other systems, but even there, the proof is usually lost due to practical considerations. There are systems similar to RSA, such as one by Michael O. Rabin that is provably secure provided factoring n = pq is impossible, but the more practical system RSA has never been proved secure in this sense. The discrete logarithm problem is the basis for believing some other cryptosystems are secure, and again, there are related, less practical systems that are provably secure relative to the discrete log problem.

As well as being aware of cryptographic history, cryptographic algorithm and system designers must also sensibly consider probable future developments while working on their designs. For instance, continuous improvements in computer processing power have increased the scope of brute-force attacks, so when specifying key lengths, the required key lengths are similarly advancing. The potential effects of quantum computing are already being considered by some cryptographic system designers developing post-quantum cryptography; the announced imminence of small implementations of these machines may be making the need for this preemptive caution rather more than merely speculative.

Essentially, prior to the early 20th century, cryptography was chiefly concerned with linguistic and lexicographic patterns. Since then the emphasis has shifted, and cryptography now makes extensive use of mathematics, including aspects of information theory, computational complexity, statistics, combinatorics, abstract algebra, number theory, and finite mathematics generally. Cryptography is also a branch of engineering, but an unusual one since it deals with active, intelligent, and malevolent opposition other kinds of engineering (e.g., civil or chemical engineering) need deal only with neutral natural forces. There is also active research examining the relationship between cryptographic problems and quantum physics.

Modern Cryptography

The modern field of cryptography can be divided into several areas of study. The chief ones are discussed here.

Symmetric-key Cryptography

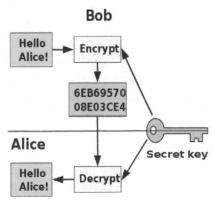

Symmetric-key cryptography, where a single key is used for encryption and decryption

Symmetric-key cryptography refers to encryption methods in which both the sender and receiver share the same key (or, less commonly, in which their keys are different, but related in an easily computable way). This was the only kind of encryption publicly known until June 1976.

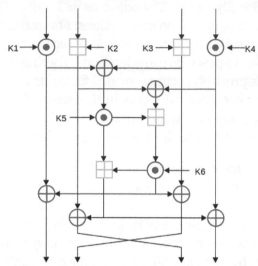

One round (out of 8.5) of the IDEA cipher, used in some versions of PGP for
high-speed encryption of, for instance, e-mail

Symmetric key ciphers are implemented as either block ciphers or stream ciphers. A block cipher enciphers input in blocks of plaintext as opposed to individual characters, the input form used by a stream cipher.

The Data Encryption Standard (DES) and the Advanced Encryption Standard (AES) are block cipher designs that have been designated cryptography standards by the US government (though DES's designation was finally withdrawn after the AES was adopted). Despite its deprecation as an official standard, DES (especially its still-approved and much more secure triple-DES variant) remains quite popular; it is used across a wide range of applications, from ATM encryption to e-mail privacy and secure remote access. Many other block ciphers have been designed and released, with considerable variation in quality. Many have been thoroughly broken, such as FEAL.

Stream ciphers, in contrast to the 'block' type, create an arbitrarily long stream of key material, which is combined with the plaintext bit-by-bit or character-by-character, somewhat like the one-time pad. In a stream cipher, the output stream is created based on a hidden internal state that changes as the cipher operates. That internal state is initially set up using the secret key material. RC4 is a widely used stream cipher. Block ciphers can be used as stream ciphers.

Cryptographic hash functions are a third type of cryptographic algorithm. They take a message of any length as input, and output a short, fixed length hash, which can be used in (for example) a digital signature. For good hash functions, an attacker cannot find two messages that produce the same hash. MD4 is a long-used hash function that is now broken; MD5, a strengthened variant of MD4, is also widely used but broken in practice. The US National Security Agency developed the Secure Hash Algorithm series of MD5-like hash functions: SHA-0 was a flawed algorithm that the agency withdrew; SHA-1 is widely deployed and more secure than MD5, but cryptanalysts have identified attacks against it; the SHA-2 family improves on SHA-1, but it isn't yet widely deployed; and the US standards authority thought it "prudent" from a security perspective to develop a new standard to "significantly improve the robustness of NIST's overall hash algorithm toolkit." Thus, a hash function design competition was meant to select a new U.S. national standard, to be called SHA-3, by 2012. The competition ended on October 2, 2012 when the NIST announced that Keccak would be the new SHA-3 hash algorithm. Unlike block and stream ciphers that are invertible, cryptographic hash functions produce a hashed output that cannot be used to retrieve the original input data. Cryptographic hash functions are used to verify the authenticity of data retrieved from an untrusted source or to add a layer of security.

Message authentication codes (MACs) are much like cryptographic hash functions, except that a secret key can be used to authenticate the hash value upon receipt; this additional complication blocks an attack scheme against bare digest algorithms, and so has been thought worth the effort.

Public-key Cryptography

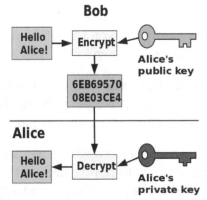

Public-key cryptography, where different keys are used for encryption and decryption

Symmetric-key cryptosystems use the same key for encryption and decryption of a message, though a message or group of messages may have a different key than others. A significant disadvantage of symmetric ciphers is the key management necessary to use them securely. Each distinct pair of communicating parties must, ideally, share a different key, and perhaps each ciphertext exchanged as well. The number of keys required increases as the square of the number of network members, which very quickly requires complex key management schemes to keep them all consistent and secret. The difficulty of securely establishing a secret key between two communicating parties, when a secure channel does not already exist between them, also presents a chicken-and-egg problem which is a considerable practical obstacle for cryptography users in the real world.

Whitfield Diffie and Martin Hellman, authors of the first published paper on public-key cryptography

In a groundbreaking 1976 paper, Whitfield Diffie and Martin Hellman proposed the notion of *public-key* (also, more generally, called *asymmetric key*) cryptography in which two different but mathematically related keys are used—a *public* key and a *private* key. A public key system is so constructed that calculation of one key (the 'private key') is computationally infeasible from the other (the 'public key'), even though they are necessarily related. Instead, both keys are generated secretly, as an interrelated pair. The historian David Kahn described public-key cryptography as "the most revolutionary new concept in the field since polyalphabetic substitution emerged in the Renaissance".

In public-key cryptosystems, the public key may be freely distributed, while its paired private key must remain secret. In a public-key encryption system, the *public key* is used for encryption, while the *private* or *secret key* is used for decryption. While Diffie and Hellman could not find such a system, they showed that public-key cryptography was indeed possible by presenting the Diffie–Hellman key exchange protocol, a solution that is now widely used in secure communications to allow two parties to secretly agree on a shared encryption key.

Diffie and Hellman's publication sparked widespread academic efforts in finding a practical public-key encryption system. This race was finally won in 1978 by Ronald Rivest, Adi Shamir, and Len Adleman, whose solution has since become known as the RSA algorithm.

The Diffie–Hellman and RSA algorithms, in addition to being the first publicly known examples of high quality public-key algorithms, have been among the most widely used. Others include the Cramer–Shoup cryptosystem, ElGamal encryption, and various elliptic curve techniques.

To much surprise, a document published in 1997 by the Government Communications Headquarters (GCHQ), a British intelligence organization, revealed that cryptographers at GCHQ had anticipated several academic developments. Reportedly, around 1970, James H. Ellis had conceived the principles of asymmetric key cryptography. In 1973, Clifford Cocks invented a solution that essentially resembles the RSA algorithm. And in 1974, Malcolm J. Williamson is claimed to have developed the Diffie–Hellman key exchange.

Public-key cryptography can also be used for implementing digital signature schemes. A digital signature is reminiscent of an ordinary signature; they both have the characteristic of being easy for a user to produce, but difficult for anyone else to forge. Digital signatures can also be permanently tied to the content of the message being signed; they cannot then be 'moved' from one document to another, for any attempt will be detectable. In digital signature schemes, there are two algorithms: one for *signing*, in which a secret key is used to process the message (or a hash of the message, or both), and one for *verification*, in which the matching public key is used with the message to check the validity of the signature. RSA and DSA are two of the most popular digital signature schemes. Digital signatures are central to the operation of public key infrastructures and many network security schemes (e.g., SSL/TLS, many VPNs, etc.).

Public-key algorithms are most often based on the computational complexity of "hard" problems, often from number theory. For example, the hardness of RSA is related to the integer factorization problem, while Diffie–Hellman and DSA are related to the discrete logarithm problem. More recently, elliptic curve cryptography has developed, a system in which security is based on number theoretic problems involving elliptic curves. Because of the difficulty of the underlying problems, most public-key algorithms involve operations such as modular multiplication and exponentiation, which are much more computationally expensive than the techniques used in most block ciphers, especially with typical key sizes. As a result, public-key cryptosystems are commonly hybrid cryptosystems, in which a fast high-quality symmetric-key encryption algorithm is used for the message itself, while the relevant symmetric key is sent with the message, but encrypted using a public-key algorithm. Similarly, hybrid signature schemes are often used, in which a cryptographic hash function is computed, and only the resulting hash is digitally signed.

Cryptanalysis

Variants of the Enigma machine, used by Germany's military and civil authorities from the late 1920s through World War II, implemented a complex electro-mechanical polyalphabetic cipher. Breaking and reading of the Enigma cipher at Poland's Cipher Bureau, for 7 years before the war, and subsequent decryption at Bletchley Park, was important to Allied victory.

The goal of cryptanalysis is to find some weakness or insecurity in a cryptographic scheme, thus permitting its subversion or evasion.

It is a common misconception that every encryption method can be broken. In connection with his WWII work at Bell Labs, Claude Shannon proved that the one-time pad cipher is unbreakable, provided the key material is truly random, never reused, kept secret from all possible attackers, and of equal or greater length than the message. Most ciphers, apart from the one-time pad, can be broken with enough computational effort by brute force attack, but the amount of effort needed may be exponentially dependent on the key size, as compared to the effort needed to make use of the cipher. In such cases, effective security could be achieved if it is proven that the effort required (i.e., "work factor", in Shannon's terms) is beyond the ability of any adversary. This means it must be shown that no efficient method (as opposed to the time-consuming brute force method) can be found to break the cipher. Since no such proof has been found to date, the one-time-pad remains the only theoretically unbreakable cipher.

There are a wide variety of cryptanalytic attacks, and they can be classified in any of several ways. A common distinction turns on what Eve (an attacker) knows and what capabilities are available. In a ciphertext-only attack, Eve has access only to the ciphertext (good modern cryptosystems are usually effectively immune to ciphertext-only attacks). In a known-plaintext attack, Eve has access to a ciphertext and its corresponding plaintext (or to many such pairs). In a chosen-plaintext attack, Eve may choose a plaintext and learn its corresponding ciphertext (perhaps many times); an example is gardening, used by the British during WWII. In a chosen-ciphertext attack, Eve may be able to *choose* ciphertexts and learn their corresponding plaintexts. Finally in a man-in-the-middle attack Eve gets in between Alice (the sender) and Bob (the recipient), accesses and modifies the traffic and then forwards it to the recipient. Also important, often overwhelmingly so, are mistakes.

Poznań monument (*center*) to Polish cryptologists whose breaking of Germany's Enigma machine ciphers, beginning in 1932, altered the course of World War II

Cryptanalysis of symmetric-key ciphers typically involves looking for attacks against the block ciphers or stream ciphers that are more efficient than any attack that could be against a perfect cipher. For example, a simple brute force attack against DES requires one known plaintext and 2^{55} decryptions, trying approximately half of the possible keys, to reach a point at which chances are better than even that the key sought will have been found. But this may not be enough assurance; a linear cryptanalysis attack against DES requires 2^{43} known plaintexts and approximately 2^{43} DES operations. This is a considerable improvement on brute force attacks.

Public-key algorithms are based on the computational difficulty of various problems. The most famous of these is integer factorization (e.g., the RSA algorithm is based on a problem related to integer factoring), but the discrete logarithm problem is also important. Much public-key cryptanalysis concerns numerical algorithms for solving these computational problems, or some of them, efficiently (i.e., in a practical time). For instance, the best known algorithms for solving the elliptic curve-based version of discrete logarithm are much more time-consuming than the best known algorithms for factoring, at least for problems of more or less equivalent size. Thus, other things being equal, to achieve an equivalent strength of attack resistance, factoring-based encryption techniques must use larger keys than elliptic curve techniques. For this reason, public-key cryptosystems based on elliptic curves have become popular since their invention in the mid-1990s.

While pure cryptanalysis uses weaknesses in the algorithms themselves, other attacks on cryptosystems are based on actual use of the algorithms in real devices, and are called *side-channel attacks*. If a cryptanalyst has access to, for example, the amount of time the device took to encrypt a number of plaintexts or report an error in a password or PIN character, he may be able to use a timing attack to break a cipher that is otherwise resistant to analysis. An attacker might also study the pattern and length of messages to derive valuable information; this is known as traffic analysis and can be quite useful to an alert adversary. Poor administration of a cryptosystem, such as permitting too short keys, will make any system vulnerable, regardless of other virtues. And, of course, social engineering, and other attacks against the personnel who work with cryptosystems or the messages they handle (e.g., bribery, extortion, blackmail, espionage, torture, ...) may be the most productive attacks of all.

Cryptographic Primitives

Much of the theoretical work in cryptography concerns cryptographic *primitives*—algorithms with basic cryptographic properties—and their relationship to other cryptographic problems. More complicated cryptographic tools are then built from these basic primitives. These primitives provide fundamental properties, which are used to develop more complex tools called *cryptosystems* or *cryptographic protocols*, which guarantee one or more high-level security properties. Note however, that the distinction between cryptographic *primitives* and cryptosystems, is quite arbitrary; for example, the RSA algorithm is sometimes considered a cryptosystem, and sometimes a primitive. Typical examples of cryptographic primitives include pseudorandom functions, one-way functions, etc.

Cryptosystems

One or more cryptographic primitives are often used to develop a more complex algorithm, called a cryptographic system, or *cryptosystem*. Cryptosystems (e.g., El-Gamal encryption) are designed to provide particular functionality (e.g., public key encryption) while guaranteeing certain security properties (e.g., chosen-plaintext attack (CPA) security in the random oracle model). Cryptosystems use the properties of the underlying cryptographic primitives to support the system's security properties. Of course, as the distinction between primitives and cryptosystems is somewhat arbitrary, a sophisticated cryptosystem can be derived from a combination of several more primitive cryptosystems. In many cases, the cryptosystem's structure involves back and forth communication among two or more parties in space (e.g., between the sender of a secure message and its receiver) or across time (e.g., cryptographically protected backup data). Such cryptosystems are sometimes called *cryptographic protocols*.

Some widely known cryptosystems include RSA encryption, Schnorr signature, El-Gamal encryption, PGP, etc. More complex cryptosystems include electronic cash systems, signcryption systems, etc. Some more 'theoretical' cryptosystems include interactive proof systems, (like zero-knowledge proofs), systems for secret sharing, etc.

Until recently, most security properties of most cryptosystems were demonstrated using empirical techniques or using ad hoc reasoning. Recently, there has been considerable effort to develop formal techniques for establishing the security of cryptosystems; this has been generally called *provable security*. The general idea of provable security is to give arguments about the computational difficulty needed to compromise some security aspect of the cryptosystem (i.e., to any adversary).

The study of how best to implement and integrate cryptography in software applications is itself a distinct field.

Legal Issues

Prohibitions

Cryptography has long been of interest to intelligence gathering and law enforcement agencies. Secret communications may be criminal or even treasonous. Because of its facilitation of privacy, and the diminution of privacy attendant on its prohibition, cryptography is also of considerable interest to civil rights supporters. Accordingly, there has been a history of controversial legal issues surrounding cryptography, especially since the advent of inexpensive computers has made wide-spread access to high quality cryptography possible.

In some countries, even the domestic use of cryptography is, or has been, restricted. Until 1999, France significantly restricted the use of cryptography domestically, though it has since relaxed many of these rules. In China and Iran, a license is still required to use cryptography. Many countries have tight restrictions on the use of cryptography. Among the more restrictive are laws in Belarus, Kazakhstan, Mongolia, Pakistan, Singapore, Tunisia, and Vietnam.

In the United States, cryptography is legal for domestic use, but there has been much conflict over legal issues related to cryptography. One particularly important issue has been the export of cryptography and cryptographic software and hardware. Probably because of the importance of cryptanalysis in World War II and an expectation that cryptography would continue to be important for national security, many Western governments have, at some point, strictly regulated export of cryptography. After World War II, it was illegal in the US to sell or distribute encryption technology overseas; in fact, encryption was designated as auxiliary military equipment and put on the United States Munitions List. Until the development of the personal computer, asymmetric key algorithms (i.e., public key techniques), and the Internet, this was not especially problematic. However, as the Internet grew and computers became more widely available, high-quality encryption techniques became well known around the globe.

Export Controls

In the 1990s, there were several challenges to US export regulation of cryptography. After the source code for Philip Zimmermann's Pretty Good Privacy (PGP) encryption program found its way onto the Internet in June 1991, a complaint by RSA Security (then called RSA Data Security, Inc.) resulted in a lengthy criminal investigation of Zimmermann by the US Customs Service and the FBI, though no charges were ever filed. Daniel J. Bernstein, then a graduate student at UC Berkeley, brought a lawsuit against the US government challenging some aspects of the restrictions based on free speech grounds. The 1995 case Bernstein v. United States ultimately resulted in a 1999 decision that printed source code for cryptographic algorithms and systems was protected as free speech by the United States Constitution.

In 1996, thirty-nine countries signed the Wassenaar Arrangement, an arms control treaty that deals with the export of arms and "dual-use" technologies such as cryptography. The treaty stipulated that the use of cryptography with short key-lengths (56-bit for symmetric encryption, 512-bit for RSA) would no longer be export-controlled. Cryptography exports from the US became less strictly regulated as a consequence of a major relaxation in 2000; there are no longer very many restrictions on key sizes in US-exported mass-market software. Since this relaxation in US export restrictions, and because most personal computers connected to the Internet include US-sourced web browsers such as Firefox or Internet Explorer, almost every Internet user worldwide has potential access to quality cryptography via their browsers (e.g., via Transport Layer Security). The Mozilla Thunderbird and Microsoft Outlook E-mail client programs similarly can transmit and receive emails via TLS, and can send and receive email encrypted with S/MIME. Many Internet users don't realize that their basic application software contains such extensive cryptosystems. These browsers and email programs are so ubiquitous that even governments whose intent is to regulate civilian use of cryptography generally don't find it practical to do much to control distribution or use of cryptography of this quality, so even when such laws are in force, actual enforcement is often effectively impossible.

NSA Involvement

NSA headquarters in Fort Meade, Maryland

Another contentious issue connected to cryptography in the United States is the influence of the National Security Agency on cipher development and policy. The NSA was involved with the design of DES during its development at IBM and its consideration by the National Bureau of Standards as a possible Federal Standard for cryptography. DES was designed to be resistant to differential cryptanalysis, a powerful and general cryptanalytic technique known to the NSA and IBM, that became publicly known only when it was rediscovered in the late 1980s. According to Steven Levy, IBM discovered differential cryptanalysis, but kept the technique secret at the NSA's request. The technique became publicly known only when Biham and Shamir re-discovered and announced it some years later. The entire affair illustrates the difficulty of determining what resources and knowledge an attacker might actually have.

Another instance of the NSA's involvement was the 1993 Clipper chip affair, an encryption microchip intended to be part of the Capstone cryptography-control initiative. Clipper was widely criticized by cryptographers for two reasons. The cipher algorithm (called Skipjack) was then classified (declassified in 1998, long after the Clipper initiative lapsed). The classified cipher caused concerns that the NSA had deliberately made the cipher weak in order to assist its intelligence efforts. The whole initiative was also criticized based on its violation of Kerckhoffs's Principle, as the scheme included a special escrow key held by the government for use by law enforcement, for example in wiretaps.

Digital Rights Management

Cryptography is central to digital rights management (DRM), a group of techniques for technologically controlling use of copyrighted material, being widely implemented and deployed at the behest of some copyright holders. In 1998, U.S. President Bill Clinton signed the Digital Millennium Copyright Act (DMCA), which criminalized all production, dissemination, and use of certain cryptanalytic techniques and technology (now known or later discovered); specifically, those that could be used to circumvent DRM technological schemes. This had a noticeable impact on the cryptography research community since an argument can be made that *any* cryptanalytic research violated, or might violate, the DMCA. Similar statutes have since been enacted in several countries and regions, including the implementation in the EU Copyright Directive. Similar restrictions are called for by treaties signed by World Intellectual Property Organization member-states.

The United States Department of Justice and FBI have not enforced the DMCA as rigorously as had been feared by some, but the law, nonetheless, remains a controversial one. Niels Ferguson, a well-respected cryptography researcher, has publicly stated that he will not release some of his research into an Intel security design for fear of prosecution under the DMCA. Cryptanalyst Bruce Schneier has argued that the DMCA encourages vendor lock-in, while inhibiting actual measures toward cyber-security. Both Alan Cox (longtime Linux kernel developer) and Edward Felten (and some of his students at Princeton) have encountered problems related to the Act. Dmitry Sklyarov was arrested during a visit to the US from Russia, and jailed for five months pending trial for alleged violations of the DMCA arising from work he had done in Russia, where the work was legal. In 2007, the cryptographic keys responsible for Blu-ray and HD DVD content scrambling were discovered and released onto the Internet. In both cases, the MPAA sent out numerous DMCA takedown notices, and there was a massive Internet backlash triggered by the perceived impact of such notices on fair use and free speech.

Forced Disclosure of Encryption Keys

In the United Kingdom, the Regulation of Investigatory Powers Act gives UK police the powers to force suspects to decrypt files or hand over passwords that protect encryption keys. Failure to comply is an offense in its own right, punishable on conviction by a two-year jail sentence or up to five years in cases involving national security. Successful prosecutions have occurred under the Act; the first, in 2009, resulted in a term of 13 months' imprisonment. Similar forced disclosure laws in Australia, Finland, France, and India compel individual suspects under investigation to hand over encryption keys or passwords during a criminal investigation.

In the United States, the federal criminal case of United States v. Fricosu addressed whether a search warrant can compel a person to reveal an encryption passphrase or password. The Electronic Frontier Foundation (EFF) argued that this is a violation of the protection from self-incrimination given by the Fifth Amendment. In 2012, the court ruled that under the All Writs Act, the defendant was required to produce an unencrypted hard drive for the court.

In many jurisdictions, the legal status of forced disclosure remains unclear.

The 2016 FBI–Apple encryption dispute concerns the ability of courts in the United States to compel manufacturers' assistance in unlocking cell phones whose contents are cryptographically protected.

As a potential counter-measure to forced disclosure some cryptographic software supports plausible deniability, where the encrypted data is indistinguishable from unused random data (for example such as that of a drive which has been securely wiped).

Symmetric-key Algorithm

Symmetric-key algorithms are algorithms for cryptography that use the same cryptographic keys for both encryption of plaintext and decryption of ciphertext. The keys may be identical or there may be a simple transformation to go between the two keys. The keys, in practice, represent a shared secret between two or more parties that can be used to maintain a private information link. This requirement that both parties have access to the secret key is one of the main drawbacks of symmetric key encryption, in comparison to public-key encryption (also known as asymmetric key encryption).

Types of Symmetric-key Algorithms

Symmetric-key encryption can use either stream ciphers or block ciphers.

- Stream ciphers encrypt the digits (typically bytes) of a message one at a time.

- Block ciphers take a number of bits and encrypt them as a single unit, padding the plaintext so that it is a multiple of the block size. Blocks of 64 bits were commonly used. The Advanced Encryption Standard (AES) algorithm approved by NIST in December 2001, and the GCM block cipher mode of operation use 128-bit blocks.

Implementations

Examples of popular symmetric algorithms include Twofish, Serpent, AES (Rijndael), Blowfish, CAST5, Kuznyechik, RC4, 3DES, Skipjack, Safer+/++ (Bluetooth), and IDEA.

Cryptographic Primitives based on Symmetric Ciphers

Symmetric ciphers are commonly used to achieve other cryptographic primitives than just encryption.

Encrypting a message does not guarantee that this message is not changed while encrypted. Hence often a message authentication code is added to a ciphertext to ensure that changes to the ciphertext will be noted by the receiver. Message authentication codes can be constructed from symmetric ciphers (e.g. CBC-MAC).

However, symmetric ciphers cannot be used for non-repudiation purposes except by involving additional parties.

Another application is to build hash functions from block ciphers.

Construction of Symmetric Ciphers

Many modern block ciphers are based on a construction proposed by Horst Feistel. Feistel's construction makes it possible to build invertible functions from other functions that are themselves not invertible.

Security of Symmetric Ciphers

Symmetric ciphers have historically been susceptible to known-plaintext attacks, chosen-plaintext attacks, differential cryptanalysis and linear cryptanalysis. Careful construction of the functions for each round can greatly reduce the chances of a successful attack.

Key Management

Key Establishment

Symmetric-key algorithms require both the sender and the recipient of a message to have the same secret key. All early cryptographic systems required one of those people to somehow receive a copy of that secret key over a physically secure channel.

Nearly all modern cryptographic systems still use symmetric-key algorithms internally to encrypt the bulk of the messages, but they eliminate the need for a physically secure channel by using Diffie–Hellman key exchange or some other public-key protocol to securely come to agreement on a fresh new secret key for each message (forward secrecy).

Key Generation

When used with asymmetric ciphers for key transfer, pseudorandom key generators are nearly always used to generate the symmetric cipher session keys. However, lack of randomness in those generators or in their initialization vectors is disastrous and has led to cryptanalytic breaks in the past. Therefore, it is essential that an implementation uses a source of high entropy for its initialization.

Reciprocal Cipher

A reciprocal cipher is a cipher where, just as one enters the plaintext into the cryptography system to get the ciphertext, one could enter the ciphertext into the same place in the system to get the plaintext. A reciprocal cipher is also sometimes referred as self-reciprocal cipher. Examples of reciprocal ciphers include:

- Beaufort cipher
- Enigma machine
- ROT13
- XOR cipher
- Vatsyayana cipher

Encryption Algorithm Example

The following steps should be followed to develop an encrypted text:

1. Generate the ASCII value of the letter

2. Generate the corresponding binary value of it (Binary value should be 8 digits e.g. for decimal 32 binary number should be 00100000)

3. Reverse the 8 digit's binary number

4. Take a 4 digits divisor (>=1000) as the Key

5. Divide the reversed number with the divisor

6. Store the remainder in first 3 digits & quotient in next 5 digits (remainder and quotient wouldn't be more than 3 digits and 5 digits long respectively. If any of these are less then 3 and 5 digits respectively we need to add required number of 0s (zeros) in the left hand side. So, this would be the cipertext i.e. encrypted text.

Now store the remainder in first 3 digits & quotient in next 5 digits.

Let us see an example to apply the above mentioned steps:

Encryption

Let, the character is "T". Now according to the steps we will get the following:

Step 1:   ASCII of "T" is 84 in decimal.

Step 2:   The Binary value of 84 is 1010100. Since it is not an 8 bit binary number we need to make it 8 bit number as per the encryption algorithm. So it would be 01010100

Step 3:   Reverse of this binary number would be 00101010

Step 4:   Let 1000 as divisor i.e. Key

Step 5:   Divide 00101010 (dividend) by 1000(divisor)

Step 6:   The remainder would be 10 and the quotient would be 101. So as per the algorithm the ciphertext would be 01000101 which is ASCII 69 in decimal i.e. "E"

Decryption algorithm

Step 1:   Multiply last 5 digits of the ciphertext by the Key

Step 2:   Add first 3 digits of the ciphertext with the result produced in the previous step

Step 3:   If the result produced in the previous step i.e. step 2 is not an 8-bit number we need to make it an 8- bit number

Step 4:   Reverse the number to get the original text i.e. the plain text

Decryption

Step 1:   Multiply last 5 digits of the ciphertext by the Key

Step 2:   Add first 3 digits of the ciphertext with the result produced in the previous step

Step 3:   If the result produced in the previous step i.e. step 2 is not an 8-bit number we need to make it an 8- bit number

Step 4:   Reverse the number to get the original text i.e. the plain text

Public-key Cryptography

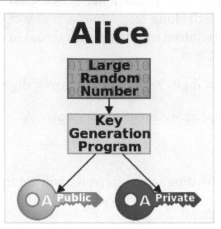

An unpredictable (typically large and random) number is used to begin
generation of an acceptable pair of keys suitable for use by an asymmetric key algorithm.

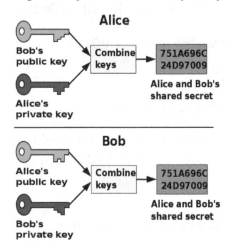

In the Diffie–Hellman key exchange scheme, each party generates a public/private key pair and distributes the public
key. After obtaining an authentic copy of each other's public keys, Alice and Bob can compute a shared secret offline.
The shared secret can be used, for instance, as the key for a symmetric cipher.

Public key cryptography, or asymmetric cryptography, is any cryptographic system that uses pairs
of keys: *public keys* which may be disseminated widely, and *private keys* which are known only to
the owner. This accomplishes two functions: authentication, which is when the public key is used
to verify that a holder of the paired private key sent the message, and encryption, whereby only the
holder of the paired private key can decrypt the message encrypted with the public key.

In a public key encryption system, any person can encrypt a message using the public key of the
receiver, but such a message can be decrypted only with the receiver's private key. For this to work
it must be computationally easy for a user to generate a public and private key-pair to be used for
encryption and decryption. The strength of a public key cryptography system relies on the degree
of difficulty (computational impracticality) for a properly generated private key to be determined
from its corresponding public key. Security then depends only on keeping the private key private,
and the public key may be published without compromising security.

Public key cryptography systems often rely on cryptographic algorithms based on mathematical problems that currently admit no efficient solution—particularly those inherent in certain integer factorization, discrete logarithm, and elliptic curve relationships. Public key algorithms, unlike symmetric key algorithms, do *not* require a secure channel for the initial exchange of one (or more) secret keys between the parties.

Because of the computational complexity of asymmetric encryption, it is usually used only for small blocks of data, typically the transfer of a symmetric encryption key (e.g. a session key). This symmetric key is then used to encrypt the rest of the potentially long message sequence. The symmetric encryption/decryption is based on simpler algorithms and is much faster.

In a public key signature system, a person can combine a message with a private key to create a short *digital signature* on the message. Anyone with the corresponding public key can combine a message, a putative digital signature on it, and a known public key to verify whether the signature was valid—made by the owner of the corresponding private key. Changing the message, even replacing a single letter, will cause verification to fail: in a secure signature system, it is computationally infeasible for anyone who does not know the private key to deduce it from the public key or from any number of signatures, or to find a valid signature on any message for which a signature has not hitherto been seen. Thus the authenticity of a message can be demonstrated by the signature, provided the owner of the private key keeps the private key secret.

Public key algorithms are fundamental security ingredients in cryptosystems, applications and protocols. They underpin various Internet standards, such as Transport Layer Security (TLS), S/MIME, PGP, and GPG. Some public key algorithms provide key distribution and secrecy (e.g., Diffie–Hellman key exchange), some provide digital signatures (e.g., Digital Signature Algorithm), and some provide both (e.g., RSA).

Public key cryptography finds application in, among others, the information technology security discipline, information security. Information security (IS) is concerned with all aspects of protecting electronic information assets against security threats. Public key cryptography is used as a method of assuring the confidentiality, authenticity and non-repudiability of electronic communications and data storage.

Description

Two of the best-known uses of public key cryptography are:

- *Public key encryption*, in which a message is encrypted with a recipient's public key. The message cannot be decrypted by anyone who does not possess the matching private key, who is thus presumed to be the owner of that key and the person associated with the public key. This is used in an attempt to ensure confidentiality.

- *Digital signatures*, in which a message is signed with the sender's private key and can be verified by anyone who has access to the sender's public key. This verification proves that the sender had access to the private key, and therefore is likely to be the person associated with the public key. This also ensures that the message has not been tampered with, as a signature is mathematically bound to the message it originally was made with, and verification will fail for practically any other message, no matter how similar to the original message.

An analogy to public key encryption is that of a locked mail box with a mail slot. The mail slot is exposed and accessible to the public – its location (the street address) is, in essence, the public key. Anyone knowing the street address can go to the door and drop a written message through the slot. However, only the person who possesses the key can open the mailbox and read the message.

An analogy for digital signatures is the sealing of an envelope with a personal wax seal. The message can be opened by anyone, but the presence of the unique seal authenticates the sender.

A central problem with the use of public key cryptography is confidence/proof that a particular public key is authentic, in that it is correct and belongs to the person or entity claimed, and has not been tampered with or replaced by a malicious third party. The usual approach to this problem is to use a public key infrastructure (PKI), in which one or more third parties – known as certificate authorities – certify ownership of key pairs. PGP, in addition to being a certificate authority structure, has used a scheme generally called the "web of trust", which decentralizes such authentication of public keys by a central mechanism, and substitutes individual endorsements of the link between user and public key. To date, no fully satisfactory solution to the "public key authentication problem" has been found.

History

During the early history of cryptography, two parties would rely upon a key that they would exchange by means of a secure, but non-cryptographic, method such as a face-to-face meeting or a trusted courier. This key, which both parties kept absolutely secret, could then be used to exchange encrypted messages. A number of significant practical difficulties arise with this approach to distributing keys.

In his 1874 book *The Principles of Science*, William Stanley Jevons wrote:

Can the reader say what two numbers multiplied together will produce the number 8616460799? I think it unlikely that anyone but myself will ever know.

Here he described the relationship of one-way functions to cryptography, and went on to discuss specifically the factorization problem used to create a trapdoor function. In July 1996, mathematician Solomon W. Golomb said: "Jevons anticipated a key feature of the RSA Algorithm for public key cryptography, although he certainly did not invent the concept of public key cryptography." (In 1869, Jevons had also invented a computing machine he called a "Logic Piano".)

Classified Discovery

In 1970, James H. Ellis, a British cryptographer at the UK Government Communications Headquarters (GCHQ), conceived of the possibility of "non-secret encryption", (now called public key cryptography), but could see no way to implement it. In 1973, his colleague Clifford Cocks implemented what has become known as the RSA encryption algorithm, giving a practical method of "non-secret encryption", and in 1974, another GCHQ mathematician and cryptographer, Malcolm

J. Williamson, developed what is now known as Diffie–Hellman key exchange. The scheme was also passed to the USA's National Security Agency. With a military focus, and low computing power, the power of public key cryptography was unrealised in both organisations:

I judged it most important for military use ... if you can share your key rapidly and electronically, you have a major advantage over your opponent. Only at the end of the evolution from Berners-Lee designing an open internet architecture for CERN, its adaptation and adoption for the Arpanet ... did public key cryptography realise its full potential.

—Ralph Benjamin

Their discovery did not become public knowledge for 27 years, until the research was declassified by the British government in 1997.

Public Discovery

In 1976, an asymmetric key cryptosystem was published by Whitfield Diffie and Martin Hellman who, influenced by Ralph Merkle's work on public key distribution, disclosed a method of public key agreement. This method of key exchange, which uses exponentiation in a finite field, came to be known as Diffie–Hellman key exchange. This was the first published practical method for establishing a shared secret-key over an authenticated (but not confidential) communications channel without using a prior shared secret. Merkle's "public key-agreement technique" became known as Merkle's Puzzles, and was invented in 1974 and published in 1978.

In 1977, a generalization of Cocks' scheme was independently invented by Ron Rivest, Adi Shamir and Leonard Adleman, all then at MIT. The latter authors published their work in 1978, and the algorithm came to be known as RSA, from their initials. RSA uses exponentiation modulo a product of two very large primes, to encrypt and decrypt, performing both public key encryption and public key digital signature. Its security is connected to the extreme difficulty of factoring large integers, a problem for which there is no known efficient general technique. In 1979, Michael O. Rabin published a related cryptosystem that is probably secure as long as the factorization of the public key remains difficult – it remains an assumption that RSA also enjoys this security.

Since the 1970s, a large number and variety of encryption, digital signature, key agreement, and other techniques have been developed in the field of public key cryptography. The ElGamal cryptosystem, invented by Taher ElGamal relies on the similar and related high level of difficulty of the discrete logarithm problem, as does the closely related DSA, which was developed at the US National Security Agency (NSA) and published by NIST as a proposed standard.

The introduction of elliptic curve cryptography by Neal Koblitz and Victor Miller, independently and simultaneously in the mid-1980s, has yielded new public key algorithms based on the discrete logarithm problem. Although mathematically more complex, elliptic curves provide smaller key sizes and faster operations for approximately equivalent estimated security.

Typical Use

Public key cryptography is often used to secure electronic communication over an open networked environment such as the Internet, without relying on a hidden or covert channel, even for key exchange.

Open networked environments are susceptible to a variety of communication security problems, such as man-in-the-middle attacks and spoofs. Communication security typically includes requirements that the communication must not be readable during transit (preserving confidentiality), the communication must not be modified during transit (preserving the integrity of the communication), the communication must originate from an identified party (sender authenticity), and the recipient must not be able to repudiate or deny receiving the communication. Combining public key cryptography with an Enveloped Public Key Encryption (EPKE) method, allows for the secure sending of a communication over an open networked environment. In other words, even if an adversary listens to an entire conversation including the key exchange, the adversary would not be able to interpret the conversation.

The distinguishing technique used in public key cryptography is the use of asymmetric key algorithms, where a key used by one party to perform encryption is not the same as the key used by another in decryption. Each user has a pair of cryptographic keys – a public encryption key and a private decryption key. For example, a key pair used for digital signatures consists of a private signing key and a public verification key. The public key may be widely distributed, while the private key is known only to its proprietor. The keys are related mathematically, but the parameters are chosen so that calculating the private key from the public key is unfeasible.

In contrast, symmetric key algorithms use a *single* secret key, which must be shared and kept private by both the sender (for encryption) and the receiver (for decryption). To use a symmetric encryption scheme, the sender and receiver must securely share a key in advance.

Because symmetric key algorithms are nearly always much less computationally intensive than asymmetric ones, it is common to exchange a key using a key-exchange algorithm, then transmit data using that key and a symmetric key algorithm. PGP and the SSL/TLS family of schemes use this procedure, and are thus called *hybrid cryptosystems*.

Security

Some encryption schemes can be proven secure on the basis of the presumed difficulty of a mathematical problem, such as factoring the product of two large primes or computing discrete logarithms. Note that "secure" here has a precise mathematical meaning, and there are multiple different (meaningful) definitions of what it means for an encryption scheme to be "secure". The "right" definition depends on the context in which the scheme will be deployed.

The most obvious application of a public key encryption system is confidentiality – a message that a sender encrypts using the recipient's public key can be decrypted only by the recipient's paired private key. This assumes, of course, that no flaw is discovered in the basic algorithm used.

Another application in public key cryptography is the digital signature. Digital signature schemes can be used for sender authentication and non-repudiation. The sender computes a digital signature for the message to be sent, then sends the signature (together with the message) to the intended receiver. Digital signature schemes have the property that signatures can be computed only with the knowledge of the correct private key. To verify that a message has been signed by a user and has not been modified, the receiver needs to know only the corresponding public key. In some cases (e.g., RSA), a single algorithm can be used to both encrypt and create digital signatures. In other cases (e.g., DSA), each algorithm can only be used for one specific purpose.

To achieve both authentication and confidentiality, the sender should include the recipient's name in the message, sign it using his private key, and then encrypt both the message and the signature using the recipient's public key.

These characteristics can be used to construct many other (sometimes surprising) cryptographic protocols and applications, such as digital cash, password-authenticated key agreement, multi-party key agreement, time-stamping services, non-repudiation protocols, etc.

Practical Considerations

Enveloped Public Key Encryption

Enveloped Public Key Encryption (EPKE) is the method of applying public key cryptography and ensuring that an electronic communication is transmitted confidentially, has the contents of the communication protected against being modified (communication integrity) and cannot be denied from having been sent (non-repudiation). This is often the method used when securing communication on an open networked environment such by making use of the Transport Layer Security (TLS) or Secure Sockets Layer (SSL) protocols.

EPKE consists of a two-stage process that includes both Public Key Encryption (PKE) and a digital signature. Both Public Key Encryption and digital signatures make up the foundation of Enveloped Public Key Encryption.

For EPKE to work effectively, it is required that:

- Every participant in the communication has their own unique pair of keys. The first key that is required is a public key and the second key that is required is a private key.

- Each person's own private and public keys must be mathematically related where the private key is used to decrypt a communication sent using a public key and vice versa. Some well-known asymmetric encryption algorithms are based on the RSA cryptosystem.

- The private key must be kept absolutely private by the owner, though the public key can be published in a public directory such as with a certification authority.

To send a message using EPKE, the sender of the message first signs the message using their own private key, this ensures non-repudiation of the message. The sender then encrypts their digitally signed message using the receiver's public key thus applying a digital envelope to the message. This step ensures confidentiality during the transmission of the message. The receiver of the message then uses their private key to decrypt the message thus removing the digital envelope and then uses the sender's public key to decrypt the sender's digital signature. At this point, if the message has been unaltered during transmission, the message will be clear to the receiver.

Due to the computationally complex nature of RSA-based asymmetric encryption algorithms, the time taken to encrypt large documents or files to be transmitted can be relatively long. To speed up the process of transmission, instead of applying the sender's digital signature to the large documents or files, the sender can rather hash the documents or files using a cryptographic hash function and then digitally sign the generated hash value, therefore enforcing non-repudiation. Hashing is a much faster computation to complete as opposed to using an RSA-based digital signature algorithm alone. The sender would then sign the newly generated hash value and encrypt the original documents or files with the receiver's public key. The transmission would then take place securely and with confidentiality and non-repudiation still intact. The receiver would then verify the signature and decrypt the encrypted documents or files with their private key.

Note: The sender and receiver do not usually carry out the process mentioned above manually though, but rather rely on sophisticated software to automatically complete the EPKE process.

Public Key Encryption

The goal of Public Key Encryption (PKE) is to ensure that the communication being sent is kept confidential during transit.

To send a message using PKE, the sender of the message uses the public key of the receiver to encrypt the contents of the message. The encrypted message is then transmitted electronically to the receiver and the receiver can then use their own matching private key to decrypt the message.

The encryption process of using the receiver's public key is useful for preserving the confidentiality of the message as only the receiver has the matching private key to decrypt the message. Therefore, the sender of the message cannot decrypt the message once it has been encrypted using the receiver's public key. However, PKE does not address the problem of non-repudiation, as the message could have been sent by anyone that has access to the receiver's public key.

Digital Signatures

A digital signature is meant to prove a message came from a particular sender; neither can anyone impersonate the sender nor can the sender deny having sent the message. This is useful for example when making an electronic purchase of shares, allowing the receiver to prove who requested the purchase. Digital signatures do not provide confidentiality for the message being sent.

The message is signed using the sender's private signing key. The digitally signed message is then sent to the receiver, who can then use the sender's public key to verify the signature.

Certification Authority

In order for Enveloped Public Key Encryption to be as secure as possible, there needs to be a "gatekeeper" of public and private keys, or else anyone could create key pairs and masquerade as the intended sender of a communication, proposing them as the keys of the intended sender. This digital key "gatekeeper" is known as a certification authority. A certification authority is a trusted third party that can issue public and private keys, thus certifying public keys. It also works as a depository to store key chain and enforce the trust factor.

Postal Analogies

An analogy that can be used to understand the advantages of an asymmetric system is to imagine two people, Alice and Bob, who are sending a secret message through the public mail. In this example, Alice wants to send a secret message to Bob, and expects a secret reply from Bob.

With a symmetric key system, Alice first puts the secret message in a box, and locks the box using a padlock to which she has a key. She then sends the box to Bob through regular mail. When Bob receives the box, he uses an identical copy of Alice's key (which he has somehow obtained previously, maybe by a face-to-face meeting) to open the box, and reads the message. Bob can then use the same padlock to send his secret reply.

In an asymmetric key system, Bob and Alice have separate padlocks. First, Alice asks Bob to send his open padlock to her through regular mail, keeping his key to himself. When Alice receives it she uses it to lock a box containing her message, and sends the locked box to Bob. Bob can then unlock the box with his key and read the message from Alice. To reply, Bob must similarly get Alice's open padlock to lock the box before sending it back to her.

The critical advantage in an asymmetric key system is that Bob and Alice never need to send a copy of their keys to each other. This prevents a third party – perhaps, in this example, a corrupt postal worker who opens unlocked boxes – from copying a key while it is in transit, allowing the third party to spy on all future messages sent between Alice and Bob. So, in the public key scenario, Alice and Bob need not trust the postal service as much. In addition, if Bob were careless and allowed someone else to copy *his* key, Alice's messages to *Bob* would be compromised, but Alice's messages to *other people* would remain secret, since the other people would be providing different padlocks for Alice to use.

Another kind of asymmetric key system, called a three-pass protocol, requires neither party to even touch the other party's padlock (or key to get access); Bob and Alice have separate padlocks. First, Alice puts the secret message in a box, and locks the box using a padlock to which only she has a key. She then sends the box to Bob through regular mail. When Bob receives the box, he adds his own padlock to the box, and sends it back to Alice. When Alice receives the box with the two padlocks, she removes her padlock and sends it back to Bob. When Bob receives the box with only his padlock on it, Bob can then unlock the box with his key and read the message from Alice. Note that, in this scheme, the order of decryption is NOT the same as the order of encryption – this is only possible if commutative ciphers are used. A commutative cipher is one in which the order of encryption and decryption is interchangeable, just as the order of multiplication is interchangeable (i.e., $A*B*C = A*C*B = C*B*A$). This method is secure for certain choices of commutative ciphers, but insecure for others (e.g., a simple XOR). For example, let $E_1()$ and $E_2()$ be two encryption functions, and let "M" be the message so that if Alice encrypts it using $E_1()$ and sends $E_1(M)$ to Bob. Bob then again encrypts the message as $E_2(E_1(M))$ and sends it to Alice. Now, Alice decrypts $E_2(E_1(M))$ using $E_1()$. Alice will now get $E_2(M)$, meaning when she sends this again to Bob, he will be able to decrypt the message using $E_2()$ and get "M". Although none of the keys were ever exchanged, the message "M" may well be a key (e.g., Alice's Public key). This three-pass protocol is typically used during key exchange.

Actual Algorithms: Two Linked Keys

Not all asymmetric key algorithms operate in this way. In the most common, Alice and Bob each own *two* keys, one for encryption and one for decryption. In a secure asymmetric key encryption scheme, the private key should not be deducible from the public key. This makes possible public key encryption, since an encryption key can be published without compromising the security of messages encrypted with that key.

In other schemes, either key can be used to encrypt the message. When Bob encrypts a message with his private key, only his public key will successfully decrypt it, authenticating Bob's authorship of the message. In the alternative, when a message is encrypted with the public key, only the private key can decrypt it. In this arrangement, Alice and Bob can exchange secret messages with no prior secret agreement, each using the other's public key to encrypt, and each using his own to decrypt.

Weaknesses

Among symmetric key encryption algorithms, only the one-time pad can be proven to be secure against any adversary – no matter how much computing power is available. However, there is no public key scheme with this property, since all public key schemes are susceptible to a "brute-force key search attack". Such attacks are impractical if the amount of computation needed to succeed – termed the "work factor" by Claude Shannon – is out of reach of all potential attackers. In many cases, the work factor can be increased by simply choosing a longer key. But other algorithms may have much lower work factors, making resistance to a brute-force attack irrelevant. Some special and specific algorithms have been developed to aid in attacking some public key encryption algorithms – both RSA and ElGamal encryption have known attacks that are much faster than the brute-force approach. These factors have changed dramatically in recent decades, both with the decreasing cost of computing power and with new mathematical discoveries.

Aside from the resistance to attack of a particular key pair, the security of the certification hierarchy must be considered when deploying public key systems. Some certificate authority – usually a purpose-built program running on a server computer – vouches for the identities assigned to specific private keys by producing a digital certificate. Public key digital certificates are typically valid for several years at a time, so the associated private keys must be held securely over that time. When a private key used for certificate creation higher in the PKI server hierarchy is compromised, or accidentally disclosed, then a "man-in-the-middle attack" is possible, making any subordinate certificate wholly insecure.

Major weaknesses have been found for several formerly promising asymmetric key algorithms. The 'knapsack packing' algorithm was found to be insecure after the development of a new attack. Recently, some attacks based on careful measurements of the exact amount of time it takes known hardware to encrypt plain text have been used to simplify the search for likely decryption keys. Thus, mere use of asymmetric key algorithms does not ensure security. A great deal of active research is currently underway to both discover, and to protect against, new attack algorithms.

Another potential security vulnerability in using asymmetric keys is the possibility of a "man-in-the-middle" attack, in which the communication of public keys is intercepted by a third party (the "man in the middle") and then modified to provide different public keys instead. Encrypted messages and responses must also be intercepted, decrypted, and re-encrypted by the attacker using the correct public keys for different communication segments, in all instances, so as to avoid suspicion. This attack may seem to be difficult to implement in practice, but it is not impossible when using insecure media (e.g., public networks, such as the Internet or wireless forms of communications) – for example, a malicious staff member at Alice or Bob's Internet Service Provider (ISP) might find it quite easy to carry out. In the earlier postal analogy, Alice would have to have a way to make sure that the lock on the returned packet really belongs to Bob before she removes her lock and sends the packet back. Otherwise, the lock could have been put on the packet by a corrupt postal worker pretending to be Bob, so as to fool Alice.

One approach to prevent such attacks involves the use of a certificate authority, a trusted third party responsible for verifying the identity of a user of the system. This authority issues a tamper-resistant, non-spoofable digital certificate for the participants. Such certificates are signed data blocks stating that this public key belongs to that person, company, or other entity. This approach also has its weaknesses – for example, the certificate authority issuing the certificate must be trusted to have properly checked the identity of the key-holder, must ensure the correctness of the public key when it issues a certificate, must be secure from computer piracy, and must have made arrangements with all participants to check all their certificates before protected communications can begin. Web browsers, for instance, are supplied with a long list of "self-signed identity certificates" from PKI providers – these are used to check the *bona fides* of the certificate authority and then, in a second step, the certificates of potential communicators. An attacker who could subvert any single one of those certificate authorities into issuing a certificate for a bogus public key could then mount a "man-in-the-middle" attack as easily as if the certificate scheme were not used at all. In an alternate scenario rarely discussed, an attacker who penetrated an authority's servers and obtained its store of certificates and keys (public and private) would be able to spoof, masquerade, decrypt, and forge transactions without limit.

Despite its theoretical and potential problems, this approach is widely used. Examples include SSL and its successor, TLS, which are commonly used to provide security for web browser transactions (for example, to securely send credit card details to an online store).

Computational Cost

The public key algorithms known thus far are relatively computationally costly compared with most symmetric key algorithms of apparently equivalent security. The difference factor is the use of typically quite large keys. This has important implications for their practical use. Most are used in hybrid cryptosystems for reasons of efficiency – in such a cryptosystem, a shared secret key ("session key") is generated by one party, and this much briefer session key is then encrypted by each recipient's public key. Each recipient then uses his own private key to decrypt the session key. Once all parties have obtained the session key, they can use a much faster symmetric algorithm to encrypt and decrypt messages. In many of these schemes, the session key is unique to each message exchange, being pseudo-randomly chosen for each message.

Associating Public Keys with Identities

The binding between a public key and its "owner" must be correct, or else the algorithm may function perfectly and yet be entirely insecure in practice. As with most cryptography applications, the protocols used to establish and verify this binding are critically important. Associating a public key with its owner is typically done by protocols implementing a public key infrastructure – these allow the validity of the association to be formally verified by reference to a trusted third party in the form of either a hierarchical certificate authority (e.g., X.509), a local trust model (e.g., SPKI), or a web of trust scheme, like that originally built into PGP and GPG, and still to some extent usable with them. Whatever the cryptographic assurance of the protocols themselves, the association between a public key and its owner is ultimately a matter of subjective judgment on the part of the trusted third party, since the key is a mathematical entity, while the owner – and the connection between owner and key – are not. For this reason, the formalism of a public key infrastructure must provide for explicit statements of the policy followed when making this judgment. For example, the complex and never fully implemented X.509 standard allows a certificate authority to identify its policy by means of an object identifier, which functions as an index into a catalog of registered policies. Policies may exist for many different purposes, ranging from anonymity to military classifications.

Relation to Real World Events

A public key will be known to a large and, in practice, unknown set of users. All events requiring revocation or replacement of a public key can take a long time to take full effect with all who must be informed (i.e., all those users who possess that key). For this reason, systems that must react to events in real time (e.g., safety-critical systems or national security systems) should not use public key encryption without taking great care. There are four issues of interest:

Privilege of Key Revocation

A malicious (or erroneous) revocation of some (or all) of the keys in the system is likely, or in the second case, certain, to cause a complete failure of the system. If public keys can be revoked individually, this is a possibility. However, there are design approaches that can reduce the practical chance of this occurring. For example, by means of certificates, we can create what is called a "compound principal" – one such principal could be "Alice and Bob have Revoke Authority". Now, only Alice and Bob (in concert) can revoke a key, and neither Alice nor Bob can revoke keys alone. However, revoking a key now requires both Alice *and* Bob to be available, and this creates a problem of reliability. In concrete terms, from a security point of view, there is now a "single point of failure" in the public key revocation system. A successful Denial of Service attack against either Alice or Bob (or both) will block a required revocation. In fact, any partition of authority between Alice and Bob will have this effect, regardless of how it comes about.

Because the principle allowing revocation authority for keys is very powerful, the mechanisms used to control it should involve both as many participants as possible (to guard against malicious attacks of this type), while at the same time as few as possible (to ensure that a key can be revoked without dangerous delay). Public key certificates that include an expiration date are unsatisfactory in that the expiration date may not correspond with a real-world revocation but at least such certificates need not all be tracked down system-wide, nor must all users be in constant contact with the system at all times.

Distribution of a New Key

After a key has been revoked, or when a new user is added to a system, a new key must be distributed in some predetermined manner. Assume that Carol's key has been revoked (e.g., by exceeding its expiration date, or because of a compromise of Carol's matching private key). Until a new key has been distributed, Carol is effectively "out of contact". No one will be able to send her messages without violating system protocols (i.e., without a valid public key, no one can encrypt messages to her), and messages from her cannot be signed, for the same reason. Or, in other words, the "part of the system" controlled by Carol is, in essence, unavailable. Security requirements have been ranked higher than system availability in such designs.

One could leave the power to create (and certify) keys (as well as to revoke them) in the hands of each user – the original PGP design did so – but this raises problems of user understanding and operation. For security reasons, this approach has considerable difficulties – if nothing else, some users will be forgetful, or inattentive, or confused. On the one hand, a message revoking a public key certificate should be spread as fast as possible, while on the other hand, parts of the system might be rendered inoperable *before* a new key can be installed. The time window can be reduced to zero by always issuing the new key together with the certificate that revokes the old one, but this requires co-location of authority to both revoke keys and generate new keys.

It is most likely a system-wide failure if the (possibly combined) principal that issues new keys fails by issuing keys improperly. This is an instance of a "common mutual exclusion" – a design can make the reliability of a system high, but only at the cost of system availability (and *vice versa*).

Spreading the Revocation

Notification of a key certificate revocation must be spread to all those who might potentially hold it, and as rapidly as possible.

There are but two means of spreading information (i.e., a key revocation) in a distributed system: either the information is "pushed" to users from a central point (or points), or else it is "pulled" from a central point(or points) by the end users.

Pushing the information is the simplest solution, in that a message is sent to all participants. However, there is no way of knowing whether all participants will actually *receive* the message. If the number of participants is large, and some of their physical or network distances are great, then the probability of complete success (which is, in ideal circumstances, required for system security) will be rather low. In a partly updated state, the system is particularly vulnerable to "denial of service" attacks as security has been breached, and a vulnerability window will continue to exist as long as some users have not "gotten the word". Put another way, pushing certificate revocation messages is neither easy to secure, nor very reliable.

The alternative to pushing is pulling. In the extreme, all certificates contain all the keys needed to verify that the public key of interest (i.e., the one belonging to the user to whom one wishes to send a message, or whose signature is to be checked) is still valid. In this case, at least some use of the system will be blocked if a user cannot reach the verification service (i.e., one of the systems that can establish the current validity of another user's key). Again, such a system design can be made as reliable as one wishes, at the cost of lowering security – the more servers to check for the possibility of a key revocation, the longer the window of vulnerability.

Another trade-off is to use a somewhat less reliable, but more secure, verification service, but to include an expiration date for each of the verification sources. How long this "timeout" should be is a decision that requires a trade-off between availability and security that will have to be decided in advance, at the time of system design.

Recovery from a Leaked Key

Assume that the principal authorized to revoke a key has decided that a certain key must be revoked. In most cases, this happens after the fact – for instance, it becomes known that at some time in the past an event occurred that endangered a private key. Let us denote the time at which it is decided that the compromise occurred as T.

Such a compromise has two implications. First, messages encrypted with the matching public key (now or in the past) can no longer be assumed to be secret. One solution to avoid this problem is to use a protocol that has perfect forward secrecy. Second, signatures made with the *no-longer-trusted-to-be-actually-private key* after time T can no longer be assumed to be authentic without additional information (i.e., who, where, when, etc.) about the events leading up to the digital signature. These will not always be available, and so all such digital signatures will be less than credible. A solution to reduce the impact of leaking a private key of a signature scheme is to use timestamps.

Loss of secrecy and/or authenticity, even for a single user, has system-wide security implications, and a strategy for recovery must thus be established. Such a strategy will determine who has authority to, and under what conditions one must, revoke a public key certificate. One must also decide how to spread the revocation, and ideally, how to deal with all messages signed with the key since time T (which will rarely be known precisely). Messages sent to that user (which require the proper – now compromised – private key to decrypt) must be considered compromised as well, no matter when they were sent.

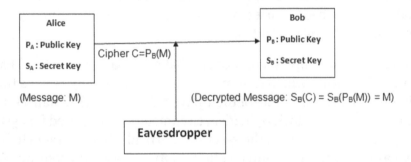

Suppose Alice wants to send some message M to Bob. But she cannot allow any other person to know the content of M. So she has to send her message in an encrypted format that can be decrypted only by Bob and not by any third party / eavesdropper. In public key cryptosystem this is achieved as follows:

Each party has a pair of public and secret key. So Bob had public key P_B and secret key S_B. All public keys of different parties are maintained in a public directory. So Alice first finds the public key P_B of Bob from the public directory. She then encrypts the message M with the public key P_B and obtains the encrypted message or cipher-text $C = P_B(M)$. This cipher-text C is sent to Bob across the communication channel. After Bob receives the cipher-text C he decrypts using his secret key S_B to get $S_B(C) = S_B(P_B(M)) = M$, the original message back.

So in this cryptosystem we have to ensure two things :

i. S_B should be the inverse of P_B.

ii. In spite of the knowledge of P_B it is computationally infeasible to an eavesdropper to determine S_B.

One important issue that is left is how a message M is represented. It is usually represented by an integer obtained as below.

M: "I am fine."

In the above message there are 9 distinct alphabets including blank. So we can use a number system of base 9 and assign the code to each alphabet as follows:

Alphabet	Code
.	0
I	1
a	2
e	3
f	4
i	5
m	6
n	7
" "	8

So the message string M is mapped to the integer: $9^{10} \times 1 + 9^9 \times 8 + 9^7 \times 2 + 9^6 \times 6 + 9^5 \times 8 + 9^4 \times 4 + 9^3 \times 5 + 9^2 \times 7 + 9^1 \times 3 + 9^0 \times 0$. We can uniquely determine the string M back given this integer in base 9.

Digital Signatures

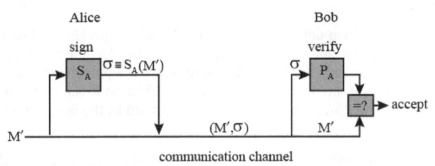

communication channel

Alice signs the message M' by appending her digital signature $\sigma = S_A(M')$ to it. She transmits the message/signature pair (M', σ) to Bob, who verifies it by checking the equation $M' = P_A(\sigma)$. If the equation holds, he accepts (M', σ) as a message that has been signed by Alice.

- Alice computes her digital signature s for the message M' using her secret key S_A and the equation $\sigma = S_A(M')$.

- Alice sends the message/signature pair (M', σ) to Bob.

- When Bob receives (M',σ), he can verify that it originated from Alice by using Alice's public key to verify the equation $M' = P_A(\sigma)$. (Presumably, M' contains Alice's name, so Bob knows whose public key to use.) If the equation holds, then Bob concludes that the message M' was actually signed by Alice. If the equation doesn't hold, Bob concludes either that the message M' or the digital signature s was corrupted by transmission errors or that the pair (M',σ) is an attempted forgery. Digital signature provides both authentication of the signer's identity

Sometimes a variation of the above approach is used for digital signatures. Here a one-way hash function h () is used. The hash function h () is public. These hash functions are called cryptographic has functions. Given a message M it is easy to compute h (M) but it is computationally infeasible to find two messages M and M' such that h (M) = h (M') . So Alice applies her secret key S_A over h (M') and not over M'. So the digital signature $\sigma = S_A(h (M'))$. Now she sends the pair (M',σ) to Bob. Bob cannot compute $h^{-1}()$. So in the first step he applies Alice's public key P_A over s to obtain $P_A(\sigma) = P_A(\sigma_A(h (M')))= h (M')$. In the second step Bob applies the public hash function over the first component of the pair (M', σ), i.e., M'to obtain h (M'). Bob accepts the signature as valid if and only if the results obtained in the two steps are equal. Otherwise he rejects the signature. This may happen either due to error in transmission or due to tampering by an eavesdropper. So he will ask Alice to retransmit the message-signature pair again.

RSA (Cryptosystem)

RSA is one of the first practical public-key cryptosystems and is widely used for secure data transmission. In such a cryptosystem, the encryption key is public and differs from the decryption key which is kept secret. In RSA, this asymmetry is based on the practical difficulty of factoring the product of two large prime numbers, the factoring problem. RSA is made of the initial letters of the surnames of Ron Rivest, Adi Shamir, and Leonard Adleman, who first publicly described the algorithm in 1977. Clifford Cocks, an English mathematician working for the UK intelligence agency GCHQ, had developed an equivalent system in 1973, but it was not declassified until 1997.

A user of RSA creates and then publishes a public key based on two large prime numbers, along with an auxiliary value. The prime numbers must be kept secret. Anyone can use the public key to encrypt a message, but with currently published methods, if the public key is large enough, only someone with knowledge of the prime numbers can feasibly decode the message. Breaking RSA encryption is known as the RSA problem; whether it is as hard as the factoring problem remains an open question.

RSA is a relatively slow algorithm, and because of this it is less commonly used to directly encrypt user data. More often, RSA passes encrypted shared keys for symmetric key cryptography which in turn can perform bulk encryption-decryption operations at much higher speed.

History

The idea of an asymmetric public-private key cryptosystem is attributed to Whitfield Diffie and Martin Hellman, who published the concept in 1976. They also introduced digital signatures and attempted to apply number theory; their formulation used a shared secret key created from exponentiation of some number, modulo a prime numbers. However, they left open the problem of realizing a one-way function, possibly because the difficulty of factoring was not well studied at the time.

Ron Rivest, Adi Shamir, and Leonard Adleman (R.S.A.) at MIT made several attempts over the course of a year to create a one-way function that is hard to invert. Rivest and Shamir, as computer scientists, proposed many potential functions while Adleman, as a mathematician, was responsible for finding their weaknesses. They tried many approaches including "knapsack-based" and "permutation polynomials". For a time they thought it was impossible for what they wanted to achieve due to contradictory requirements. In April 1977, they spent Passover at the house of a student and drank a good deal of Manischewitz wine before returning to their home at around midnight. Rivest, unable to sleep, lay on the couch with a math textbook and started thinking about their one-way function. He spent the rest of the night formalizing his idea and had much of the paper ready by daybreak. The algorithm is now known as RSA – the initials of their surnames in same order as their paper.

Adi Shamir, one of the authors of RSA: Rivest, Shamir and Adleman

Clifford Cocks, an English mathematician working for the UK intelligence agency GCHQ, described an equivalent system in an internal document in 1973. However, given the relatively expensive computers needed to implement it at the time, it was mostly considered a curiosity and, as far as is publicly known, was never deployed. His discovery, however, was not revealed until 1997 due to its secret classification.

Kid-RSA (KRSA) is a simplified public-key cipher published in 1997, designed for educational purposes. Some people feel that learning Kid-RSA gives insight into RSA and other public-key ciphers, analogous to simplified DES.

Patent

MIT was granted U.S. Patent 4,405,829 for a "Cryptographic communications system and method" that used the algorithm, on September 20, 1983. Though the patent was going to expire on September 21, 2000 (the term of patent was 17 years at the time), the algorithm was released to the public domain by RSA Security on September 6, 2000, two weeks earlier. Since a paper describing the algorithm had been published in August 1977, prior to the December 1977 filing date of the patent application, regulations in much of the rest of the world precluded patents elsewhere and only the US patent was granted. Had Cocks' work been publicly known, a patent in the US would not have been possible either.

From the DWPI's abstract of the patent,

The system includes a communications channel coupled to at least one terminal having an encoding device and to at least one terminal having a decoding device. A message-to-be-transferred is enciphered to ciphertext at the encoding terminal by encoding the message as a number M in a predetermined set. That number is then raised to a first predetermined power (associated with the intended receiver) and finally computed. The remainder or residue, C, is... computed when the exponentiated number is divided by the product of two predetermined prime numbers (associated with the intended receiver).

Operation

The RSA algorithm involves four steps: key generation, key distribution, encryption and decryption.

A basic principle behind RSA is the observation that it is practical to find three very large positive integers e, d and n such that with modular exponentiation for all integer m:

$$(m^e)^d \equiv m \pmod{n}$$

and that even knowing e and n or even m it can be extremely difficult to find d.

Additionally, for some operations it is convenient that the order of the two exponentiations can be changed and that this relation also implies:

$$(m^d)^e \equiv m \pmod{n}$$

RSA involves a *public key* and a *private key*. The public key can be known by everyone and is used for encrypting messages. The intention is that messages encrypted with the public key can only be decrypted in a reasonable amount of time using the private key. The public key is represented by the integers n and e; and, the private key, by the integer d (although n is also used during the decryption process; so, it might be considered a part of the private key, too). m represents the message (previously prepared with certain technique explained below).

Key Generation

The keys for the RSA algorithm are generated the following way:

1. Choose two distinct prime numbers p and q.

    *   For security purposes, the integers p and q should be chosen at random, and should be similar in magnitude but 'differ in length by a few digits' to make factoring harder. Prime integers can be efficiently found using a primality test.

2. Compute $n = pq$.

    * n is used as the modulus for both the public and private keys. Its length, usually expressed in bits, is the key length.

3. Compute $\lambda(n) = \mathrm{lcm}(\lambda(p), \lambda(q)) = \mathrm{lcm}(p - 1, q - 1)$, where λ is Carmichael's totient function. This value is kept private.

4. Choose an integer e such that $1 < e < \lambda(n)$ and $\gcd(e, \lambda(n)) = 1$; i.e., e and $\lambda(n)$ are coprime.

5. Determine d as $d \equiv e^{-1} \pmod{\lambda(n)}$; i.e., d is the modular multiplicative inverse of e (modulo $\lambda(n)$).

- This is more clearly stated as: solve for d given $d{\cdot}e \equiv 1 \pmod{\lambda(n)}$.

- e having a short bit-length and small Hamming weight results in more efficient encryption – most commonly $2^{16} + 1 = 65{,}537$. However, much smaller values of e (such as 3) have been shown to be less secure in some settings.

- e is released as the public key exponent.

- d is kept as the private key exponent.

The *public key* consists of the modulus n and the public (or encryption) exponent e. The *private key* consists of the modulus n and the private (or decryption) exponent d, which must be kept secret. p, q, and $\lambda(n)$ must also be kept secret because they can be used to calculate d.

Alternatively, as in the original RSA paper, the Euler totient function $\phi(n) = (p-1)(q-1)$ can be used instead of $\lambda(n)$ for calculating the private exponent d. This works because $\phi(n)$ is always divisible by $\lambda(n)$ (a consequence of applying Lagrange's theorem to the multiplicative group of integers modulo pq), and thus any d satisfying $d{\cdot}e \equiv 1 \pmod{\phi(n)}$ also satisfies $d{\cdot}e \equiv 1 \pmod{\lambda(n)}$. However, computing d modulo $\phi(n)$ will sometimes yield a result that is larger than necessary (i.e. $d > \lambda(n)$). Most RSA implementations will accept exponents generated using either method (if they use the private exponent d at all, rather than using the optimized decryption method based on the Chinese remainder theorem described below), but some standards like FIPS 186-4 may require that $d < \lambda(n)$. Any "oversized" private exponents not meeting that criterion may always be reduced modulo $\lambda(n)$ to obtain a smaller equivalent exponent.

Since any common factors of $(p-1)$ and $(q-1)$ are present in the factorisation of $n-1 = pq-1 = (p-1)(q-1) + (p-1) + (q-1)$, it is recommended that $(p-1)$ and $(q-1)$ have only very small common factors, if any besides the necessary 2.

Note: The authors of the original RSA paper carry out the key generation by choosing d and then computing e as the modular multiplicative inverse of d (modulo $\phi(n)$). Since it is beneficial to use a small value for e (i.e. 65,537) in order to speed up the encryption function, current implementations of RSA, such as PKCS#1 choose e and compute d instead.

Key Distribution

Suppose that Bob wants to send a secret message to Alice. If they decide to use RSA, Bob must know Alice's public key to encrypt the message and, Alice must use her private key to decrypt the message. To enable Bob to send his encrypted messages, Alice transmits her public key (n, e) to Bob via a reliable, but not necessarily secret route. Alice's private key (d), is never distributed.

Encryption

After Bob obtains Alice's public key, he can send a message M to Alice.

To do it, he first turns M (strictly speaking, the un-padded plaintext) into an integer m (strictly speaking, the padded plaintext), such that $0 \le m < n$ by using an agreed-upon reversible protocol known as a padding scheme. He then computes the ciphertext c, using Alice's public key e, corresponding to

$$c \equiv m^e \pmod{n}$$

This can be done reasonably quickly, even for 500-bit numbers, using modular exponentiation. Bob then transmits c to Alice.

Decryption

Alice can recover m from c by using her private key exponent d by computing

$$c^d \equiv (m^e)^d \equiv m \pmod{n}$$

Given m, she can recover the original message M by reversing the padding scheme.

Example

Here is an example of RSA encryption and decryption. The parameters used here are artificially small, but one can also use OpenSSL to generate and examine a real keypair.

1. Choose two distinct prime numbers, such as

   $p = 61$ and $q = 53$

2. Compute $n = pq$ giving

   $n = 61 \times 53 = 3233$

3. Compute the totient of the product as $\lambda(n) = \mathrm{lcm}(p - 1, q - 1)$ giving

   $\lambda(3233) = \mathrm{lcm}(60, 52) = 780$

4. Choose any number $1 < e < 780$ that is coprime to 780. Choosing a prime number for e leaves us only to check that e is not a divisor of 780.

   Let $e = 17$

5. Compute d, the modular multiplicative inverse of e (mod $\lambda(n)$) yielding,

   $d = 413$

Worked example for the modular multiplicative inverse:

$$d \times e \bmod (n) = 1$$

$$413 \times 17 \bmod 780 = 1$$

The public key is ($n = 3233$, $e = 17$). For a padded plaintext message m, the encryption function is

$$c(m) = m^{17} \bmod 3233$$

The private key is ($n = 3233$, $d = 413$). For an encrypted ciphertext c, the decryption function is

$$m(c) = c^{413} \bmod 3233$$

For instance, in order to encrypt $m = 65$, we calculate

$$c = 65^{17} \bmod 3233 = 2790$$

To decrypt $c = 2790$, we calculate

$$m = 2790^{413} \bmod 3233 = 65$$

Both of these calculations can be computed efficiently using the square-and-multiply algorithm for modular exponentiation. In real-life situations the primes selected would be much larger; in our example it would be trivial to factor n, 3233 (obtained from the freely available public key) back to the primes p and q. e, also from the public key, is then inverted to get d, thus acquiring the private key.

Practical implementations use the Chinese remainder theorem to speed up the calculation using modulus of factors (mod pq using mod p and mod q).

The values d_p, d_q and q_{inv}, which are part of the private key are computed as follows:

$$d_p = d \bmod (p-1) = 2753 \bmod (61-1) = 53$$
$$d_q = d \bmod (q-1) = 2753 \bmod (53-1) = 49$$
$$q_{inv} = q^{-1} \bmod p = 53^{-1} \bmod 61 = 38$$
$$\Rightarrow (q_{inv} \times q) \bmod p = 38 \times 53 \bmod 61 = 1$$

Here is how d_p, d_q and q_{inv} are used for efficient decryption. (Encryption is efficient by choice of a suitable d and e pair)

$$m_1 = c^{d_p} \bmod p = 2790^{53} \bmod 61 = 4$$
$$m_2 = c^{d_q} \bmod q = 2790^{49} \bmod 53 = 12$$
$$h = (q_{inv} \times (m_1 - m_2)) \bmod p = (38 \times -8) \bmod 61 = 1$$
$$m = m_2 + h \times q = 12 + 1 \times 53 = 65$$

Code

A working example in JavaScript using BigInteger.js. This code should not be used in production, as bigInt.randBetween() uses Math.random(), which is not a cryptographically secure pseudorandom number generator.

```
'use strict';

/**
```

```
 * RSA hash function reference implementation.

 * Uses BigInteger.js https://github.com/peterolson/BigInteger.js

 * Code originally based on https://github.com/kubrickology/Bitcoin-explained/
blob/master/RSA.js

 *

 * @namespace

 */

var RSA = {};

/**

 * Generates a k-bit RSA public/private key pair

 * https://en.wikipedia.org/wiki/RSA_(cryptosystem)#Code

 *

 * @param    {keysize} int, bitlength of desired RSA modulus n (should be even)

 * @returns {array} Result of RSA generation (object with three bigInt members:
n, e, d)

 */

RSA.generate = function (keysize) {

    /**

     * Generates a random k-bit prime greater than √2 × 2^(k-1)

     *

     * @param    {bits} int, bitlength of desired prime

     * @returns {bigInt} a random generated prime

     */

    function random_prime(bits) {

        var min = bigInt(6074001000).shiftLeft(bits-33); // min ≈ √2 × 2^(bits - 1)

        var max = bigInt.one.shiftLeft(bits).minus(1);    // max = 2^(bits) - 1

        while (true) {

            var p = bigInt.randBetween(min, max);  // WARNING: not a cryptograph-
ically secure RNG!

            if (p.isProbablePrime(256)) return p;

        }

    }


    // set up variables for key generation
```

```
    var e = bigInt(65537),          // use fixed public exponent

        p, q, lambda;


    // generate p and q such that λ(n) = lcm(p - 1, q - 1) is coprime with e and
|p-q| >= 2^(keysize/2 - 100)
    do {

        p = random_prime(keysize / 2);

        q = random_prime(keysize / 2);

        lambda = bigInt.lcm(p.minus(1), q.minus(1));

        } while (bigInt.gcd(e, lambda).notEquals(1) || p.minus(q).abs().shif-
tRight(keysize/2-100).isZero());


    return {
      n: p.multiply(q),    // public key (part I)

        e: e,              // public key (part II)

        d: e.modInv(lambda) // private key d = e^(-1) mod λ(n)

    };
};


/**

 * Encrypt

 *

 * @param    {m} int / bigInt: the 'message' to be encoded

 * @param    {n} int / bigInt: n value returned from RSA.generate() aka public
key (part I)

 * @param    {e} int / bigInt: e value returned from RSA.generate() aka public
key (part II)

 * @returns {bigInt} encrypted message

 */
RSA.encrypt = function(m, n, e){

    return bigInt(m).modPow(e, n);

};


/**

 * Decrypt
```

```
 *

 * @param    {c} int / bigInt: the 'message' to be decoded (encoded with RSA.
encrypt())

 * @param    {d} int / bigInt: d value returned from RSA.generate() aka private
key

 * @param    {n} int / bigInt: n value returned from RSA.generate() aka public
key (part I)

 * @returns {bigInt} decrypted message

 */

RSA.decrypt = function(c, d, n){

     return bigInt(c).modPow(d, n);

};
```

Signing Messages

Suppose Alice uses Bob's public key to send him an encrypted message. In the message, she can claim to be Alice but Bob has no way of verifying that the message was actually from Alice since anyone can use Bob's public key to send him encrypted messages. In order to verify the origin of a message, RSA can also be used to sign a message.

Suppose Alice wishes to send a signed message to Bob. She can use her own private key to do so. She produces a hash value of the message, raises it to the power of d (modulo n) (as she does when decrypting a message), and attaches it as a "signature" to the message. When Bob receives the signed message, he uses the same hash algorithm in conjunction with Alice's public key. He raises the signature to the power of e (modulo n) (as he does when encrypting a message), and compares the resulting hash value with the message's actual hash value. If the two agree, he knows that the author of the message was in possession of Alice's private key, and that the message has not been tampered with since.

Proofs of Correctness

Proof using Fermat'S Little Theorem

The proof of the correctness of RSA is based on Fermat's little theorem. This theorem states that if p is prime and p does not divide an integer a then

$$a^{p-1} \equiv 1 \pmod{p}$$

We want to show that $m^{ed} \equiv m \pmod{pq}$ for every integer m when p and q are distinct prime numbers and e and d are positive integers satisfying

$$ed \equiv 1 \pmod{(p-1)(q-1)}.$$

Write

$$ed - 1 = h(p-1) = k(q-1)$$

for some nonnegative integers h and k.

To check whether two numbers, like m^{ed} and m, are congruent mod pq it suffices (and in fact is equivalent) to check they are congruent mod p and mod q separately. (This is part of the Chinese remainder theorem, although it is not the significant part of that theorem.) To show $m^{ed} \equiv m$ (mod p), we consider two cases: $m \equiv 0$ (mod p) and $m \not\equiv 0$ (mod p).

In the first case, m is a multiple of p, thus m^{ed} is a multiple of p, so $m^{ed} \equiv 0 \equiv m$ (mod p). In the second case

$$m^{ed} = m^{ed-1}m = m^{h(p-1)}m = (m^{p-1})^h m \equiv 1^h m \equiv m \quad (\text{mod } p)$$

where we used Fermat's little theorem to replace m^{p-1} mod p with 1.

The verification that $m^{ed} \equiv m$ (mod q) proceeds in a similar way, treating separately the cases $m \equiv 0$ (mod q) and $m \not\equiv 0$ (mod q).

In the first case m^{ed} is a multiple of q, so $m^{ed} \equiv 0 \equiv m$ (mod q). In the second case

$$m^{ed} = m^{ed-1}m = m^{k(q-1)}m = (m^{q-1})^k m \equiv 1^k m \equiv m \quad (\text{mod } q)$$

This completes the proof that, for any integer m, and integers e, d such that ,

$$ed \equiv 1 \quad (\text{mod}(p-1)(q-1)),$$
$$(m^e)^d \equiv m \quad (\text{mod } pq).$$

Proof using Euler's Theorem

Although the original paper of Rivest, Shamir, and Adleman used Fermat's little theorem to explain why RSA works, it is common to find proofs that rely instead on Euler's theorem.

We want to show that $m^{ed} \equiv m$ (mod n), where $n = pq$ is a product of two different prime numbers and e and d are positive integers satisfying $ed \equiv 1$ (mod $\phi(n)$). Since e and d are positive, we can write $ed = 1 + h\phi(n)$ for some non-negative integer h. *Assuming* that m is relatively prime to n, we have

$$m^{ed} = m^{1+h\varphi(n)} = m(m^{\varphi(n)})^h \equiv m(1)^h \equiv m \quad (\text{mod } n)$$

where the second-last congruence follows from Euler's theorem.

More generally, for any e and d satisfying $ed \equiv 1$ (mod $\lambda(n)$), the same conclusion follows from Carmichael's generalization of Euler's theorem, which states that $m^{\lambda(n)} \equiv 1$ (mod n) for all m relatively prime to n.

When m is not relatively prime to n, the argument just given is invalid. This is highly improbable (only a proportion of $1/p + 1/q - 1/(pq)$ numbers have this property), but even in this case the desired congruence is still true. Either $m \equiv 0$ (mod p) or $m \equiv 0$ (mod q), and these cases can be treated using the previous proof.

Padding

Attacks Against Plain RSA

There are a number of attacks against plain RSA as described below.

- When encrypting with low encryption exponents (e.g., $e = 3$) and small values of the m, (i.e., $m < n^{1/e}$) the result of m^e is strictly less than the modulus n. In this case, ciphertexts can be easily decrypted by taking the eth root of the ciphertext over the integers.

- If the same clear text message is sent to e or more recipients in an encrypted way, and the receivers share the same exponent e, but different p, q, and therefore n, then it is easy to decrypt the original clear text message via the Chinese remainder theorem. Johan Håstad noticed that this attack is possible even if the cleartexts are not equal, but the attacker knows a linear relation between them. This attack was later improved by Don Coppersmith.

- Because RSA encryption is a deterministic encryption algorithm (i.e., has no random component) an attacker can successfully launch a chosen plaintext attack against the cryptosystem, by encrypting likely plaintexts under the public key and test if they are equal to the ciphertext. A cryptosystem is called semantically secure if an attacker cannot distinguish two encryptions from each other even if the attacker knows (or has chosen) the corresponding plaintexts. As described above, RSA without padding is not semantically secure.

- RSA has the property that the product of two ciphertexts is equal to the encryption of the product of the respective plaintexts. That is $m_1^e m_2^e \equiv (m_1 m_2)^e \pmod{n}$. Because of this multiplicative property a chosen-ciphertext attack is possible. E.g., an attacker, who wants to know the decryption of a ciphertext $c \equiv m^e \pmod{n}$ may ask the holder of the private key d to decrypt an unsuspicious-looking ciphertext $c' \equiv cr^e \pmod{n}$ for some value r chosen by the attacker. Because of the multiplicative property c' is the encryption of $mr \pmod{n}$. Hence, if the attacker is successful with the attack, he will learn $mr \pmod{n}$ from which he can derive the message m by multiplying mr with the modular inverse of r modulo n.

Padding Schemes

To avoid these problems, practical RSA implementations typically embed some form of structured, randomized padding into the value m before encrypting it. This padding ensures that m does not fall into the range of insecure plaintexts, and that a given message, once padded, will encrypt to one of a large number of different possible ciphertexts.

Standards such as PKCS#1 have been carefully designed to securely pad messages prior to RSA encryption. Because these schemes pad the plaintext m with some number of additional bits, the size of the un-padded message M must be somewhat smaller. RSA padding schemes must be carefully designed so as to prevent sophisticated attacks which may be facilitated by a predictable message structure. Early versions of the PKCS#1 standard (up to version 1.5) used a construction that appears to make RSA semantically secure. However, at Eurocrypt 2000, Coron et al. showed that for some types of messages, this padding does not provide a high enough level of security. Furthermore, at Crypto 1998, Bleichenbacher showed that this version is vulnerable to a practical adaptive chosen ciphertext attack. Later versions of the standard include Optimal Asymmetric Encryption

Padding (OAEP), which prevents these attacks. As such, OAEP should be used in any new application, and PKCS#1 v1.5 padding should be replaced wherever possible. The PKCS#1 standard also incorporates processing schemes designed to provide additional security for RSA signatures, e.g. the Probabilistic Signature Scheme for RSA (RSA-PSS).

Secure padding schemes such as RSA-PSS are as essential for the security of message signing as they are for message encryption. Two US patents on PSS were granted (USPTO 6266771 and USPTO 70360140); however, these patents expired on 24 July 2009 and 25 April 2010, respectively. Use of PSS no longer seems to be encumbered by patents. Note that using different RSA key-pairs for encryption and signing is potentially more secure.

Security and Practical Considerations

Using the Chinese Remainder Algorithm

For efficiency many popular crypto libraries (like OpenSSL, Java and .NET) use the following optimization for decryption and signing based on the Chinese remainder theorem. The following values are precomputed and stored as part of the private key:

- p and q: the primes from the key generation,

- $d_P = d \pmod{p-1}$,

- $d_Q = d \pmod{q-1}$ and

- $q_{\text{inv}} = q^{-1} \pmod{p}$.

These values allow the recipient to compute the exponentiation $m = c^d \pmod{pq}$ more efficiently as follows:

- $m_1 = c^{d_P} \pmod{p}$

- $m_2 = c^{d_Q} \pmod{q}$

- $h = q_{\text{inv}}(m_1 - m_2) \pmod{p}$ (if $m_1 < m_2$ then some libraries compute h as

$$q_{\text{inv}}\left[\left(m_1 + \left\lceil \frac{q}{p} \right\rceil p\right) - m_2\right] \pmod{p})$$

- $m = m_2 + hq$

This is more efficient than computing exponentiation by squaring even though two modular exponentiations have to be computed. The reason is that these two modular exponentiations both use a smaller exponent and a smaller modulus.

Integer Factorization and RSA Problem

The security of the RSA cryptosystem is based on two mathematical problems: the problem of factoring large numbers and the RSA problem. Full decryption of an RSA ciphertext is thought to be infeasible on the assumption that both of these problems are hard, i.e., no efficient algorithm exists for solving them. Providing security against *partial* decryption may require the addition of a secure padding scheme.

The RSA problem is defined as the task of taking eth roots modulo a composite n: recovering a value m such that $c \equiv m^e \pmod{n}$, where (n, e) is an RSA public key and c is an RSA ciphertext. Currently the most promising approach to solving the RSA problem is to factor the modulus n. With the ability to recover prime factors, an attacker can compute the secret exponent d from a public key (n, e), then decrypt c using the standard procedure. To accomplish this, an attacker factors n into p and q, and computes $\text{lcm}(p - 1, q - 1)$ which allows the determination of d from e. No polynomial-time method for factoring large integers on a classical computer has yet been found, but it has not been proven that none exists.

Multiple polynomial quadratic sieve (MPQS) can be used to factor the public modulus n. The time taken to factor 128-bit and 256-bit n on a desktop computer (Processor: Intel Dual-Core i7-4500U 1.80GHz) are respectively 2 seconds and 35 minutes.

Bits	Time
128	Less than 2 seconds
192	16 seconds
256	35 minutes
260	1 hour

A tool called yafu can be used to optimize this process. The automation within YAFU is state-of-the-art, combining factorization algorithms in an intelligent and adaptive methodology that minimizes the time to find the factors of arbitrary input integers. Most algorithm implementations are multi-threaded, allowing YAFU to fully utilize multi- or many-core processors (including SNFS, GNFS, SIQS, and ECM). The time taken to factor n using yafu on the same computer was reduced to 103.1746 seconds. Yafu requires the GGNFS binaries to factor N that are 320 bits or larger. It took about 5720s to factor *320bit-N* on the same computer.

Bits	Time	Memory used
128	0.4886 seconds	0.1 MiB
192	3.9979 seconds	0.5 MiB
256	103.1746 seconds	3 MiB
300	1175.7826 seconds	10.9 MiB

In 2009, Benjamin Moody factored an RSA-512 bit key in 73 days using only public software (GGNFS) and his desktop computer (dual-core Athlon64 at 1,900 MHz). Just under 5 gigabytes of disk was required and about 2.5 gigabytes of RAM for the sieving process. The first RSA-512 factorization in 1999 required the equivalent of 8,400 MIPS years over an elapsed time of about 7 months.

Rivest, Shamir and Adleman note that Miller has shown that – assuming the Extended Riemann Hypothesis – finding d from n and e is as hard as factoring n into p and q (up to a polynomial time difference). However, Rivest, Shamir and Adleman note hat they have not found a proof that inverting RSA is equally hard as factoring.

As of 2010, the largest factored RSA number was 768 bits long. Its factorization, by a state-of-the-art distributed implementation, took around fifteen hundred CPU years (two years of real time, on many hundreds of computers). No larger RSA key is publicly known to have been factored. In practice, RSA keys are typically 1024 to 4096 bits long. Some experts believe that 1024-bit keys may become breakable in the near future or may already be breakable by a sufficiently well-funded attacker (though this is disputed); few see any way that 4096-bit keys could be broken in the foreseeable future. Therefore, it is generally presumed that RSA is secure if n is sufficiently large. If n is 300 bits or shorter, it can be factored in a few hours on a personal computer, using software already freely available. Keys of 512 bits have been shown to be practically breakable in 1999 when RSA-155 was factored by using several hundred computers and are now factored in a few weeks using common hardware. Exploits using 512-bit code-signing certificates that may have been factored were reported in 2011. A theoretical hardware device named TWIRL and described by Shamir and Tromer in 2003 called into question the security of 1024 bit keys. It is currently recommended that n be at least 2048 bits long.

In 1994, Peter Shor showed that a quantum computer (if one could ever be practically created for the purpose) would be able to factor in polynomial time, breaking RSA.

Faulty Key Generation

Finding the large primes p and q is usually done by testing random numbers of the right size with probabilistic primality tests which quickly eliminate virtually all non-primes.

Numbers p and q should not be 'too close', lest the Fermat factorization for n be successful, if $p - q$, for instance is less than $2n^{1/4}$ (which for even small 1024-bit values of n is $3{\times}10^{77}$) solving for p and q is trivial. Furthermore, if either $p - 1$ or $q - 1$ has only small prime factors, n can be factored quickly by Pollard's $p - 1$ algorithm, and these values of p or q should therefore be discarded as well.

It is important that the private exponent d be large enough. Michael J. Wiener showed that if p is between q and $2q$ (which is quite typical) and $d < n^{1/4}/3$, then d can be computed efficiently from n and e.

There is no known attack against small public exponents such as $e = 3$, provided that proper padding is used. Coppersmith's Attack has many applications in attacking RSA specifically if the public exponent e is small and if the encrypted message is short and not padded. 65537 is a commonly used value for e; this value can be regarded as a compromise between avoiding potential small exponent attacks and still allowing efficient encryptions (or signature verification). The NIST Special Publication on Computer Security (SP 800-78 Rev 1 of August 2007) does not allow public exponents e smaller than 65537, but does not state a reason for this restriction.

Importance of Strong Random Number Generation

A cryptographically strong random number generator, which has been properly seeded with adequate entropy, must be used to generate the primes p and q. An analysis comparing millions of public keys gathered from the Internet was carried out in early 2012 by Arjen K. Lenstra, James P.

Hughes, Maxime Augier, Joppe W. Bos, Thorsten Kleinjung and Christophe Wachter. They were able to factor 0.2% of the keys using only Euclid's algorithm.

They exploited a weakness unique to cryptosystems based on integer factorization. If $n = pq$ is one public key and $n' = p'q'$ is another, then if by chance $p = p'$ (but q is not equal to q'), then a simple computation of $\gcd(n,n') = p$ factors both n and n', totally compromising both keys. Lenstra et al. note that this problem can be minimized by using a strong random seed of bit-length twice the intended security level, or by employing a deterministic function to choose q given p, instead of choosing p and q independently.

Nadia Heninger was part of a group that did a similar experiment. They used an idea of Daniel J. Bernstein to compute the GCD of each RSA key n against the product of all the other keys n' they had found (a 729 million digit number), instead of computing each $\gcd(n,n')$ separately, thereby achieving a very significant speedup since after one large division the GCD problem is of normal size.

Heninger says in her blog that the bad keys occurred almost entirely in embedded applications, including "firewalls, routers, VPN devices, remote server administration devices, printers, projectors, and VOIP phones" from over 30 manufacturers. Heninger explains that the one-shared-prime problem uncovered by the two groups results from situations where the pseudorandom number generator is poorly seeded initially and then reseeded between the generation of the first and second primes. Using seeds of sufficiently high entropy obtained from key stroke timings or electronic diode noise or atmospheric noise from a radio receiver tuned between stations should solve the problem.

Strong random number generation is important throughout every phase of public key cryptography. For instance, if a weak generator is used for the symmetric keys that are being distributed by RSA, then an eavesdropper could bypass the RSA and guess the symmetric keys directly.

Timing Attacks

Kocher described a new attack on RSA in 1995: if the attacker Eve knows Alice's hardware in sufficient detail and is able to measure the decryption times for several known ciphertexts, she can deduce the decryption key d quickly. This attack can also be applied against the RSA signature scheme. In 2003, Boneh and Brumley demonstrated a more practical attack capable of recovering RSA factorizations over a network connection (e.g., from a Secure Sockets Layer (SSL)-enabled webserver) This attack takes advantage of information leaked by the Chinese remainder theorem optimization used by many RSA implementations.

One way to thwart these attacks is to ensure that the decryption operation takes a constant amount of time for every ciphertext. However, this approach can significantly reduce performance. Instead, most RSA implementations use an alternate technique known as cryptographic blinding. RSA blinding makes use of the multiplicative property of RSA. Instead of computing c^d (mod n), Alice first chooses a secret random value r and computes $(r^e c)^d$ (mod n). The result of this computation after applying Euler's Theorem is rc^d (mod n) and so the effect of r can be removed by multiplying by its inverse. A new value of r is chosen for each ciphertext. With blinding applied, the decryption time is no longer correlated to the value of the input ciphertext and so the timing attack fails.

Adaptive Chosen Ciphertext Attacks

In 1998, Daniel Bleichenbacher described the first practical adaptive chosen ciphertext attack, against RSA-encrypted messages using the PKCS #1 v1 padding scheme (a padding scheme randomizes and adds structure to an RSA-encrypted message, so it is possible to determine whether a decrypted message is valid). Due to flaws with the PKCS #1 scheme, Bleichenbacher was able to mount a practical attack against RSA implementations of the Secure Socket Layer protocol, and to recover session keys. As a result of this work, cryptographers now recommend the use of provably secure padding schemes such as Optimal Asymmetric Encryption Padding, and RSA Laboratories has released new versions of PKCS #1 that are not vulnerable to these attacks.

Side-channel Analysis Attacks

A side-channel attack using branch prediction analysis (BPA) has been described. Many processors use a branch predictor to determine whether a conditional branch in the instruction flow of a program is likely to be taken or not. Often these processors also implement simultaneous multithreading (SMT). Branch prediction analysis attacks use a spy process to discover (statistically) the private key when processed with these processors.

Simple Branch Prediction Analysis (SBPA) claims to improve BPA in a non-statistical way. In their paper, "On the Power of Simple Branch Prediction Analysis", the authors of SBPA (Onur Aciicmez and Cetin Kaya Koc) claim to have discovered 508 out of 512 bits of an RSA key in 10 iterations.

A power fault attack on RSA implementations has been described in 2010. The authors recovered the key by varying the CPU power voltage outside limits; this caused multiple power faults on the server.

RSA Public Key Cryptosystem

The cryptosystem is set up as follows:

1. Choose two large random and distinct primes p and q 100 – 200 digit each roughly of the same size.

2. Compute n = pq

3. Compute $\Phi(n) = n(1-1/p)(1-1/q) = (p-1)(q-1)$.

4. Pick an integer e that is relatively prime to $\Phi(n)$, i.e., gcd$(e, \Phi(n)) = 1$.

5. Compute d the multiplicative inverse of e modulo $\Phi(n)$, i.e., ed $\equiv$ 1 mod $\Phi(n)$.

6. Publish the pair (e, n) as the RSA public key.

7. Retain the pair (d, n) as the RSA secret key.

Suppose Alice wants to send a message M to Bob. Assume M<n. So Alice encrypts M with the public key d of Bob to obtain the cipher-text C = M^d mod n. She sends C to Bob. Bob decrypts the cipher C using his secret key d to get C^d mod n $\equiv M^{ed}$ mod n $\equiv$ M mod n. Eve knows C, e and n. But to deter-

mine M she has to determine d for which she has to compute $\Phi(n)$. Since $\Phi(n) = n\,(1\text{-}1/\,p\,)(1\text{-}1/\,q\,)$ = $(\,p\,\text{-}1)(\,q\,\text{-}1)$, for Bob it is easy to compute $\Phi(n)$ since he knows both p and q . But this computation for Eve requires factoring n . So it is computationally infeasible for Eve to determine d .

Correctness of RSA is established via following argument:

We know $M \in Z_n$ since $M \in Z \in \wedge\ M < n$.

Since e and d are multiplicative inverses we have $ed \equiv 1 \bmod \Phi\,(n)$, i.e., $ed = 1 + k\,(p\,\text{-}1)(q\,\text{-}1)$ for some integer k .

Now if $M \neq 0 \bmod p$, we have:

$$M^{ed} \quad \equiv M(M^{k(\,p\,\text{-}1)(\,q\,\text{-}1))} \qquad \bmod p$$

$$\equiv M(M^{(\,p\,\text{-}1)k(\,q\,\text{-}1)} \qquad \bmod p$$

$$\equiv M(1)^{k(\,q\,\text{-}1)} \qquad \bmod p \ [\text{Applying Fermat's Theorem}]$$

$$\equiv M \quad \bmod p$$

Again if $M \equiv 0 \bmod p$ then trivially $M^{ed} \equiv M \bmod p$.

Thus for all $M \in Z_n$ we have:

$$M^{ed} \equiv M \bmod p \text{-------------} (1)$$

Similarly for all $M \in Z_n$ we have:

$$M^{ed} \equiv M \bmod q \text{------------} (2)$$

Combining (1) and (2) using Chinese Remainder Theorem we have:

$$M^{ed} \equiv M \bmod n$$

for all M.

Computationally hard assumption for RSA algorithm is the difficulty of factoring the modulus n . If n can be factorized in polynomial time to obtain p and q then the attacker can break the cipher in polynomial time. This is because the attacker will know $\Phi\,(\,n\,) = (\,p\,\text{-}1)(\,q\,\text{-}1)$ and then by using EXTENDED-EUCLID algorithm d can be computed. Conversely if the attacker can figure out the decryption key d then the attacker can come to know $k\,\Phi\,(n)$ since $ed \equiv 1 \bmod \Phi\,(\,n\,) \Rightarrow ed = 1 + k\,\Phi\,(\,n\,)$ for some integer k .

RSA is frequently used in hybrid mode with fast non-public key cryptosystem. It is combined with cryptosystems for which encryption and decryption keys are identical like DES or AES. RSA is used to transmit the key. But the original message is encrypted as a symmetric cipher. Suppose the key required for symmetric encryption is K. So the message M is encrypted with K to obtain the symmetric cipher E(K, M). But the receiving party Bob doesn't know K. So the sender Alice encrypts K in RSA with receiver's public key P_B to obtain $P_B\,(K)$. She then sends to Bob E(K, M) || $P_B\,(K)$. Bob after receiving applies his own secret key S_B over $P_B\,(K)$ to obtain K. He then applies K over the first component for symmetric decryption to retrieve M.

Choice of the Public Key: To speed up the modular exponentiation operation it is desirable that the public key has lot of 0 bits. Usual choice of public key is of the form 2^k+1 since this will have exactly two zeros. Common choice of public keys are 3, 17 and 65537 (= $2^{16}+1$).

If the public key is very small then RSA is vulnerable to the following attack:

Suppose the encryption / public key is e = 3 used by three different users A, B and C having 3 distinct moduli namely n_1, n_2 and n_3. Suppose the sender X wants to send the same message M to A, B and C. So he encrypts all of them with the same public key e and computes the cipher texts C_A = M^e mod n_1, C_B = M^e mod n_2 and C_C = M^e mod n_3 respectively.

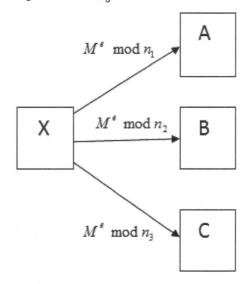

Suppose it happens to be n_1, n_2 and n_3 are pairwise relatively prime and $n_1 {}^* n_2 {}^* n_3 > M^e$. This can only happen if e is very small. In our case let us assume $M^3 < n_1 {}^* n_2 {}^* n_3$ since e = 3 though M^3 is larger than each n_1, n_2 and n_3. Then using Chinese Remainder Theorem the attacker can easily compute M^3 and thus can determine M after computing the cube root.

Operations using the secret key:

For the decryption operation we perform the following modular exponentiation operation to retrieve the original message M:

M = C^d mod n where C is the cipher text, d is the secret key and n = p×q where p and q are two large primes. To speed up this operation we compute:

V_p = C^d mod p and V_q = C^d mod q

From these using to compute C^d mod n we have to use Chinese Remainder Theorem.

So we compute:

X_p = q x (q^{-1} mod p) and X_q = p x (p^{-1} mod q)

Now we retrieve M as follows:

M = ($V_p X_p$ + $V_q X_q$) mod n

To speed up the two modular exponentiation operations to compute V_p and V_q we can make use of Fermat's theorem as follows:

$a^b \bmod p = a^y \bmod p$

where $b = (p-1)x + y$ since $a^{p-1} \equiv 1 \bmod p$.

Attacks on RSA:

There are several attacks on RSA public key cryptosystem. They are categorized as follows:

1. Brute Force Attack: Here the attacker tries with different secret keys.

2. Mathematical Attacks: Most of these approaches finally broil down to factoring RSA modulus.

3. Timing Attack: This attack uses the timing difference of modular exponentiation algorithm depending on the number of 0 bits and 1 bits in the secret key. We will elaborate on this later.

4. Chosen Cipher Text Attack (CCA).

Mathematical Attack:

Here we prove that if the attacker can figure out the secret key d in polynomial time then we have a randomized polynomial time algorithm to factor n.

Choose a random number $r \in Z_n^*$. Since both e and d are known we know $ed - 1 = k.\Phi(n)$. Thus from Euler's theorem $r^{ed-1} \equiv 1 \bmod n$. The goal here is to obtain a non-trivial square root of 1. For this we keep on computing $r^{\frac{ed-1}{2}}, r^{\frac{ed-1}{4}}, \ldots$ and so on till we get either -1 or a non-trivial square root of 1 or $\frac{ed-1}{2^l}$ is no longer divisible by 2. If we obtain -1 or $\frac{ed-1}{2^l}$ is no longer divisible by 2 we repeat the above procedure selecting a new random number r. Otherwise if we get a non-trivial square root of 1, i.e., x such that $x^2 \equiv 1 \bmod n$ and $x \neq \pm 1$ then gcd $(x+1, n)$ or gcd $(x-1, n)$ will give a non-trivial factor of n (i.e., 1 or n). Thus we have a randomized polynomial time algorithm to factorize n.

Chosen Cipher Text Attack:

Here the attacker Eve gets holds of a cipher text C that was sent by Alice to Bob. Let M be the corresponding plaintext. Thus M = Ce mod n. The attack proceeds as follows:

1. Eve selects a random number r, such that $1 < r < n-1$ and $\gcd(r,n) = 1$.

2. Eve computes $X = r^e C \bmod n$ and submits to Bob as a chosen cipher text.

3. Eve receives back the signed message from Bob $Y = X^d \bmod n = rM \bmod n$.

4. Since Eve know r^{-1} she retrieves the message $M = r^{-1}Y \bmod n$.

Remedies:

To overcome this attack the plaintext is usually padded prior to encryption. Method like optimal asymmetric encryption scheme (OAEP) has been proposed to overcome such attacks.

Attacks on RSA & Remedies

Timing Attack:

This attack was first suggested by Paul Kocher in 1995. He showed that it is possible to find out the secret key by careful examination of the computation times in a series of decryption procedure. The method uses the weakness of modular exponentiation algorithm and can be used to attack not only RSA but also any other cryptographic algorithms that use modular exponentiation that includes algorithms based on discrete log computation.

Suppose Eve sends to Bob several ciphertexts y. After decryption of each ciphertext Bob sends the acknowledgement back to Eve. Thus Eve comes to know the decryption time of each ciphertext. From this timing information Eve has to figure out the decryption exponent d.

We need to assume that Eve knows the hardware being used to to calculate y^d (mod n). Eve can use this information to calculate the computation time of various steps that occur in this process.

Let $d=b_1b_2...b_w$ be written in binary. Let y and n be integers. We perform the modular exponentiation using the following algorithm:

1. Start with k=1 and s_1=1.

2. If b_k==1, let $r_k \equiv s_k$ y(mod n). If b_k == 0, let $r_k=s_k$.

3. Let $s_{k+1} \equiv r_k^2$ (mod n).

4. If k==w, stop. If k<w, add 1 to k and go to (3).

Finally $r_w \equiv y^d$ (mod n).

Here we note that the multiplication s_k y occurs only when the bit b_k==1. In practice there is a large variation in timing of this multiplication operation.

Now we need to introduce few notations from Probability & Statistics. Let t denote the random variable for the time taken for the decryption of a ciphertext y.

Let t_1, t_2, ..., t_n denote the decryption time of ciphertexts y_1, y_2, ..., y_n. The mean is denoted by :

$$\text{Mean}(t) = m = \frac{t_1 + t_2 + ... + t_n}{n}$$

The variance of the random variable t is denoted by:

$$Var(t) = \frac{(t_1 - m)^2 + (t_2 - m)^2 + ... + (t_n - m)^2}{n}$$

If we break up the computation time t_i for the decryption of the ciphertext y_i into two independent random processes with computation times t_i' and t_i'' respectively such that $t_i = t_i' + t_i''$, then Var(t_i) = Var(t_i') + Var(t_i'').

Eve knows t_1, t_2, ..., t_n. Suppose she knows bits $b_1b_2...b_{k-1}$ of the secret key d. Since she knows the hardware she can figure out the time required for computing r_1, r_2, ...r_{k-1} in the modular exponentiation algorithm. Also she can determine the time to calculate $s_{k+1} \equiv r_k^2 \pmod n$ when $b_k == 0$ since $r_k = s_k$. Thus she knows the remaining computation time x_i for each ciphertext y_i to compute $r_k, \ldots, r_w$.

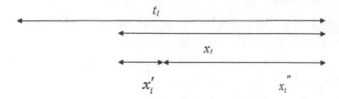

Let x_i' be the computation time for $s_k \, y \pmod n$ if the bit $b_k == 1$. Eve still doesn't know b_k. Let $x_i'' = x_i - x_i'$. Eve computes $Var(x_i)$ and $Var(x_i'')$. If $Var(x_i) > Var(x_i'')$ Eve concludes $b_k = 1$ else $b_k = 0$. After determining b_k Eve proceeds in the same manner to determine the remaining bits of the secret key.

Correctness Proof: If $b_k = 1$ then the multiplication $s_k \, y \pmod n$ indeed occurs. It is reasonable to assume x_i' and x_i'' are independent and thus:

$Var(x_i) = Var(x_i') + Var(x_i'') > Var(x_i'')$.

If $b_k = 0$ then the multiplication does not occur and $= Var(x_i') \cong 0$. Thus

$$Var(x_i) = Var(x_i') + Var(x_i'') \cong Var(x_i).$$

Remedies:

i) Constant Exponentiation Time: Timing attack can be avoided if Bob sends the acknowledgement back after the same fixed amount of time for each ciphertext. This solves the problem but the performance is degraded.

ii) Random Delay: Here Bob sends back the acknowledgement after adding a random delay after the end of each modular exponentiation computation. This is susceptible to attack since the attacker can compensate the added random delay considering it as fluctuation over the d.c (average) component.

iii) Blinding: This proceeds as follows:

  1. Bob selects a random number r, such that $1 < r < n-1$ and $gcd(r,n) = 1$.

  2. Bob computes $X = r^e \, C \bmod n$, where e is the public key.

  3. Bob Computes $Y = X^d \bmod n = rM \bmod n$.

  4. Since Bob knows r^{-1} he retrieves the message $M = r^{-1} Y \bmod n$.

This process prevents the attacker in knowing what cipher text bits are being processed and prevents bit by bit analysis that is essential for the timing attack.

Rabin Cryptosystem:

Rabin cryptosystem is described as follows:

Let n be the product of two distinct primes p and q, $p, q \equiv 3 \pmod 4$

Let P, C $\in Z_n$, where P is the plaintext and C is the cipher text.

Define

K = {(n, p, q, B) : 0 ≤ B ≤ n-1}

For K = (n, p, q, B), define

$e_K(x) = x(x+B) \bmod n$

and

$$d_K(y) = \left(\sqrt{\frac{B^2}{4} + y} - \frac{B}{2} \right) \bmod n$$

The values n and B are public, while p and q are secret.

The encryption function e_K is not an injection, so decryption cannot be done in an unambiguous fashion. In fact, there are four possible plaintexts that could be the encryption of any given ciphertext. It is easy to verify that if ω is a nontrivial square root of 1 modulo n, then there are four decryptions of $e_K(x)$ for any x$\in Z_n$:

$$x, -x, \omega\left(x + \frac{B}{2} \right) - \frac{B}{2}, -\omega\left(x + \frac{B}{2} \right) - \frac{B}{2}$$

Example:

$$e\left(\omega\left(x + \frac{B}{2} \right) - \frac{B}{2} \right) = \left(\omega\left(x + \frac{B}{2} \right) - \frac{B}{2} \right)\left(\omega\left(x + \frac{B}{2} \right) + \frac{B}{2} \right) = \omega^2\left(x + \frac{B}{2} \right)^2 - \left(\frac{B}{2} \right)^2 = x^2 + Bx = e(x)$$

So the decryption process won't be unique unless the plaintext contains sufficient redundancy to eliminate three pf these four values.

The decryption process is analyzed as follows:

Given a ciphertext y, the plaintext x is determined by the solving the equation

$x^2 + Bx \equiv y \pmod{n}$

Substituting $x = x_1 - B/2$, the above equation reduces to

$x_1^2 - Bx_1 + B^2/4 + Bx_1 - B^2/2 - y \equiv 0 \pmod{n}$

or

$x_1^2 \equiv B^2/4 + y \pmod{n}$

Let C = $B^2/4 + y$, then we can rewrite the congruence as

$x_1^2 \equiv C \pmod{n}$

So, decryption reduces to extracting square roots modulo n. This is equivalent to solving the two congruences

$$x_1^2 \equiv C \ (\text{mod } p)$$

and

$$x_1^2 \equiv C \ (\text{mod } q)$$

Now there are two square roots of C modulo p and two square roots of C modulo q. Using the Chinese remainder theorem, these can be combined to yield four solutions modulo n. Also it can be determined by Euler's criterion if C is a quadratic residue modulo p (and modulo q). Infact, C will be a quadratic residue modulo p (and modulo q) if encryption is performed correctly.

When $p \equiv 3 \ (\text{mod } 4)$, there is a simple formula to compute square roots of quadratic residues modulo p. Suppose C is a quadratic residue and $p \equiv 3 \ (\text{mod } 4)$. Then we have that

$$\pm C^{(p+1)/4} \text{ mod } p \equiv C^{(p+1)/2} (\text{mod } p)$$
$$\equiv C^{(p-1)/2} C (\text{mod } p)$$
$$\equiv C (\text{mod } p)$$

Here, we again make use of Euler's criterion, which says that if C is a quadratic residue modulo p, then $C^{(p-1)/2} \equiv 1 \ (\text{mod } p)$. Hence the two square roots of C modulo p are $\pm C^{(p+1)/4} \text{ mod } p$. In a similar fashion, the two square roots of C modulo q are $\pm C^{(q+1)/4} \text{ mod } q$. One can then obtain the four square roots x_1 of C modulo n using the Chinese Remainder Theorem

Example:

Let us illustrate the encryption and decryption procedures for the Rabin cryptosystem with a toy example. Suppose n = 77 = 7 x 11 and B = 9. Then the encryption function is

$$e_K(x) = x^2 + 9x \text{mod } 77$$

and the decryption function is

$$d_K(y) = \left(\sqrt{1+y} - 43 \right) \text{mod } 77$$

Suppose the ciphertext y = 22. Compute the square roots of 23 modulo 7 and modulo 11. Since 7 and 11 are both congruent to 3 mod 4, using the formula derived above, we have

$$23^{(7+1)/4} \equiv 22 \equiv 4 \ mod \ 7$$
$$23^{(11+1)/4} \equiv 13 \equiv 1 \ mod \ 11$$

Using Chinese Remainder Theorem, we compute the four square roots of 23 modulo 77 to be ± 10 and ± 32 mod 77.

Finally, the four possible plaintexts are

$$10 - 63 \bmod 77 = 44$$

$$67 - 43 \bmod 77 = 24$$

$$32 - 43 \bmod 77 = 66$$

$$45 - 43 \bmod 77 = 2$$

The computationally hard problem in this cryptosystem is the difficulty of factoring the modulus n. In contrary let us assume that the adversary can figure out the square roots modulo n. Since n is the product of two primes there will be 4 square roots x_1 , x_2 , x_3 and x_4 such that $x_1^2 \equiv x_2^2 \equiv x_3^2 \equiv x_4^2 \bmod n$. Among these 4 square roots there will be a pair such that $x_i \bmod n \neq \pm x_j \bmod n$ for some i , j $\in$ [1..4]. Then gcd (x_i + x_j , n) or gcd (x_i - x_j , n) will give a non trivial factor of n. Thus if we can break the cryptosystem in polynomial time we will be able to factor n in polynomial time.

References

- "Case Closed on Zimmermann PGP Investigation". IEEE Computer Society's Technical Committee on Security and Privacy. 14 February 1996. Retrieved 26 March 2015

- Goldwasser, S.; Micali, S.; Rackoff, C. (1989). "The Knowledge Complexity of Interactive Proof Systems". SIAM Journal on Computing. 18 (1): 186–208. doi:10.1137/0218012

- Menezes, A. J.; van Oorschot, P. C.; Vanstone, S. A. Handbook of Applied Cryptography. ISBN 0-8493-8523-7. Archived from the original on 7 March 2005

- "Cryptology (definition)". Merriam-Webster's Collegiate Dictionary (11th ed.). Merriam-Webster. Retrieved 26 March 2015

- Sharbaf, M.S. (2011-11-01). "Quantum cryptography: An emerging technology in network security". 2011 IEEE International Conference on Technologies for Homeland Security (HST): 13–19. doi:10.1109/THS.2011.6107841

- Coppersmith, D. (May 1994). "The Data Encryption Standard (DES) and its strength against attacks" (PDF). IBM Journal of Research and Development. 38 (3): 243–250. doi:10.1147/rd.383.0243. Retrieved 26 March 2015

- Oded Goldreich, Foundations of Cryptography, Volume 1: Basic Tools, Cambridge University Press, 2001, ISBN 0-521-79172-3

- "FIPS PUB 197: The official Advanced Encryption Standard" (PDF). Computer Security Resource Center. National Institute of Standards and Technology. Retrieved 26 March 2015

- Al-Kadi, Ibrahim A. (April 1992). "The origins of cryptology: The Arab contributions". Cryptologia. 16 (2): 97–126. doi:10.1080/0161-119291866801

- Biham, E.; Shamir, A. (1991). "Differential cryptanalysis of DES-like cryptosystems" (PDF). Journal of Cryptology. Springer-Verlag. 4 (1): 3–72. doi:10.1007/bf00630563. Retrieved 26 March 2015

- Gannon, James (2001). Stealing Secrets, Telling Lies: How Spies and Codebreakers Helped Shape the Twentieth Century. Washington, D.C.: Brassey's. ISBN 1-57488-367-4

- "NIST Selects Winner of Secure Hash Algorithm (SHA-3) Competition". Tech Beat. National Institute of Standards and Technology. October 2, 2012. Retrieved 26 March 2015

- Shamir, A. (1979). "How to share a secret". Communications of the ACM. Association for Computing Machinery. 22: 612–613. doi:10.1145/359168.359176

- Ayushi (2010). "A Symmetric Key Cryptographic Algorithm" (PDF). International Journal of Computer Applications. 1-No 15

- Shannon, Claude; Weaver, Warren (1963). The Mathematical Theory of Communication. University of Illinois Press. ISBN 0-252-72548-4

- Wayner, Peter (24 December 1997). "British Document Outlines Early Encryption Discovery". New York Times. Retrieved 26 March 2015

- Rivest, R.; Shamir, A.; Adleman, L. (February 1978). "A Method for Obtaining Digital Signatures and Public-Key Cryptosystems" (PDF). Communications of the ACM. 21 (2): 120–126. doi:10.1145/359340.359342

- Coppersmith, Don (1997). "Small Solutions to Polynomial Equations, and Low Exponent RSA Vulnerabilities". Journal of Cryptology. 10 (4): 233–260. doi:10.1007/s001459900030

- Delfs, Hans & Knebl, Helmut (2007). "Symmetric-key encryption". Introduction to cryptography: principles and applications. Springer. ISBN 9783540492436

- Ingold, John (January 4, 2012). "Password case reframes Fifth Amendment rights in context of digital world". The Denver Post. Retrieved 26 March 2015

- Håstad, Johan (1986). "On using RSA with Low Exponent in a Public Key Network". Advances in Cryptology — CRYPTO '85 Proceedings. Lecture Notes in Computer Science. 218. pp. 403–408. doi:10.1007/3-540-39799-X_29

4

Elliptic Curves: An Integrated Study

Elliptic curves are very important for the subject of number theory. Elliptical curve cryptography is based on the theory of elliptic curves. It is used to make cryptographic keys more efficient and faster. These keys are generated through the properties of elliptic curve equations. This chapter discusses elliptic curves based cryptography in a critical manner providing key analysis to the subject matter.

Elliptic Curves

An elliptic curve is defined by an equation in two variables, with coefficients. For cryptography, the variables and coefficients are restricted to elements in a finite field.

Note : Elliptic curves are not ellipses. They are so named because they are described by cubic equations, similar to those used for calculating the circumference of an ellipse.

Definition : Let K be a field of characteristic $\neq 2,3$ and let $x^3 + ax + b$ (where $a,b \in K$) be a cubic polynomial with no multiple roots. An elliptic curve over K is the set of points (x,y) with $x,y \in K$ which satisfy the equation

$$y^2 = x^3 + ax + b$$

together with a single element 0 and called the "point at infinity".

If K is a field of characteristic 2, then an elliptic curve over K is the set of points satisfying an equation of type either

$$y^2 + cy = x^3 + ax + b$$

or else,

$$y^2 + xy = x^3 + ax^2 + b$$

If K is a field of characteristic 3, then an elliptic curve over is the set of points satisfying the equation

$$y^3 = x^3 + ax^2 + bx + c$$

Figure shows two examples of elliptic curves. Now, consider the set of points E (a,b) consisting of all of the points (x,y) that satisfy Equation $y^2 = x^3 + ax + b$ together with the element O. Using a different value of the pair (a,b) results in a different set E (a,b).

Using this terminology, the two curves in Figure depict the sets $E(-1,0)$ and $E(1,1)$, respectively.

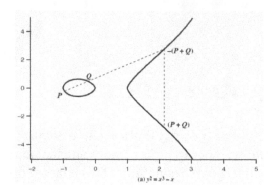 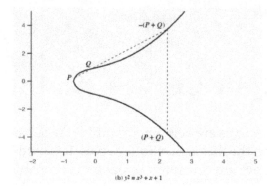

(a) $y^2 = x^3 - x$ (b) $y^2 = x^3 + x + 1$

Examples of Elliptic Curves

Geometric Description of Addition :

A group can be defined based on the set E (a,b) for specific values of a and b in Equation $y^2 = x^3 + ax + b$, provided the following condition is met:

$$4a^3 + 27b^2 \neq 0$$

To define a group, we define an operation, called addition and denoted by +, for the set E (a,b), where a and b satisfy Equation $4a^3 + 27b^2 \neq 0$. In geometric terms, the rules for addition can be stated as follows: If three points on an elliptic curve lie on a straight line, their sum is O.

From this definition, we can define the rules of addition over an elliptic curve:

i. O serves as the additive identity. Thus $O = -O$ and for any point P on the elliptic curve, $P + O = P$. In what follows, assume $P \neq O$ and $Q \neq O$.

ii.   The negative of a point P is the point with the same x coordinate but the negative of the y coordinate; that is; if $P = (x, y)$ then $-P = (x, -y)$. Note that these two points can be joined by a vertical line. Note that $P + (-P) = P - P = O$.

iii. To add two points P and Q with different x coordinate, draw a straight line between them and find the third point of intersection R that is the point of intersection (unless the line is tangent to the curve at either P or Q, in which case we take $R = P$ or $R = Q$, respectively). To form a group structure, we need to define addition on these three points as follows: $P + Q = -R$ .That is, we define $P + Q$ to the mirror image (with respect to the axis) of the third points of intersection. Figure illustrates this construction.

iv.   The geometric interpretation of the preceding item also applies to two points, P and $-P$, with the same x coordinate. The points are joined by a vertical line, which can be viewed as also intersecting the curve at the infinity point. We therefore have $P + -P = O$.

v.   To double a point Q, draw the tangent line and fine the other point of intersection S. Then $Q + Q = 2Q = -S$.

Let $(x_1, y_1), (x_2, y_2)$ and $(x_3, -y_3)$ denote the coordinates of P, Q, and R respectively. We want to express x_3 and y_3 in terms of x_1, y_1, x_2, y_2.

Let $y = \alpha x + \beta$ be the equation of the line passing through P and Q.

$$\therefore \alpha = \frac{y_2 - y_1}{(x_2 - x_1)}$$

The equation of the elliptic curve $y^2 = x^3 + ax + b$ is

$$(\alpha x + \beta)^2 = x^3 + ax + b$$

$$\Rightarrow x^3 - (\alpha x + \beta)^2 + ax + b = 0$$

Roots of the equation are x_1, x_2, x_3.

$$(x - \alpha)(x - \beta)(x - \gamma) = 0$$

$$\Rightarrow x^3 - (\alpha + \beta + \gamma)x^2 + (\alpha\beta + \beta\gamma + \gamma\alpha)x - \alpha\beta\gamma = 0$$

$$Sum\ of\ the\ roots = (\alpha + \beta + \gamma)$$

Addition of two points:

$$x_1 + x_2 + x_3 = \alpha^2$$

$$\therefore x_3 = \alpha^2 - x_1 - x_2$$

$$y_3 = \alpha x_3 + \beta$$

$$y_1 = \alpha x_1 + \beta$$

$$\therefore \beta = y_1 - \alpha x_1$$

$$y_3 = \alpha x_3 + y_1 - \alpha x_1$$

$$\therefore y_3 = \alpha(x_3 - x_1) + y_1$$

$$\therefore -y_3 = \alpha(x_1 - x_3) - y_1$$

$$-R = (x_3, y_3)$$

$$x_3 = \left(\frac{y_2 - y_1}{x_2 - x_1}\right)^2 - x_1 - x_2$$

$$y_3 = \left(\frac{y_2 - y_1}{x_2 - x_1}\right)(x_1 - x_3) - y_1$$

$$y^2 = x^3 + ax + b \qquad P = Q = (x_1, y_1)$$

$$\therefore 2y\frac{dy}{dx} = 3x^2 + a$$

$$\therefore \frac{dy}{dx} = \frac{3x^2 + a}{2y} = \alpha$$

$$x_3 = \left(\frac{3x_1^2 + a}{2y_1}\right)^2 - 2x_1$$

$$y_3 = \left(\frac{3x_1^2 + a}{2y_1}\right)(x_1 - x_3) - y_1$$

$R = (x_3, -y_3)$ is the point of intersection of the tangent at P and the elliptic curve.

Example : On the elliptic curve $y^2 = x^3 - 36x$ let $P = (-3, 9)$ and $Q = (-2, 8)$. Find $P + Q$ and $2P$.

Solution.

$$P = (-3, 9) \qquad Q = (-2, 8)$$

For finding $P + Q$,

$$\alpha = \frac{8 - 9}{-2 + 3} = \frac{-1}{1} = -1$$

$$x_3 = \alpha^2 - x_1 - x_2$$

$$= 1 + 3 + 2$$

$$= 6$$

$$y_3 = \alpha(x_3 - x_1) - y_1$$

$$= -1(-3 - 6) - 9$$

$$= 9 - 9$$

$$= 0$$

$$\therefore P + Q = (6, 0)$$

For finding $2P$,

$$\alpha = \frac{3x_1^2 - 36}{2y_1}$$

$$= \frac{3(9) - 36}{2(9)}$$

$$= -\frac{1}{2}$$

$$x_3 = \alpha^2 - 2x_1$$

$$= \frac{1}{4} - 2(-3)$$

$$= \frac{25}{4}$$

$$y_3 = -y_1 + \alpha(x_1 - x_3)$$
$$= -9 + \left(-\frac{1}{2}\right)\left(-3 - \frac{25}{4}\right)$$
$$= -\frac{35}{8}$$
$$\therefore 2P = \left(\frac{25}{4}, -\frac{35}{8}\right)$$

Elliptic curves over Z_p :

For elliptic curves over Z_p, we have

$$y^2 = (x^3 + ax + b) \bmod p$$

Now consider the set $E_p(a,b)$ consisting of all pairs of integers (x, y) that satisfy above equation , together with a point at infinity O. The coefficients a and b and the variables x and y are all elements of Z_p.

It can be shown that a finite abelian group can be defined based on the set $E_p(a,b)$ provided that $(x^3 + ax + b) \bmod p$ has no repeated factors. This is equivalent to the condition

$$(4a^3 + 27b^2) \bmod p \neq 0 \bmod p$$

For example, let $a = 1, b = 1$ and $p = 23$ that is, the elliptic curve

$E_{23}(1,1): y^2 = x^3 + x + 1 (\bmod 23)$. For the set $E_{23}(1,1)$, we are only interested in the nonnegative integers in the quadrant from $(0,0)$ through $(p-1, p-1)$ that satisfy the equation mod p. Table lists the points (other than O) that are part of $E_{23}(1,1)$. Figure plots the points of $E_{23}(1,1)$.

In case of the finite group $E_p(a,b)$, the number of points N is bounded by

$$p + 1 - 2\sqrt{p} \leq N \leq p + 1 + 2\sqrt{p}$$

Table : Points on the Elliptic curve $E_{23}(1,1)$ other than O

(0, 1)	(6, 4)	(12, 19)
(0.22)	(6.19)	(13.7)
(1, 7)	(7, 11)	(13, 16)
(1, 16)	(7, 12)	(17, 3)
(3, 10)	(9, 7)	(17, 20)
(3, 13)	(9, 16)	(18, 3)
(4, 0)	(11, 3)	(18, 20)
(5, 4)	(11, 20)	(19, 5)
(5, 19)	(12, 4)	(19, 18)

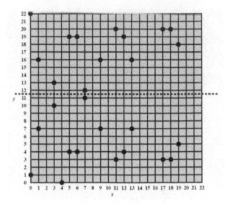

The Elliptic Curve $E_{23}(1, 1)$

Elliptic Curve Discrete Logarithm Problem

The Elliptic Curve cryptosystem (*ECC*) have the potential to provide relatively small block size, high security public key schemes that can be efficiently implemented. The Elliptic Curve Discrete Logarithm problem (*ECDL P*) is based on the fact that given m.P for some integer m and some point P on the Elliptic Curve where P is known, we have to find v alue of m. The smaller key size of Elliptic Curve Cryptosystem makes possible much more compact implementations for a given level of security , which means faster cryptographic operations, running on smaller chips or more compact software. We main-ly concentrate on the Elliptic Curve whose equation is given by $y^2 = x^3 + Ax + B$ defined over a finite field F_p for prime p for A , B in the field. The ECC transforms data into some point representation of the Elliptic Curve. It relies on calculating the multiple of a point P as m.P which is public and it is difficult to find integer m from P and m.P. This is the Elliptic Curve Discrete Logarithm Problem (*ECDL P*). It basically defines a group by the operator addition on the points found on the Elliptic Curve.

Informally a zero-knowledge proof system allows one person to convince another person of some fact without revealing any information about the proof. There are usually two participants, the prover and the verifier. The prover would like to prevent the verifier from gaining any useful infor-mation while participating in the protocol.

An Elliptic Curve is defined on a field. The field may be finite or infinite. We will draw our attention towards finite fields. It is denoted by F_q having q elements where $q = p^r$ having p as the character-istic of the field F_q and r as any positive integer. We will mainly consider for the curve where q = p i.e. r = 1. The points on the curve whose x and y values are in the field are taken into account. The ECC transforms the data into some point representation. The points form an Abelian Group w.r.t. the operator addition. There is one point indicated by O called the identity element.

The Order of a point is defined as the number of times the point must be added in order to give the identity element i.e. the point O.

The Generator of the group is a point whose Order is equal to the number of points that are in the group.

The basis of ECC is The Elliptic Curve Discrete Logarithm Problem i.e. the ECDL P.

The Elliptic Curve Discrete Logarithm problem or ECDLP is defined as follows:

Given points P and Q on E_p(A, B) such that the equation m.P = Q holds. Compute k given P and Q.

Zero-knowledge Proof

In cryptography, a zero-knowledge proof or zero-knowledge protocol is a method by which one party (the *prover*) can prove to another party (the *verifier*) that a given statement is true, without conveying any information apart from the fact that the statement is indeed true.

If proving the statement requires knowledge of some secret information on the part of the prover, the definition implies that the verifier will not be able to prove the statement in turn to anyone else, since the verifier does not possess the secret information. Notice that the statement being proved must include the assertion that the prover has such knowledge (otherwise, the statement would not be proved in zero-knowledge, since at the end of the protocol the verifier would gain the additional information that the prover has knowledge of the required secret information). If the statement consists *only* of the fact that the prover possesses the secret information, it is a special case known as *zero-knowledge proof of knowledge*, and it nicely illustrates the essence of the notion of zero-knowledge proofs: proving that one has knowledge of certain information is trivial if one is allowed to simply reveal that information; the challenge is proving that one has such knowledge without revealing the secret information or anything else.

For zero-knowledge proofs of knowledge, the protocol must necessarily require interactive input from the verifier, usually in the form of a challenge or challenges such that the responses from the prover will convince the verifier if and only if the statement is true (i.e., if the prover does have the claimed knowledge). This is clearly the case, since otherwise the verifier could record the execution of the protocol and replay it to someone else: if this were accepted by the new party as proof that the replaying party knows the secret information, then the new party's acceptance is either justified—the replayer *does* know the secret information—which means that the protocol leaks knowledge and is not zero-knowledge, or it is spurious—i.e. leads to a party accepting someone's proof of knowledge who does not actually possess it.

Some forms of non-interactive zero-knowledge proofs of knowledge exist, but the validity of the proof relies on computational assumptions (typically the assumptions of an ideal cryptographic hash function).

Abstract Example

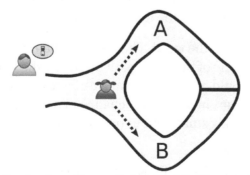

Peggy randomly takes either path A or B, while Victor waits outside

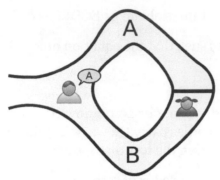

Victor chooses an exit path

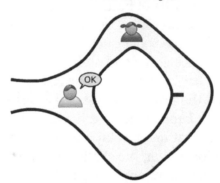

Peggy reliably appears at the exit Victor names

There is a well-known story presenting the fundamental ideas of zero-knowledge proofs, first published by Jean-Jacques Quisquater and others in their paper "How to Explain Zero-Knowledge Protocols to Your Children". It is common practice to label the two parties in a zero-knowledge proof as Peggy (the prover of the statement) and Victor (the verifier of the statement).

In this story, Peggy has uncovered the secret word used to open a magic door in a cave. The cave is shaped like a ring, with the entrance on one side and the magic door blocking the opposite side. Victor wants to know whether Peggy knows the secret word; but Peggy, being a very private person, does not want to reveal her knowledge (the secret word) to Victor or to reveal the fact of her knowledge to the world in general.

They label the left and right paths from the entrance A and B. First, Victor waits outside the cave as Peggy goes in. Peggy takes either path A or B; Victor is not allowed to see which path she takes. Then, Victor enters the cave and shouts the name of the path he wants her to use to return, either A or B, chosen at random. Providing she really does know the magic word, this is easy: she opens the door, if necessary, and returns along the desired path.

However, suppose she did not know the word. Then, she would only be able to return by the named path if Victor were to give the name of the same path by which she had entered. Since Victor would choose A or B at random, she would have a 50% chance of guessing correctly. If they were to repeat this trick many times, say 20 times in a row, her chance of successfully anticipating all of Victor's requests would become vanishingly small (about one in a million).

Thus, if Peggy repeatedly appears at the exit Victor names, he can conclude that it is very probable—astronomically probable—that Peggy does in fact know the secret word.

One side note with respect to third party observers: Even if Victor is wearing a hidden camera that records the whole transaction, the only thing the camera will record is in one case Victor shouting "A!" and Peggy appearing at A or in the other case Victor shouting "B!" and Peggy appearing at B. A recording of this type would be trivial for any two people to fake (requiring only that Peggy and Victor agree beforehand on the sequence of A's and B's that Victor will shout). Such a recording will certainly never be convincing to anyone but the original participants. In fact, even a person who was present as an observer *at the original experiment* would be unconvinced, since Victor and Peggy might have orchestrated the whole "experiment" from start to finish.

Further notice that if Victor chooses his A's and B's by flipping a coin on-camera, this protocol loses its zero-knowledge property; the on-camera coin flip would probably be convincing to any person watching the recording later. Thus, although this does not reveal the secret word to Victor, it does make it possible for Victor to convince the world in general that Peggy has that knowledge—counter to Peggy's stated wishes. However, digital cryptography generally "flips coins" by relying on a pseudo-random number generator, which is akin to a coin with a fixed pattern of heads and tails known only to the coin's owner. If Victor's coin behaved this way, then again it would be possible for Victor and Peggy to have faked the "experiment", so using a pseudo-random number generator would not reveal Peggy's knowledge to the world in the same way using a flipped coin would.

Definition

A zero-knowledge proof must satisfy three properties:

1. Completeness: if the statement is true, the honest verifier (that is, one following the protocol properly) will be convinced of this fact by an honest prover.

2. Soundness: if the statement is false, no cheating prover can convince the honest verifier that it is true, except with some small probability.

3. Zero-knowledge: if the statement is true, no cheating verifier learns anything other than the fact that the statement is true. In other words, just knowing the statement (not the secret) is sufficient to imagine a scenario showing that the prover knows the secret. This is formalized by showing that every cheating verifier has some *simulator* that, given only the statement to be proved (and no access to the prover), can produce a transcript that "looks like" an interaction between the honest prover and the cheating verifier.

The first two of these are properties of more general interactive proof systems. The third is what makes the proof zero-knowledge.

Zero-knowledge proofs are not proofs in the mathematical sense of the term because there is some small probability, the *soundness error*, that a cheating prover will be able to convince the verifier of a false statement. In other words, zero-knowledge proofs are probabilistic "proofs" rather than deterministic proofs. However, there are techniques to decrease the soundness error to negligibly small values.

A formal definition of zero-knowledge has to use some computational model, the most common one being that of a Turing machine. Let P, V, and S be turing machines. An interactive proof system with (P,V) for a language L is zero-knowledge if for any probabilistic polynomial time (PPT) verifier $\hat{V}$ there exists an expected PPT simulator S such that

$$\forall x \in L, z \in \{0,1\}^{*}, \text{View}_{\hat{V}}[P(x) \leftrightarrow \hat{V}(x,z)] = S(x,z)$$

The prover P is modeled as having unlimited computation power (in practice, P usually is a probabilistic Turing machine). Intuitively, the definition states that an interactive proof system (P,V) is zero-knowledge if for any verifier $\hat{V}$ there exists an efficient simulator S that can reproduce the conversation between P and $\hat{V}$ on any given input. The auxiliary string z in the definition plays the role of "prior knowledge". The definition implies that $\hat{V}$ cannot use any prior knowledge string z to mine information out of its conversation with P because we demand that if S is also given this prior knowledge then it can reproduce the conversation between $\hat{V}$ and P just as before.

The definition given is that of perfect zero-knowledge. Computational zero-knowledge is obtained by requiring that the views of the verifier $\hat{V}$ and the simulator are only computationally indistinguishable, given the auxiliary string.

Practical Examples

Discrete Log of a given Value

We can extend these ideas to a more realistic cryptography application. Peggy wants to prove to Victor that she knows the discrete log of a given value in a given group. For example, given a value y, a large prime p and a generator g, she wants to prove that she knows a value x such that $g^{x} \bmod p = y$, without revealing x. Indeed, revealing x could be used as a proof of identity, in that Peggy could have such knowledge because she chose a random value x that she didn't reveal to anyone, computed $y = g^{x} \bmod p$ and distributed the value of y to all potential verifiers, such that at a later time, proving knowledge of x is equivalent to proving identity as Peggy.

The protocol proceeds as follows: in each round, Peggy generates a random number r, computes $C = g^{r} \bmod p$ and discloses this to Victor. After receiving C, Victor randomly issues one of the following two requests: he either requests that Peggy discloses the value of r, or the value of $(x+r) \bmod (p-1)$. With either answer, Peggy is only disclosing a random value, so no information is disclosed by a correct execution of one round of the protocol.

Victor can verify either answer; if he requested r, he can then compute $g^{r} \bmod p$ and verify that it matches C. If he requested $(x+r) \bmod (p-1)$, he can verify that C is consistent with this, by computing $g^{(x+r)\bmod (p-1)} \bmod p$ and verifying that it matches $C \cdot y \bmod p$. If Peggy indeed knows the value of x, she can respond to either one of Victor's possible challenges.

If Peggy knew or could guess which challenge Victor is going to issue, then she could easily cheat and convince Victor that she knows x when she does not: if she knows that Victor is going to request r, then she proceeds normally: she picks r, computes $C = g^{r} \bmod p$ and discloses C to Victor; she will be able to respond to Victor's challenge. On the other hand, if she knows that Victor will request $(x+r) \bmod (p-1)$, then she picks a random value $r^{'}$, computes $C' = g^{r'} \cdot (g^{x})^{-1} \bmod p$, and disclose C' to Victor as the value of C that he is expecting. When Victor challenges her to reveal $(x+r) \bmod (p-1)$, she reveals $r^{'}$, for which Victor will verify consistency, since he will in turn compute $g^{r'} \bmod p$, which matches $C' \cdot y$, since Peggy multiplied by the inverse of y.

However, if in either one of the above scenarios Victor issues a challenge other than the one she was expecting and for which she manufactured the result, then she will be unable to respond to the challenge under the assumption of infeasibility of solving the discrete log for this group. If she picked r and disclosed $C = g^r \bmod p$, then she will be unable to produce a valid $(x + r) \bmod (p - 1)$ that would pass Victor's verification, given that she does not know x. And if she picked a value r' that poses as $(x + r) \bmod (p - 1)$, then she would have to respond with the discrete log of the value that she disclosed – a value that she obtained through arithmetic with known values, and not by computing a power with a known exponent.

Thus, a cheating prover has a 0.5 probability of successfully cheating in one round. By executing a large enough number of rounds, the probability of a cheating prover succeeding can be made arbitrarily low.

Hamiltonian Cycle for a Large Graph

The following scheme is due to Manuel Blum.

In this scenario, Peggy knows a Hamiltonian cycle for a large graph G. Victor knows G but not the cycle (e.g., Peggy has generated G and revealed it to him.) Finding a Hamiltonian cycle given a large graph is believed to be computationally infeasible, since its corresponding decision version is known to be NP-complete. Peggy will prove that she knows the cycle without simply revealing it (perhaps Victor is interested in buying it but wants verification first, or maybe Peggy is the only one who knows this information and is proving her identity to Victor).

To show that Peggy knows this Hamiltonian cycle, she and Victor play several rounds of a game.

- At the beginning of each round, Peggy creates H, a graph which is isomorphic to G (i.e. H is just like G except that all the vertices have different names). Since it is trivial to translate a Hamiltonian cycle between isomorphic graphs with known isomorphism, if Peggy knows a Hamiltonian cycle for G she also must know one for H.

- Peggy commits to H. She could do so by using a cryptographic commitment scheme. Alternatively, she could number the vertices of H, then for each edge of H write a small piece of paper containing the two vertices of the edge and then put these pieces of paper upside down on a table. The purpose of this commitment is that Peggy is not able to change H while at the same time Victor has no information about H.

- Victor then randomly chooses one of two questions to ask Peggy. He can either ask her to show the isomorphism between H and G, or he can ask her to show a Hamiltonian cycle in H.

- If Peggy is asked to show that the two graphs are isomorphic, she first uncovers all of H (e.g. by turning all pieces of papers that she put on the table) and then provides the vertex translations that map G to H. Victor can verify that they are indeed isomorphic.

- If Peggy is asked to prove that she knows a Hamiltonian cycle in H, she translates her Hamiltonian cycle in G onto H and only uncovers the edges on the Hamiltonian cycle. This is enough for Victor to check that H does indeed contain a Hamiltonian cycle.

Completeness

If Peggy does know a Hamiltonian cycle in G, she can easily satisfy Victor's demand for either the graph isomorphism producing H from G (which she had committed to in the first step) or a Hamiltonian cycle in H (which she can construct by applying the isomorphism to the cycle in G).

Zero-knowledge

Peggy's answers do not reveal the original Hamiltonian cycle in G. Each round, Victor will learn only H's isomorphism to G or a Hamiltonian cycle in H. He would need both answers for a single H to discover the cycle in G, so the information remains unknown as long as Peggy can generate a distinct H every round. If Peggy does not know of a Hamiltonian Cycle in G, but somehow knew in advance what Victor would ask to see each round then she could cheat. For example, if Peggy knew ahead of time that Victor would ask to see the Hamiltonian Cycle in H then she could generate a Hamiltonian cycle for an unrelated graph. Similarly, if Peggy knew in advance that Victor would ask to see the isomorphism then she could simply generate an isomorphic graph H (in which she also does not know a Hamiltonian Cycle). Victor could simulate the protocol by himself (without Peggy) because he knows what he will ask to see. Therefore, Victor gains no information about the Hamiltonian cycle in G from the information revealed in each round.

Soundness

If Peggy does not know the information, she can guess which question Victor will ask and generate either a graph isomorphic to G or a Hamiltonian cycle for an unrelated graph, but since she does not know a Hamiltonian cycle for G she cannot do both. With this guesswork, her chance of fooling Victor is 2^{-n}, where n is the number of rounds. For all realistic purposes, it is infeasibly difficult to defeat a zero knowledge proof with a reasonable number of rounds in this way.

Variants of Zero-knowledge

Different variants of zero-knowledge can be defined by formalizing the intuitive concept of what is meant by the output of the simulator "looking like" the execution of the real proof protocol in the following ways:

- We speak of *perfect zero-knowledge* if the distributions produced by the simulator and the proof protocol are distributed exactly the same. This is for instance the case in the first example above.

- *Statistical zero-knowledge* means that the distributions are not necessarily exactly the same, but they are statistically close, meaning that their statistical difference is a negligible function.

- We speak of *computational zero-knowledge* if no efficient algorithm can distinguish the two distributions.

Applications

Research in zero-knowledge proofs has been motivated by authentication systems where one party wants to prove its identity to a second party via some secret information (such as a password) but doesn't want the second party to learn anything about this secret. This is called a "zero-knowledge proof of knowledge". However, a password is typically too small or insufficiently random to be used in many schemes for zero-knowledge proofs of knowledge. A zero-knowledge password proof is a special kind of zero-knowledge proof of knowledge that addresses the limited size of passwords.

One of the uses of zero-knowledge proofs within cryptographic protocols is to enforce honest behavior while maintaining privacy. Roughly, the idea is to force a user to prove, using a zero-knowledge proof, that its behavior is correct according to the protocol. Because of soundness, we know that the user must really act honestly in order to be able to provide a valid proof. Because of zero knowledge, we know that the user does not compromise the privacy of its secrets in the process of providing the proof.

In 2016, the Princeton Plasma Physics Laboratory and Princeton University demonstrated a novel technique that may have applicability to future nuclear disarmament talks.

History and Results

Zero-knowledge proofs were first conceived in 1985 by Shafi Goldwasser, Silvio Micali, and Charles Rackoff in their paper "The Knowledge Complexity of Interactive Proof-Systems". This paper introduced the IP hierarchy of interactive proof systems and conceived the concept of *knowledge complexity*, a measurement of the amount of knowledge about the proof transferred from the prover to the verifier. They also gave the first zero-knowledge proof for a concrete problem, that of deciding quadratic nonresidues mod m (this more or less means that there isn't any number x where x^2 is "equivalent" to some given number). Together with a paper by László Babai and Shlomo Moran, this landmark paper invented interactive proof systems, for which all five authors won the first Gödel Prize in 1993.

In their own words, Goldwasser, Micali, and Rackoff say:

Of particular interest is the case where this additional knowledge is essentially 0 and we show that [it] is possible to interactively prove that a number is quadratic non residue mod m releasing 0 additional knowledge. This is surprising as no efficient algorithm for deciding quadratic residuosity mod m is known when m's factorization is not given. Moreover, all known *NP* proofs for this problem exhibit the prime factorization of m. This indicates that adding interaction to the proving process, may decrease the amount of knowledge that must be communicated in order to prove a theorem.

The quadratic nonresidue problem has both an NP and a co-NP algorithm, and so lies in the interj174 of NP and co-NP. This was also true of several other problems for which zero-knowledge proofs were subsequently discovered, such as an unpublished proof system by Oded Goldreich verifying that a two-prime modulus is not a Blum integer.

Oded Goldreich, Silvio Micali, and Avi Wigderson took this one step further, showing that, assuming the existence of unbreakable encryption, one can create a zero-knowledge proof system for the NP-complete graph coloring problem with three colors. Since every problem in NP can be efficiently reduced to this problem, this means that, under this assumption, all problems in NP have zero-knowledge proofs. The reason for the assumption is that, as in the above example, their protocols require encryption. A commonly cited sufficient condition for the existence of unbreakable encryption is the existence of one-way functions, but it is conceivable that some physical means might also achieve it.

On top of this, they also showed that the graph nonisomorphism problem, the complement of the graph isomorphism problem, has a zero-knowledge proof. This problem is in co-NP, but is not currently known to be in either NP or any practical class. More generally, Goldreich, Goldwasser et al. would go on to show that, also assuming unbreakable encryption, there are zero-knowledge proofs for *all* problems in IP = PSPACE, or in other words, anything that can be proved by an interactive proof system can be proved with zero knowledge.

Not liking to make unnecessary assumptions, many theorists sought a way to eliminate the necessity of one way functions. One way this was done was with *multi-prover interactive proof systems*, which have multiple independent provers instead of only one, allowing the verifier to "cross-examine" the provers in isolation to avoid being misled. It can be shown that, without any intractability assumptions, all languages in NP have zero-knowledge proofs in such a system.

It turns out that in an Internet-like setting, where multiple protocols may be executed concurrently, building zero-knowledge proofs is more challenging. The line of research investigating concurrent zero-knowledge proofs was initiated by the work of Dwork, Naor, and Sahai. One particular development along these lines has been the development of witness-indistinguishable proof protocols. The property of witness-indistinguishability is related to that of zero-knowledge, yet witness-indistinguishable protocols do not suffer from the same problems of concurrent execution.

Another variant of zero-knowledge proofs are non-interactive zero-knowledge proofs. Blum, Feldman, and Micali showed that a common random string shared between the prover and the verifier is enough to achieve computational zero-knowledge without requiring interaction.

Definition 2.4. The Zero Knowledge Proof is defined as follows:

There are usually two participants, the prover and the verifier. The prover knows some fact and wishes to prove that to the verifier. The prover and the verifier will be allowed to perform alternatively the following computations:

1. Receive message from the other party.

2. Perform a private computation.

3. Send a message to the other party.

A typical round of the protocol will consist of a challenge by the verifier and a response by the prover. At the end the verifier either accepts or rejects.

Definition 2.5. The Birthday Paradox is defined as follows :

How many people must there be in a room before there is a 50% chance that two of them were born on the same day of the year.

The above problem can be stated in a different way as follows :

Given a random variable that is an integer with uniform distributions between 1 and n and a selection of k instances (k = n) of the random variable, what is the probability $p(n, k)$ that there is at least one duplicate ? The Birthday Paradox is a special case where n = 365 and asks for the value of k such that $p(n, k) > 0.5$. The answer to this problem is

$k \approx O(\sqrt{n})$.

The Modular Linear Equation is stated as $ax = b \pmod{n}$ where a > 0 and n > 0.

Review of Existing Results

Let E be an Elliptic Curve defined over a finite field with F_p having equation $y^2 = x^3 + Ax + B$, where A & B satisfies the inequality $4A^3 + 27B^2 = 0$. We can find the number of points on the curve by checking the Legendre Symbol for y^2 for each value of x. The number of points will be denoted by $\#E(F_p)$.

The Hasses's theorem provides some limit on the number of points on an Elliptic Curve defined over a finite field. It states that $|p + 1 - \#E(F_p)| \leq 2\sqrt{p}$.

Theorem: The Equation $ax \equiv b \pmod{n}$ is solvable for the unknown x if and only if

$\gcd(a, n) | b$.

Theorem: The Equation $ax \equiv b \pmod{n}$ either has d distinct solutions modulo n, where $d = \gcd(a, n)$, or it has no solutions.

Theorem: Let $d = \gcd(a, n)$, and suppose that $d = ax^f + ny^f$ for some integers x^f and y^f. If $d | b$, then the equation $ax \equiv b \pmod{n}$ has as one of it's solutions the value x_0, where $x_0 = x^f(b/d) \bmod n$.

Theorem: Suppose that the equation $ax \equiv b \pmod{n}$ is solvable (that is, $d | b$, where $d = \gcd(a, n)$) and that x_0 is any solution to this equation. Then, this equation has exactly d distinct solutions, modulo n, given by $x_i = x_0 + i(n/d)$ for $i = 0, 1, 2, 3, \ldots, d - 1$.

Corollary: For any n > 1, if $\gcd(a, n) = 1$, then the equation $ax \equiv b \pmod{n}$ has a unique solution, modulo n. In particular if b = 1 then $x = a^{-1} n \in Z^*$.

Theorem: In a coin toss, if the probability of obtaining a head is p then it is expected that after $1/p$ tosses the first head is obtained.

Theorem: $\forall n > 1, \varphi(n)/n = \Omega(\log \log n / \log n)$.

First we will provide a Zero Knowledge Proof for Elliptic Curve Discrete Logarithm Problem (ECDL P) and explain the properties.

Properties of Zero Knowledge Interactive Proof

A Zero Knowledge Interactive Proof (ZKIP) or Zero Knowledge Protocol is an iterative method for one party to prove to another that a (usually mathematical) statement is true without revealing anything other than the veracity of the statement. A Zero Knowledge Interactive Proof must satisfy three properties :

1. Completeness : If the statement is true, the honest verifier (that is, one following the protocol

property) will be convinced of this fact by an honest prover.

2. Soundness : If the statement is false, no cheating prover can convince the honest verifier that it is true except with small probability.

3. Zero-Knowledge : If the statement is true, no cheating verifier learns anything other than this fact.

Now we will give the Zero Knowledge Proof for Elliptic Curve Discrete Logarithm Prob- lem(EC-DLP) and prove the properties. Let the prover be Alice and the verifier be Bob. Let the Elliptic Curve be denoted by $E_p(A, B)$ and let n be the number of points on the Elliptic Curve. Let $P \in E_p(A, B)$ be a generator of the group. So Alice wants to convince Bob that she knows the value of m where $Q = mP$ without disclosing m. It can be achieved by following steps :

1. Alice picks random integer k with $1 = k = p-1$ where p is the characteristic of the field and sends $R = kP$ to Bob.

2. Bob picks random integer r with $1 = r = p-1$ and sends it to Alice.

3. Alice computes $Y = (k-mr) \mod n$ where n is the number of points on the curve i.e. $\# E(F_p) = n$, and sends it to Alice.

4. Bob verifies if $R == YP + rQ$.

If step 4 is satisfied then Bob accepts else rejects. Now we will verify the three properties stated previously for the protocol as follows :

1. Completeness : Given $Q = mP$. We have to show that if Alice knows value of m , then Bob is convinced that Alice knows it.

   Since Alice knows value of m , all four steps in the protocol can be carried out. At step 3 Alice computes $Y = (k - mr) \mod n$ and sends it to Bob. At step 4, Bob verifies $YP + rQ = R$ or not.Now $YP + rQ = (k - mr) P + rQ = kP - rmP + rQ = kP - rQ + rQ = kP = R$ (verified).

So Bob is convinced that Alice knows m.

2. Soundness : Here we have to show that if Alice does not know value of m then she can't convince Bob that she knows it or succeeds with a very small probability.

   Now suppose Alice doesn't know value of m and wants to convince Bob that she knows it. The only way that Alice can convince Bob is in step 3 of the protocol Alice should send such a value for Y such that Y P should have value R- rQ , so that after adding rQ Bob will get R.

   i.e. $YP = R-rQ$

   i.e. $YP = kP - rmP$

   i.e. $YP = (k - mr)P$

   i.e. $Y= (k -mr) \mod n$

   Now Alice has values of k, r but she doesn't have the value of m. So it can't find value of k-mr. So she can't cheat.

3. Zero-Knowledge : Here we have to show that no information is released in the protocol.

Now in one session of the protocol Bob/Eavesdropper E has the following information:

P, Q, R = kP, r, Y = (k - mr) mod n.

Now from Y = (k - mr) mod n, in order to find out value of m it knows value of r. So the only thing left is to know k. But to find k the only way is to solve the ECDLP , R = kP for k. So Bob/Eavesdropper can't know value of m. So the proof is a Perfect Zero-Knowledge.

Attack on the Zero Knowledge Protocol

During the whole protocol the Eavesdropper E has the following information :

point P (known)

point Q = mP (known)

point R = k P (known) (k unknown)

number r (known)

number Y = (k - mr) mod n (known, m unknown)

From it the Eavsdropper can't find any useful information. But the attack is possible if the attacker uses information from multiple sessions of the challenge-response protocol. Now suppose in one session

$$Y_1 = (k - mr_1) \mod n$$

In another session Alice use the same k to compute R and thus

$$Y_2 = (k - mr_2) \mod n$$

So from above two euations ? $Y_1 - Y_2 = m(r_2 - r_1) \mod n$

$$\Rightarrow m (r_2 - r_1) = (Y_1 - Y_2) \mod n$$

So $r_2 - r_1$ is known, and $Y_1 - Y_2$ is known. So we can solve form by using Theorem. Here in the Modular Linear Equation $ax \equiv b \mod n$, $a = (r_2 - r_1)$, $b = (Y_1 - Y_2)$, $x = m$ and the number of solutions = gcd(a, n). The attack proceeds as follows :

In step 1 of the protocol Eavesdropper E gets the value of $R_i = k_i P(i = 1 , 2 , 3 , ...)$ where i denotes the session numbers of the challenge-response protocol. Suppose at some session j, E discovers $R_j = R_l$, for some l < j. Thus we have :

$k_j P = k_l P \Rightarrow (k_j - k_l)P = O$. We will assume P is either the generator or a point on the Elliptic Curve with high order. Otherwise ECDLP can be easily solved by any brute force method. Thus we can safely assume without loss of generality $O(P) >> k_j - k_l$. Thus the only way the equality holds if $k_j = k_l$. Thus the entire problem reduces to solving the Modular Linear Equation ($\Rightarrow m (r_2 - r_1) = (Y_1 - Y_2) \mod n$). From Corollary ($\Rightarrow m (r_2 - r_1) = (Y_1 - Y_2) \mod n$) of Modular Linear Equation we hence

$m = (Y_1 - Y_2)(r_2 - r_1) - 1 \mod n$.

As stated in Corollary, $(r_2 - r_1)$-1 would be uniquely defined if gcd $(r_2 - r_1, n) = 1$.

Let $\Delta = r_2 - r_1$. Thus gcd$(\Delta, n) = 1$. W e can adopt the following randomized algorithm

to compute Δ and thus r_2 from r_1.

Algorithm 1 RAND (n)

1: Pick a random number x from $(2 , 3 , ..., n - 1)$.

2: Compute gcd(x, n).

3: if gcd (x, n) = 1 then

4: Set $\Delta \leftarrow x$.

5: else

6: goto step 1.

7: end if

8: Return Δ.

We know that $|Zn^*| = \Phi (n)$. Thus the tptal number of integers less than n and relatively prime w.r.t n is $\Phi(n)$. Thus the probability that the selected number $x \in Z n^*$ in RAND step 1 is $\Phi (n)/ n$. Thus from Theorem after expected $n / \Phi(n) \in O (\log n / \log\log n)$ iterations we will get $x \in Z n^*$. Thus the expected time complexity of RAND is $O (\log n / \log\log n)$ assuming the time complexity to compute gcd(x, n) is $O (\log n)$. Thus in sessions i and j attacker will use a random number r_1 and $r_2 = r_1 + \Delta$. Now we can clearly see that this attack will fail if Alice chooses different values of k at each session. But in step 1 of the protocol Alice picks up k with $1 \le k \le p-1$ at random. Thus from Birthday Paradox after $O (\sqrt{p})$ sessions Alice will pick up k used in some earlier session with high probability. Thus after $O (\sqrt{p})$ sessions of the challenge response protocol with high probability an Eavesdropper can compute the value m for ECDLP.

Solution to Overcome the Above Attack

In this section we will provide a solution i.e., a modified Zero Knowledge Proof for the ECDLP that overcomes the above attack and prove the required properties i.e., Completeness, Soundness, and Zero-Knowledge, as explained previously. We also provide an explanation of how it overcomes the above attack.

Let the prover be Alice and the verifier be Bob. Let the Elliptic Curve be denoted by $E_p(A, B)$ and let n be the number of points on the Elliptic Curve. Let $P \in E_p(A, B)$ be a generator of the group. So Alice wants to convince Bob that she knows the value of m where Q = mP without disclosing m. It can be achieved by following steps :

1. Alice picks random integers k_1 and k_2 with $1 \le k_1, k_2 \le p - 1$ where p is the characteristic of the field and sends $R_1 = k_1 P$ and $R_2 = k_2 Q$ to Bob.

2. Bob picks random integer r with $1 \le r \le p - 1$ and sends it to Alice.

3. Alice computes $Y = (mrk_2 - k_1)$ mod n where n is the number of points on the curve i.e. $\#E(F_p) =$ n , and sends it to Alice.

4. Bob verifies if $YP + R_1 == rR_2$.

If step 4 is satisfied then Bob accepts else rejects. Now we will verify the three properties stated previously for the protocol as follows :

1. Completeness : Given $Q = mP$. We have to show that if Alice knows value of m , then Bob is convinced that Alice knows it.

   Since Alice knows value of m , all four steps in the protocol can be carried out. At step 3 Alice computes $Y = (mrk_2 - k_1)$ mod n and sends it to Bob. At step 4, Bob verifies $YP + R_1 = rR_2$ or not.

   Now $YP + R_1 = (mrk_2 - k_1)P + k_1P$

   $= mrk_2P - k_1P + k_1P$

   $= mrk_2P$

   $= rk_2Q$ (Replacing mP by Q)

   $= rR_2$ (Replacing k_2Q by R_2) (Verified). So Bob is convinced that Alice knows m.

2. Soundness : Here we have to show that if Alice does not know value of m then she can't convince Bob that she knows it or succeeds with a very small probability.

   Now suppose Alice doesn't know value of m and wants to convince Bob that she knows it. The only way that Alice can convince Bob is in step 3 of the protocol Alice should send such a value for Y such that YP should have value $rR_2 - R_1$, so that after adding R_1 Bob will get rR_2.

   i.e. $YP = rR_2 - R_1$ i.e. $YP = k_2rQ - k_1P$ i.e. $YP = mrk_2P - k_1P$

   i.e. $Y = (mrk_2 - k_1)$ mod n

   Now Alice has values of r, k_2, k_1 but she doesn't have the value of m. So it can't find value of $(mrk_2 - k_1)$. So she can't cheat.

3. Zero-Knowledge : Here we have to show that no information is released in the protocol.

Now in one session of the protocol Bob/Eavesdropper E has the following information :

$P, Q, R_1 = k_1P , R_2 = k_2Q, Y = (mrk_2 - k_1)$ mod n.

Now $Y = (mrk_2 - k_1)$ mod n. From this modular equation to find out value of m the known quantities are r and Y. In this modular linear equation $Y = (mrk_2 - k_1)$ mod n we have 3 unknowns m, k_1, and k_2. Thus 2 ECDLPs $R_1 = k_1P$ and $R_2 = k_2Q$ reduces to solving $Y = (mrk_2 - k_1)$ mod n. Thus in other words if there is an efficient way of obtaining k_1 and k_2 from the modular linear equation $Y = (mrk_2 - k_1)$ mod n then there is an efficient solution to 2 ECDLPs $R_1 = k_1P$ and $R_2 = k_2Q$. Hence solving the modular linear equation $Y = (mrk_2 - k_1)$ mod n is at least as hard as solving ECDLPs $R_1 = k_1P$ and $R_2 = k_2Q$. So Bob/Eavesdropper can't know value of m. So the proof is a Perfect Zero-Knowledge.

Now we will explain how the attack is avoided. Now suppose as earlier Bob / E gets Y_1 and Y_2 as follows :

$Y_1 = (mr_1k_{12} - k) \bmod n$ and $Y_2 = (mr_2k_{22} - k) \bmod n$ i.e., in both sessions R_1 values are same. Here k_{12} and k_{22} indicate the k_2 values in both sessions. Now subtracting as previously we will get $Y_1 - Y_2 = m(r_1k_{12} - r_2k_{22}) \bmod n$. But as it doesn't know the value of k_{12} and k_{22}, so it can't solve for the Modular Linear Equation. Even if R_2 is same in both cases with $R_2 = k_2Q$ then it will get the final subtraction result as $Y_1 - Y_2 = mk_2(r_1 - r_2) \bmod n$. So solving it will give the value of mk_2. Again if we can obtain m efficiently we have an efficient solution to the ECDLP $R_2 = k_2Q$. Thus again we have a reduction from ECDLP to the problem of computing m from mk_2. So this proof system is not susceptible to the previous attack.

The Elliptic Curve cryptosystem (*ECC*) can play an important role in asymmetric cryp- tography. ECC is a stronger option than the RSA and Discrete Logarithm systems for the future. Here we have presented a Zero Knowledge In teractive Proof for *ECDLP* where the elliptic curve is of the form $E_p(A, B)$ where p is a prime. The re- sult can be easily generalized to $E_q(A, B)$ for composite q where $q = p^r$. Given a guess of m for *ECDLP* we can easily verify in polynomial time whether $P = m.Q$. This shows $ECDLP \in NP \subseteq PSPACE = IP$. This confirms with our result that shows $ECDLP \in IP$. Subsequently we have also presented an attack on the Zero Knowledge Pro-tocol using Birthday Paradox. Lastly we modified the Zero Knowledge Proof to overcome this attack.

Non-interactive Zero-knowledge Proof

Non-interactive zero-knowledge proofs are a variant of zero-knowledge proofs in which no interaction is necessary between prover and verifier. Blum, Feldman, and Micali showed that a common reference string shared between the prover and the verifier is enough to achieve computational zero-knowledge without requiring interaction. Goldreich and Oren gave impossibility results for one shot zero-knowledge protocols in the standard model. In 2003, Goldwasser and Kalai published an instance of an identification scheme for which any hash function will yield an insecure digital signature scheme. These results are not contradictory, as the impossibility result of Goldreich and Oren does not hold in the common reference string model or the random oracle model. Non-interactive zero-knowledge proofs however show a separation between the cryptographic tasks that can be achieved in the standard model and those that can be achieved in 'more powerful' extended models.

The model influences the properties that can be obtained from a zero-knowledge protocol. Pass showed that in the common reference string model non-interactive zero-knowledge protocols do not preserve all of the properties of interactive zero-knowledge protocols; e.g., they do not preserve deniability.

Non-interactive zero-knowledge proofs can also be obtained in the random oracle model using the Fiat–Shamir heuristic.

Definition

Originally, non-interactive zero-knowledge was only defined as a single theorem proof system. In such a system each proof requires its own fresh common reference string. A common reference string in general is not a random string. It may, for instance, consist of randomly chosen group elements that all protocol parties use. Although the group elements are random, the reference string is not as it contains a certain structure (e.g., group elements) that is distinguishable from randomness. Subsequently, Feige, Lapidot, and Shamir introduced multi-theorem zero-knowledge proofs as a more versatile notion for non-interactive zero knowledge proofs.

In this model the prover and the verifier are in possession of a reference string sampled from a distribution, D, by a trusted setup $\sigma \leftarrow \text{Setup}(1^k)$. To prove statement $y \in L$ with witness w, the prover runs $\pi \leftarrow \text{Prove}(\sigma, y, w)$ and sends the proof, π, to the verifier. The verifier accepts if $\text{Verify}(\sigma, y, \pi) = \text{accept}$, and rejects otherwise. To account for the fact that σ may influence the statements that are being proven, the witness relation can be generalized to $(y, w) \in R_\sigma$ parameterized by σ.

Completeness

Verification succeeds for all $\sigma \in \text{Setup}(1^k)$ and every $(y, w) \in R_\sigma$.

More formally, for all k, all $\sigma \in \text{Setup}(1^k)$, and all $(y, w) \in R_\sigma$:

$$\Pr[\pi \leftarrow \text{Prove}(\sigma, y, w) : \text{Verify}(\sigma, y, \pi) = \text{accept}] = 1$$

Soundness

Soundness requires that no prover can make the verifier accept a wrong statement $y \notin L$ except with some small probability. The upper bound of this probability is referred to as the soundness error of a proof system.

More formally, for every malicious prover, $\tilde{P}$, there exists a negligible function, ν, such that

$$\Pr\left[\sigma \leftarrow \text{Setup}(1^k), (y, \pi) \leftarrow \tilde{P}(\sigma) : y \notin L \wedge \text{Verify}(\sigma, y, \pi) = \text{accept}\right] = \nu(k).$$

The above definition requires the soundness error to be negligible in the security parameter, k. By increasing k the soundness error can be made arbitrary small. If the soundness error is 0 for all k, we speak of *perfect soundness*.

Multi-theorem Zero-knowledge

A non-interactive proof system $(\text{Setup}, \text{Prove}, \text{Verify})$ is multi-theorem zero-knowledge, if there exists a simulator, $\text{Sim} = (\text{Sim}_1, \text{Sim}_2)$, such that for all non-uniform polynomial time adversaries, $\mathcal{A}$,

$$\Pr\left[\sigma \leftarrow \text{Setup}(1^k) : \mathcal{A}^{\text{Prove}(\sigma, \cdot, \cdot)}(\sigma) = 1\right] \equiv \Pr\left[(\sigma, \tau) \leftarrow \text{Sim}_1 : \mathcal{A}^{\text{Sim}(\sigma, \tau, \cdot, \cdot)}(\sigma) = 1\right]$$

Here $\text{Sim}(\sigma, \tau, y, w)$ outputs $\text{Sim}_2(\sigma, \tau, y)$ for $(y, w) \in R_\sigma$ and both oracles output *failure* otherwise.

Pairing-based Non-interactive Proofs

Pairing-based cryptography has led to several cryptographic advancements. One of these advancements is more powerful and more efficient non-interactive zero-knowledge proofs. The seminal idea was to hide the values for the evaluation of the pairing in a commitment. Using different commitment schemes, this idea was used to build zero-knowledge proof systems under the sub-group hiding and under the decisional linear assumption. These proof systems prove circuit satisfiability, and thus by the Cook–Levin theorem allow proving membership for every language in NP. The size of the common reference string and the proofs is relatively small; however, transforming a statement into a boolean circuit incurs considerable overhead.

Proof systems under the sub-group hiding, decisional linear assumption, and external Diffie–Hellman assumption that allow directly proving the pairing product equations that are common in pairing-based cryptography have been proposed.

Under strong knowledge assumptions, it is known how to create sublinear-length computationally sound proof systems for NP-complete languages. More precisely, the proof in such proof systems consists only of a small number of bilinear group elements.

Elliptic Curve Cryptography

Elliptic curve cryptography (ECC) is an approach to public-key cryptography based on the algebraic structure of elliptic curves over finite fields. ECC requires smaller keys compared to non-ECC cryptography (based on plain Galois fields) to provide equivalent security.

Elliptic curves are applicable for key agreement, digital signatures, pseudo-random generators and other tasks. Indirectly, they can be used for encryption by combining the key agreement with a symmetric encryption scheme. They are also used in several integer factorization algorithms based on elliptic curves that have applications in cryptography, such as Lenstra elliptic curve factorization.

Rationale

Public-key cryptography is based on the intractability of certain mathematical problems. Early public-key systems are secure assuming that it is difficult to factor a large integer composed of two or more large prime factors. For elliptic-curve-based protocols, it is assumed that finding the discrete logarithm of a random elliptic curve element with respect to a publicly known base point is infeasible: this is the "elliptic curve discrete logarithm problem" (ECDLP). The security of elliptic curve cryptography depends on the ability to compute a point multiplication and the inability to compute the multiplicand given the original and product points. The size of the elliptic curve determines the difficulty of the problem.

The primary benefit promised by elliptic curve cryptography is a smaller key size, reducing storage and transmission requirements, i.e. that an elliptic curve group could provide the same level of security afforded by an RSA-based system with a large modulus and correspondingly larger key:

for example, a 256-bit elliptic curve public key should provide comparable security to a 3072-bit RSA public key.

The U.S. National Institute of Standards and Technology (NIST) has endorsed elliptic curve cryptography in its Suite B set of recommended algorithms, specifically elliptic curve Diffie–Hellman (ECDH) for key exchange and Elliptic Curve Digital Signature Algorithm (ECDSA) for digital signature. The U.S. National Security Agency (NSA) allows their use for protecting information classified up to top secret with 384-bit keys. However, in August 2015, the NSA announced that it plans to replace Suite B with a new cipher suite due to concerns about quantum computing attacks on ECC.

While the RSA patent expired in 2000, there may be patents in force covering certain aspects of ECC technology. However some argue that the US government elliptic curve digital signature standard (ECDSA; NIST FIPS 186-3) and certain practical ECC-based key exchange schemes (including ECDH) can be implemented without infringing them, including RSA Laboratories and Daniel J. Bernstein

History

The use of elliptic curves in cryptography was suggested independently by Neal Koblitz and Victor S. Miller in 1985. Elliptic curve cryptography algorithms entered wide use in 2004 to 2005.

Theory

For current cryptographic purposes, an *elliptic curve* is a plane curve over a finite field (rather than the real numbers) which consists of the points satisfying the equation

$$y^2 = x^3 + ax + b,$$

along with a distinguished point at infinity, denoted ∞. (The coordinates here are to be chosen from a fixed finite field of characteristic not equal to 2 or 3, or the curve equation will be somewhat more complicated.)

This set together with the group operation of elliptic curves is an Abelian group, with the point at infinity as identity element. The structure of the group is inherited from the divisor group of the underlying algebraic variety.

$$\mathrm{Div}^0(E) \rightarrow \mathrm{Pic}^0(E) \simeq E,$$

Cryptographic Schemes

Several discrete logarithm-based protocols have been adapted to elliptic curves, replacing the group $(\mathbb{Z}_p)^\times$ with an elliptic curve:

- The elliptic curve Diffie–Hellman (ECDH) key agreement scheme is based on the Diffie–Hellman scheme,

- The Elliptic Curve Integrated Encryption Scheme (ECIES), also known as Elliptic Curve Augmented Encryption Scheme or simply the Elliptic Curve Encryption Scheme,

- The Elliptic Curve Digital Signature Algorithm (ECDSA) is based on the Digital Signature Algorithm,

- The deformation scheme using Harrison's p-adic Manhattan metric,

- The Edwards-curve Digital Signature Algorithm (EdDSA) is based on Schnorr signature and uses twisted Edwards curves,

- The ECMQV key agreement scheme is based on the MQV key agreement scheme,

- The ECQV implicit certificate scheme.

At the RSA Conference 2005, the National Security Agency (NSA) announced Suite B which exclusively uses ECC for digital signature generation and key exchange. The suite is intended to protect both classified and unclassified national security systems and information.

Recently, a large number of cryptographic primitives based on bilinear mappings on various elliptic curve groups, such as the Weil and Tate pairings, have been introduced. Schemes based on these primitives provide efficient identity-based encryption as well as pairing-based signatures, signcryption, key agreement, and proxy re-encryption.

Implementation

Some common implementation considerations include:

Domain Parameters

To use ECC, all parties must agree on all the elements defining the elliptic curve, that is, the *domain parameters* of the scheme. The field is defined by p in the prime case and the pair of m and f in the binary case. The elliptic curve is defined by the constants a and b used in its defining equation. Finally, the cyclic subgroup is defined by its *generator* (a.k.a. *base point*) G. For cryptographic application the order of G, that is the smallest positive number n such that $nG = \infty$, is normally prime. Since n is the size of a subgroup of $E(\mathbb{F}_p)$ it follows from Lagrange's theorem that the number $h = \frac{1}{n} |E(\mathbb{F}_p)|$ is an integer. In cryptographic applications this number h, called the *cofactor*, must be small ($h \leq 4$) and, preferably, $h = 1$. To summarize: in the prime case, the domain parameters are (p, a, b, G, n, h); in the binary case, they are (m, f, a, b, G, n, h).

Unless there is an assurance that domain parameters were generated by a party trusted with respect to their use, the domain parameters *must* be validated before use.

The generation of domain parameters is not usually done by each participant because this involves computing the number of points on a curve which is time-consuming and troublesome to implement. As a result, several standard bodies published domain parameters of elliptic curves for several common field sizes. Such domain parameters are commonly known as "standard curves" or "named curves"; a named curve can be referenced either by name or by the unique object identifier defined in the standard documents:

- NIST, Recommended Elliptic Curves for Government Use (From Internet Archive Wayback Machine, current link dead)

- SECG, SEC 2: Recommended Elliptic Curve Domain Parameters

- ECC Brainpool (RFC 5639), ECC Brainpool Standard Curves and Curve Generation

SECG test vectors are also available. NIST has approved many SECG curves, so there is a significant overlap between the specifications published by NIST and SECG. EC domain parameters may be either specified by value or by name.

If one (despite the above) wants to construct one's own domain parameters, one should select the underlying field and then use one of the following strategies to find a curve with appropriate (i.e., near prime) number of points using one of the following methods:

- Select a random curve and use a general point-counting algorithm, for example, Schoof's algorithm or Schoof–Elkies–Atkin algorithm,

- Select a random curve from a family which allows easy calculation of the number of points (e.g., Koblitz curves), or

- Select the number of points and generate a curve with this number of points using *complex multiplication* technique.

Several classes of curves are weak and should be avoided:

- Curves over $\mathbb{F}_{2^m}$ with non-prime m are vulnerable to Weil descent attacks.

- Curves such that n divides $p^B - 1$ (where p is the characteristic of the field – q for a prime field, or 2 for a binary field) for sufficiently small B are vulnerable to Menezes–Okamoto–Vanstone (MOV) attack which applies usual Discrete Logarithm Problem (DLP) in a small degree extension field of $\mathbb{F}_p$ to solve ECDLP. The bound B should be chosen so that discrete logarithms in the field $\mathbb{F}_{p^B}$ are at least as difficult to compute as discrete logs on the elliptic curve $E(\mathbb{F}_q)$.

- Curves such that $| E(\mathbb{F}_q) | = q$ are vulnerable to the attack that maps the points on the curve to the additive group of $\mathbb{F}_q$

Key Sizes

Because all the fastest known algorithms that allow one to solve the ECDLP (baby-step giant-step, Pollard's rho, etc.), need $O(\sqrt{n})$ steps, it follows that the size of the underlying field should be roughly twice the security parameter. For example, for 128-bit security one needs a curve over $\mathbb{F}_q$, where $q \approx 2^{256}$. This can be contrasted with finite-field cryptography (e.g., DSA) which requires 3072-bit public keys and 256-bit private keys, and integer factorization cryptography (e.g., RSA) which requires a 3072-bit value of n, where the private key should be just as large. However the public key may be smaller to accommodate efficient encryption, especially when processing power is limited.

The hardest ECC scheme (publicly) broken to date had a 112-bit key for the prime field case and a 109-bit key for the binary field case. For the prime field case, this was broken in July 2009 using a cluster of over 200 PlayStation 3 game consoles and could have been finished in 3.5 months using this cluster when running continuously. The binary field case was broken in April 2004 using 2600 computers over 17 months.

A current project is aiming at breaking the ECC2K-130 challenge by Certicom, by using a wide range of different hardware: CPUs, GPUs, FPGA.

Projective Coordinates

A close examination of the addition rules shows that in order to add two points, one needs not only several additions and multiplications in $\mathbb{F}_q$ but also an inversion operation. The inversion (for given $x \in \mathbb{F}_q$ find $y \in \mathbb{F}_q$ such that $xy = 1$) is one to two orders of magnitude slower than multiplication. Fortunately, points on a curve can be represented in different coordinate systems which do not require an inversion operation to add two points. Several such systems were proposed: in the *projective* system each point is represented by three coordinates (X, Y, Z) using the following relation: $x = \dfrac{X}{Z}$, $y = \dfrac{Y}{Z}$; in the *Jacobian system* a point is also represented with three coordinates (X, Y, Z), but a different relation is used: $x = \dfrac{X}{Z^2}$, $y = \dfrac{Y}{Z^3}$; in the *López–Dahab system* the relation is $x = \dfrac{X}{Z}$, $y = \dfrac{Y}{Z^2}$; in the *modified Jacobian* system the same relations are used but four coordinates are stored and used for calculations (X, Y, Z, aZ^4); and in the *Chudnovsky Jacobian* system five coordinates are used (X, Y, Z, Z^2, Z^3). Note that there may be different naming conventions, for example, IEEE P1363-2000 standard uses "projective coordinates" to refer to what is commonly called Jacobian coordinates. An additional speed-up is possible if mixed coordinates are used.

Fast Reduction (NIST curves)

Reduction modulo p (which is needed for addition and multiplication) can be executed much faster if the prime p is a pseudo-Mersenne prime, that is $p \approx 2^d$; for example, $p = 2^{521} - 1$ or $p = 2^{256} - 2^{32} - 2^9 - 2^8 - 2^7 - 2^6 - 2^4 - 1$. Compared to Barrett reduction, there can be an order of magnitude speed-up. The speed-up here is a practical rather than theoretical one, and derives from the fact that the moduli of numbers against numbers near powers of two can be performed efficiently by computers operating on binary numbers with bitwise operations.

The curves over $\mathbb{F}_p$ with pseudo-Mersenne p are recommended by NIST. Yet another advantage of the NIST curves is that they use $a = -3$, which improves addition in Jacobian coordinates.

According to Bernstein and Lange, many of the efficiency-related decisions in NIST FIPS 186-2 are sub-optimal. Other curves are more secure and run just as fast.

Applications

Elliptic curves are applicable for encryption, digital signatures, pseudo-random generators and other tasks. They are also used in several integer factorization algorithms that have applications in cryptography, such as Lenstra elliptic curve factorization.

In 1999, NIST recommended 15 elliptic curves. Specifically, FIPS 186-3 has 10 recommended finite fields:

- Five prime fields $\mathbb{F}_p$ for certain primes p of sizes 192, 224, 256, 384, and 521 bits. For each of the prime fields, one elliptic curve is recommended.

- Five binary fields $\mathbb{F}_{2^m}$ for m equal 163, 233, 283, 409, and 571. For each of the binary fields, one elliptic curve and one Koblitz curve was selected.

The NIST recommendation thus contains a total of 5 prime curves and 10 binary curves. The curves were ostensibly chosen for optimal security and implementation efficiency.

In 2013, the *New York Times* stated that Dual Elliptic Curve Deterministic Random Bit Generation (or Dual_EC_DRBG) had been included as a NIST national standard due to the influence of NSA, which had included a deliberate weakness in the algorithm and the recommended elliptic curve. RSA Security in September 2013 issued an advisory recommending that its customers discontinue using any software based on Dual_EC_DRBG. In the wake of the exposure of Dual_EC_DRBG as "an NSA undercover operation", cryptography experts have also expressed concern over the security of the NIST recommended elliptic curves, suggesting a return to encryption based on non-elliptic-curve groups.

Security

Side-channel Attacks

Unlike most other DLP systems (where it is possible to use the same procedure for squaring and multiplication), the EC addition is significantly different for doubling ($P = Q$) and general addition ($P \neq Q$) depending on the coordinate system used. Consequently, it is important to counteract side channel attacks (e.g., timing or simple/differential power analysis attacks) using, for example, fixed pattern window (a.k.a. comb) methods (note that this does not increase computation time). Alternatively one can use an Edwards curve; this is a special family of elliptic curves for which doubling and addition can be done with the same operation. Another concern for ECC-systems is the danger of fault attacks, especially when running on smart cards.

Backdoors

Cryptographic experts have expressed concerns that the National Security Agency has inserted a kleptographic backdoor into at least one elliptic curve-based pseudo random generator. Internal memos leaked by former NSA contractor, Edward Snowden, suggest that the NSA put a backdoor in the Dual_EC_DRBG standard. One analysis of the possible backdoor concluded that an adversary in possession of the algorithm's secret key could obtain encryption keys given only 32 bytes of ciphertext.

The SafeCurves project has been launched in order to catalog curves that are easy to securely implement and are designed in a fully publicly verifiable way to minimize the chance of a backdoor.

Quantum Computing Attacks

In contrast with its current standing over RSA, elliptic curve cryptography is expected to be more vulnerable to an attack based on Shor's algorithm. In theory, making a practical attack feasible many years before an attack on an equivalently secure RSA scheme is possible. This is because smaller elliptic curve keys are needed to match the classical security of RSA. The work of Proos and Zalka show how a quantum computer for breaking 2048-bit RSA requires roughly 4096 qubits, while a quantum computer to break the equivalently secure 224-bit Elliptic Curve Cryptography requires between 1300 and 1600 qubits.

To avoid quantum computing concerns, an elliptic curve-based alternative to Elliptic Curve Diffie Hellman which is not susceptible to Shor's attack is the Supersingular Isogeny Diffie–Hellman Key Exchange of De Feo, Jao and Plut. It uses elliptic curve isogenies to create a drop-in replacement for the quantum attackable Diffie–Hellman and Elliptic curve Diffie–Hellman key exchanges. This key exchange uses the same elliptic curve computational primitives of existing elliptic curve cryptography and requires computational and transmission overhead similar to many currently used public key systems.

In August, 2015, NSA announced that it planned to transition "in the not distant future" to a new cipher suite that is resistant to quantum attacks. "Unfortunately, the growth of elliptic curve use has bumped up against the fact of continued progress in the research on quantum computing, necessitating a re-evaluation of our cryptographic strategy."

Patents

At least one ECC scheme (ECMQV) and some implementation techniques are covered by patents.

Alternative Representations

Alternative representations of elliptic curves include:

- Hessian curves

- Edwards curves

- Twisted curves

- Twisted Hessian curves

- Twisted Edwards curve

- Doubling-oriented Doche–Icart–Kohel curve

- Tripling-oriented Doche–Icart–Kohel curve

- Jacobian curve

- Montgomery curve

Elliptic curve cryptosystem is based Elliptic Curve Discrete Logarithm Problem , i.e., ECDLP. The problem is defined as follows:

Given points P and Q on $E_p(a, b)$ such that the equation $kP = Q$ holds. Compute k given P and Q.

Representing Plaintext Message by a Point on the Elliptic Curve

Suppose the plaintext message is an integer m. We have to represent this by a point on the elliptic curve $y^2 = x^3 + ax + b \pmod{p}$. We choose the x -coordinate of the representative point by m. But it may so happen that m³+am+b (mod p) is not a quadratic residue and thus the ordinate value is undefined.

Let K be the largest integer such that the failure probability $1/2^k$ is acceptable. We also assume that (m +1)K< p. the message m will be represented by a point with the abscissa value x = mK + j, where $0 \le j < K$. Also we assume that p = 3 mod 4. This assumption will help us in computing the square root deterministically. For j=0, 1, 2, ..., K -1 check if z=x³+ax+b (mod p) is a quadratic residue or not. If it

is a quadratic residue we compute the value of y as $Z^{\frac{P+1}{4}}$ mod p Now we represent the message by P_m= (x, y). If the test fails for all values of j then we fail to map the message to a point. Clearly the failure probability is $1/2^k$.

At the time of decryption we recover the message m from P_m= (x, y) as follows:

$$m = \left\lfloor \frac{x}{K} \right\rfloor.$$

Elliptic Curve Analogue of Diffie- Hellman Key Exchange

Publicly available information: E_p(a, b) and a point G on the curve with high order, i.e., kG = O for large k. Let n be the total number of points on the curve.

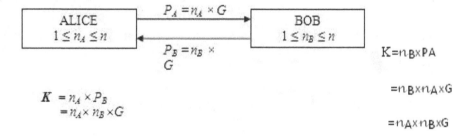

1. Alice chooses her private key n_A such that $1 \le n_A \le n$ and computes the public key P_A = n_AxG.

2. Bob chooses his private key n_B such that $1 \le n_B \le n$ and computes the public key P_B = n_BxG.

3. Alice and Bob simultaneously compute the shared key K = n_Axn_BxG after computing n_AxP_B and n_BxP_A respectively.

This key exchange scheme as mentioned earlier is susceptible to intruder-in-the-middle attack. To overcome this all messages should be authenticated by its sender.

Elliptic Curve Analogue of ElGamal Cryptosystem

Bob's Public Key: P_B

Bob's Secret Key: a where P_B =αG.

Other Publicly Available Information: Elliptic Curve E_p(a, b) and a point G of large order on the elliptic curve and the prime p.

Encryption (Sender: Alice)

Let P_m be the point on the elliptic curve corresponding to the plaintext message m.

- Alice chooses a random number k , such that $1 \leq k \leq p-1$.

- She computes the cipher text $C = \{C_1, C_2\} = \{kG, P_m + kP_B\}$.

- She sends the cipher text $C = \{C_1, C_2\}$ to Bob.

Decryption (Receiver: Bob)

After receiving the cipher text $C = \{C_1, C_2\}$

- Bob computes $\alpha C_1 = \alpha kG = k\alpha G = kP_B$

- Then Bob subtracts the result obtained in Step1 from C_2. Thus Bob computes $C_2 - kP_B = P_m$ and recovers the plaintext.

References

- Sahai, Amit; Vadhan, Salil (1 March 2003). "A complete problem for statistical zero knowledge" (PDF). Journal of the ACM. 50 (2): 196–249. doi:10.1145/636865.636868. Archived (PDF) from the original on 2015-06-25

- Blum, Manuel; Feldman, Paul; Micali, Silvio (1988). "Non-Interactive Zero-Knowledge and Its Applications". Proceedings of the twentieth annual ACM symposium on Theory of computing (STOC 1988): 103–112. doi:10.1145/62212.62222

- Goldwasser, S.; Micali, S.; Rackoff, C. (1989), "The knowledge complexity of interactive proof systems" (PDF), SIAM Journal on Computing, Philadelphia: Society for Industrial and Applied Mathematics, 18 (1): 186–208, ISSN 1095-7111, doi:10.1137/0218012

- Ben-Sasson, Eli; Chiesa, Alessandro; Garman, Christina; Green, Matthew; Miers, Ian; Tromer, Eran; Virza, Madars (18 May 2014). "Zerocash: Decentralized Anonymous Payments from Bitcoin" (PDF). IEEE. Retrieved 26 January 2016

- Chaum, David; Evertse, Jan-Hendrik; van de Graaf, Jeroen (1987). "An Improved Protocol for Demonstrating Possession of Discrete Logarithms and Some Generalizations". Advances in Cryptology – EuroCrypt '87: Proceedings. 304: 127–141. doi:10.1007/3-540-39118-5_13

- Goldreich, Oded; Micali, Silvio; Wigderson, Avi (1991). "Proofs that yield nothing but their validity". Journal of the ACM. 38 (3): 690–728. doi:10.1145/116825.116852

- Feige, Uriel; Shamir, Adi (1990). "Witness Indistinguishable and Witness Hiding Protocols". Proceedings of the twenty-second annual ACM Symposium on Theory of Computing (STOC). doi:10.1145/100216.100272

5

Fundamentals of Digital Signatures and Ciphering

A digital signature comprises of three algorithms. These three algorithms are key generations, signature verifying algorithm and signing algorithm. Digital signature is usually used for financial transactions, software distribution and contract management software. This chapter has been carefully written to provide an easy understanding of the varied facets of digital signatures and ciphering.

Digital Signature

A digital signature is a mathematical scheme for demonstrating the authenticity of digital messages or documents. A valid digital signature gives a recipient reason to believe that the message was created by a known sender (authentication), that the sender cannot deny having sent the message (non-repudiation), and that the message was not altered in transit (integrity).

Digital signatures are a standard element of most cryptographic protocol suites, and are commonly used for software distribution, financial transactions, contract management software, and in other cases where it is important to detect forgery or tampering.

Explanation

Digital signatures are often used to implement electronic signatures, a broader term that refers to any electronic data that carries the intent of a signature, but not all electronic signatures use digital signatures. In some countries, including the United States, Turkey, India, Brazil, Indonesia, Mexico, Saudi Arabia, Switzerland and the countries of the European Union, electronic signatures have legal significance.

Digital signatures employ asymmetric cryptography. In many instances they provide a layer of validation and security to messages sent through a non-secure channel: Properly implemented, a digital signature gives the receiver reason to believe the message was sent by the claimed sender. Digital seals and signatures are equivalent to handwritten signatures and stamped seals. Digital signatures are equivalent to traditional handwritten signatures in many respects, but properly implemented digital signatures are more difficult to forge than the handwritten type. Digital signature schemes, in the sense used here, are cryptographically based, and must be implemented properly to be effective. Digital signatures can also provide non-repudiation, meaning that the signer cannot successfully claim they did not sign a message, while also claiming their private key remains secret; further, some non-repudiation schemes offer a time stamp for the digital signature, so that even if the private key is exposed, the signature is valid. Digitally signed messages may be anything re-presentable as a bitstring: examples include electronic mail, contracts, or a message sent via some other cryptographic protocol.

Definition of Digital Signature

A digital signature scheme typically consists of three algorithms;

- A *key generation* algorithm that selects a *private key* uniformly at random from a set of possible private keys. The algorithm outputs the private key and a corresponding *public key*.

- A *signing* algorithm that, given a message and a private key, produces a signature.

- A *signature verifying* algorithm that, given the message, public key and signature, either accepts or rejects the message's claim to authenticity.

Two main properties are required. First, the authenticity of a signature generated from a fixed message and fixed private key can be verified by using the corresponding public key. Secondly, it should be computationally infeasible to generate a valid signature for a party without knowing that party's private key. A digital signature is an authentication mechanism that enables the creator of the message to attach a code that acts as a signature. The Digital Signature Algorithm (DSA), developed by the National Institute of Standards and Technology, is one of many examples of a signing algorithm.

In the following discussion, 1^n refers to a unary number.

Formally, a digital signature scheme is a triple of probabilistic polynomial time algorithms, (G, S, V), satisfying:

- G (key-generator) generates a public key, pk, and a corresponding private key, sk, on input 1^n, where n is the security parameter.

- S (signing) returns a tag, t, on the inputs: the private key, sk, and a string, x.

- V (verifying) outputs *accepted* or *rejected* on the inputs: the public key, pk, a string, x, and a tag, t.

For correctness, S and V must satisfy

$$\Pr\left[\,(pk, sk) \leftarrow G(1^n),\ V(\,pk, x, S(sk, x)\,) = accepted\,\right] = 1.$$

A digital signature scheme is secure if for every non-uniform probabilistic polynomial time adversary, A

$$\Pr\left[\,(pk, sk) \leftarrow G(1^n),\ (x, t) \leftarrow A^{S(sk,\,\cdot\,)}(pk, 1^n),\ x \notin Q,\ V(pk, x, t) = accepted\right] < \mathrm{negl}(n),$$

where $A^{S(sk,\,\cdot\,)}$ denotes that A has access to the oracle, $S(sk, \cdot\,)$, and Q denotes the set of the queries on S made by A, which knows the public key, pk, and the security parameter, n. Note that we require any adversary cannot directly query the string, x, on S.

History of Digital Signature

In 1976, Whitfield Diffie and Martin Hellman first described the notion of a digital signature scheme, although they only conjectured that such schemes existed. Soon afterwards, Ronald

Rivest, Adi Shamir, and Len Adleman invented the RSA algorithm, which could be used to produce primitive digital signatures (although only as a proof-of-concept – "plain" RSA signatures are not secure). The first widely marketed software package to offer digital signature was Lotus Notes 1.0, released in 1989, which used the RSA algorithm.

Other digital signature schemes were soon developed after RSA, the earliest being Lamport signatures, Merkle signatures (also known as "Merkle trees" or simply "Hash trees"), and Rabin signatures.

In 1988, Shafi Goldwasser, Silvio Micali, and Ronald Rivest became the first to rigorously define the security requirements of digital signature schemes. They described a hierarchy of attack models for signature schemes, and also presented the GMR signature scheme, the first that could be proved to prevent even an existential forgery against a chosen message attack.

How they Work

To create RSA signature keys, generate a RSA key pair containing a modulus, N, that is the product of two large primes, along with integers, e and d, such that $e\,d \equiv 1 \pmod{\phi(N)}$, where ϕ is the Euler phi-function. The signer's public key consists of N and e, and the signer's secret key contains d.

To sign a message, m, the signer computes a signature, σ, such that $\sigma \equiv m^d \pmod N$. To verify, the receiver checks that $\sigma^e \equiv m \pmod N$.

As noted earlier, this basic scheme is not very secure. To prevent attacks, one can first apply a cryptographic hash function to the message, m, and then apply the RSA algorithm described above to the result. This approach is secure assuming the hash function is a random oracle.

Most early signature schemes were of a similar type: they involve the use of a trapdoor permutation, such as the RSA function, or in the case of the Rabin signature scheme, computing square modulo composite, n. A trapdoor permutation family is a family of permutations, specified by a parameter, that is easy to compute in the forward direction, but is difficult to compute in the reverse direction without already knowing the private key ("trapdoor"). Trapdoor permutations can be used for digital signature schemes, where computing the reverse direction with the secret key is required for signing, and computing the forward direction is used to verify signatures.

Used directly, this type of signature scheme is vulnerable to a key-only existential forgery attack. To create a forgery, the attacker picks a random signature σ and uses the verification procedure to determine the message, m, corresponding to that signature. In practice, however, this type of signature is not used directly, but rather, the message to be signed is first hashed to produce a short digest that is then signed. This forgery attack, then, only produces the hash function output that corresponds to σ, but not a message that leads to that value, which does not lead to an attack. In the random oracle model, this hash-then-sign form of signature is existentially unforgeable, even against a chosen-plaintext attack.

There are several reasons to sign such a hash (or message digest) instead of the whole document.

For efficiency

> The signature will be much shorter and thus save time since hashing is generally much faster than signing in practice.

For compatibility

> Messages are typically bit strings, but some signature schemes operate on other domains (such as, in the case of RSA, numbers modulo a composite number N). A hash function can be used to convert an arbitrary input into the proper format.

For integrity

> Without the hash function, the text "to be signed" may have to be split (separated) in blocks small enough for the signature scheme to act on them directly. However, the receiver of the signed blocks is not able to recognize if all the blocks are present and in the appropriate order.

Notions of Security

In their foundational paper, Goldwasser, Micali, and Rivest lay out a hierarchy of attack models against digital signatures:

1. In a *key-only* attack, the attacker is only given the public verification key.

2. In a *known message* attack, the attacker is given valid signatures for a variety of messages known by the attacker but not chosen by the attacker.

3. In an *adaptive chosen message* attack, the attacker first learns signatures on arbitrary messages of the attacker's choice.

They also describe a hierarchy of attack results:

1. A *total break* results in the recovery of the signing key.

2. A universal forgery attack results in the ability to forge signatures for any message.

3. A selective forgery attack results in a signature on a message of the adversary's choice.

4. An existential forgery merely results in some valid message/signature pair not already known to the adversary.

The strongest notion of security, therefore, is security against existential forgery under an adaptive chosen message attack.

Applications of Digital Signatures

As organizations move away from paper documents with ink signatures or authenticity stamps, digital signatures can provide added assurances of the evidence to provenance, identity, and status of an electronic document as well as acknowledging informed consent and approval by a signatory. The United States Government Printing Office (GPO) publishes electronic versions of the budget, public and private laws, and congressional bills with digital signatures. Universities including Penn State, University of Chicago, and Stanford are publishing electronic student transcripts with digital signatures.

Below are some common reasons for applying a digital signature to communications:

Authentication

Although messages may often include information about the entity sending a message, that information may not be accurate. Digital signatures can be used to authenticate the source of messages. When ownership of a digital signature secret key is bound to a specific user, a valid signature shows that the message was sent by that user. The importance of high confidence in sender authenticity is especially obvious in a financial context. For example, suppose a bank's branch office sends instructions to the central office requesting a change in the balance of an account. If the central office is not convinced that such a message is truly sent from an authorized source, acting on such a request could be a grave mistake.

Integrity

In many scenarios, the sender and receiver of a message may have a need for confidence that the message has not been altered during transmission. Although encryption hides the contents of a message, it may be possible to *change* an encrypted message without understanding it. (Some encryption algorithms, known as nonmalleable ones, prevent this, but others do not.) However, if a message is digitally signed, any change in the message after signature invalidates the signature. Furthermore, there is no efficient way to modify a message and its signature to produce a new message with a valid signature, because this is still considered to be computationally infeasible by most cryptographic hash functions.

Non-repudiation

Non-repudiation, or more specifically *non-repudiation of origin*, is an important aspect of digital signatures. By this property, an entity that has signed some information cannot at a later time deny having signed it. Similarly, access to the public key only does not enable a fraudulent party to fake a valid signature.

Note that these authentication, non-repudiation etc. properties rely on the secret key *not having been revoked* prior to its usage. Public revocation of a key-pair is a required ability, else leaked secret keys would continue to implicate the claimed owner of the key-pair. Checking revocation status requires an "online" check; e.g., checking a certificate revocation list or via the Online Certificate Status Protocol. Very roughly this is analogous to a vendor who receives credit-cards first checking online with the credit-card issuer to find if a given card has been reported lost or stolen. Of course, with stolen key pairs, the theft is often discovered only after the secret key's use, e.g., to sign a bogus certificate for espionage purpose.

Additional Security Precautions

Putting the Private Key on a Smart Card

All public key / private key cryptosystems depend entirely on keeping the private key secret. A private key can be stored on a user's computer, and protected by a local password, but this has two disadvantages:

- the user can only sign documents on that particular computer

- the security of the private key depends entirely on the security of the computer

A more secure alternative is to store the private key on a smart card. Many smart cards are designed to be tamper-resistant (although some designs have been broken, notably by Ross Anderson and his students). In a typical digital signature implementation, the hash calculated from the document is sent to the smart card, whose CPU signs the hash using the stored private key of the user, and then returns the signed hash. Typically, a user must activate his smart card by entering a personal identification number or PIN code (thus providing two-factor authentication). It can be arranged that the private key never leaves the smart card, although this is not always implemented. If the smart card is stolen, the thief will still need the PIN code to generate a digital signature. This reduces the security of the scheme to that of the PIN system, although it still requires an attacker to possess the card. A mitigating factor is that private keys, if generated and stored on smart cards, are usually regarded as difficult to copy, and are assumed to exist in exactly one copy. Thus, the loss of the smart card may be detected by the owner and the corresponding certificate can be immediately revoked. Private keys that are protected by software only may be easier to copy, and such compromises are far more difficult to detect.

Using Smart Card Readers with a Separate Keyboard

Entering a PIN code to activate the smart card commonly requires a numeric keypad. Some card readers have their own numeric keypad. This is safer than using a card reader integrated into a PC, and then entering the PIN using that computer's keyboard. Readers with a numeric keypad are meant to circumvent the eavesdropping threat where the computer might be running a keystroke logger, potentially compromising the PIN code. Specialized card readers are also less vulnerable to tampering with their software or hardware and are often EAL3 certified.

Other Smart Card Designs

Smart card design is an active field, and there are smart card schemes which are intended to avoid these particular problems, though so far with little security proofs.

Using Digital Signatures only with Trusted Applications

One of the main differences between a digital signature and a written signature is that the user does not "see" what he signs. The user application presents a hash code to be signed by the digital signing algorithm using the private key. An attacker who gains control of the user's PC can possibly replace the user application with a foreign substitute, in effect replacing the user's own communications with those of the attacker. This could allow a malicious application to trick a user into signing any document by displaying the user's original on-screen, but presenting the attacker's own documents to the signing application.

To protect against this scenario, an authentication system can be set up between the user's application (word processor, email client, etc.) and the signing application. The general idea is to provide some means for both the user application and signing application to verify each other's integrity. For example, the signing application may require all requests to come from digitally signed binaries.

Using A Network Attached Hardware Security Module

One of the main differences between a cloud based digital signature service and a locally provided one is risk. Many risk averse companies, including governments, financial and medical institutions, and payment processors require more secure standards, like FIPS 140-2 level 3 and FIPS 201 certification, to ensure the signature is validated and secure.

WYSIWYS

Technically speaking, a digital signature applies to a string of bits, whereas humans and applications "believe" that they sign the semantic interpretation of those bits. In order to be semantically interpreted, the bit string must be transformed into a form that is meaningful for humans and applications, and this is done through a combination of hardware and software based processes on a computer system. The problem is that the semantic interpretation of bits can change as a function of the processes used to transform the bits into semantic content. It is relatively easy to change the interpretation of a digital document by implementing changes on the computer system where the document is being processed. From a semantic perspective this creates uncertainty about what exactly has been signed. WYSIWYS (What You See Is What You Sign) means that the semantic interpretation of a signed message cannot be changed. In particular this also means that a message cannot contain hidden information that the signer is unaware of, and that can be revealed after the signature has been applied. WYSIWYS is a necessary requirement for the validity of digital signatures, but this requirement is difficult to guarantee because of the increasing complexity of modern computer systems. The term WYSIWYS was coined by Peter Landrock and Torben Pedersen to describe some of the principles in delivering secure and legally binding digital signatures for Pan-European projects.

Digital Signatures versus Ink on Paper Signatures

An ink signature could be replicated from one document to another by copying the image manually or digitally, but to have credible signature copies that can resist some scrutiny is a significant manual or technical skill, and to produce ink signature copies that resist professional scrutiny is very difficult.

Digital signatures cryptographically bind an electronic identity to an electronic document and the digital signature cannot be copied to another document. Paper contracts sometimes have the ink signature block on the last page, and the previous pages may be replaced after a signature is applied. Digital signatures can be applied to an entire document, such that the digital signature on the last page will indicate tampering if any data on any of the pages have been altered, but this can also be achieved by signing with ink and numbering all pages of the contract.

Some Digital Signature Algorithms

- RSA-based signature schemes, such as RSA-PSS

- DSA and its elliptic curve variant ECDSA

- Edwards-curve Digital Signature Algorithm and its Ed25519 variant.

- ElGamal signature scheme as the predecessor to DSA, and variants Schnorr signature and Pointcheval–Stern signature algorithm

- Rabin signature algorithm

- Pairing-based schemes such as BLS

- Undeniable signatures

- Aggregate signature - a signature scheme that supports aggregation: Given n signatures on n messages from n users, it is possible to aggregate all these signatures into a single signature whose size is constant in the number of users. This single signature will convince the verifier that the n users did indeed sign the n original messages.

- Signatures with efficient protocols - are signature schemes that facilitate efficient cryptographic protocols such as zero-knowledge proofs or secure computation.

The Current State of use – Legal and Practical

All digital signature schemes share the following basic prerequisites regardless of cryptographic theory or legal provision:

1. Quality algorithms

   Some public-key algorithms are known to be insecure, as practical attacks against them having been discovered.

2. Quality implementations

   An implementation of a good algorithm (or protocol) with mistake(s) will not work.

3. Users (and their software) must carry out the signature protocol properly.

4. The private key must remain private

   If the private key becomes known to any other party, that party can produce *perfect* digital signatures of anything whatsoever.

5. The public key owner must be verifiable

   A public key associated with Bob actually came from Bob. This is commonly done using a public key infrastructure (PKI) and the public key↔user association is attested by the operator of the PKI (called a certificate authority). For 'open' PKIs in which anyone can request such an attestation (universally embodied in a cryptographically protected identity certificate), the possibility of mistaken attestation is non-trivial. Commercial PKI operators have suffered several publicly known problems. Such mistakes could lead to falsely signed, and thus wrongly attributed, documents. 'Closed' PKI systems are more expensive, but less easily subverted in this way.

Only if all of these conditions are met will a digital signature actually be any evidence of who sent the message, and therefore of their assent to its contents. Legal enactment cannot change this reality of the existing engineering possibilities, though some such have not reflected this actuality.

Legislatures, being importuned by businesses expecting to profit from operating a PKI, or by the technological avant-garde advocating new solutions to old problems, have enacted statutes and/or regulations in many jurisdictions authorizing, endorsing, encouraging, or permitting digital signatures and providing for (or limiting) their legal effect. The first appears to have been in Utah in the United States, followed closely by the states Massachusetts and California. Other countries have also passed statutes or issued regulations in this area as well and the UN has had an active model law project for some time. These enactments (or proposed enactments) vary from place to place, have typically embodied expectations at variance (optimistically or pessimistically) with the state of the underlying cryptographic engineering, and have had the net effect of confusing potential users and specifiers, nearly all of whom are not cryptographically knowledgeable. Adoption of technical standards for digital signatures have lagged behind much of the legislation, delaying a more or less unified engineering position on interoperability, algorithm choice, key lengths, and so on what the engineering is attempting to provide.

Industry Standards

Some industries have established common interoperability standards for the use of digital signatures between members of the industry and with regulators. These include the Automotive Network Exchange for the automobile industry and the SAFE-BioPharma Association for the healthcare industry.

Using Separate Key Pairs for Signing and Encryption

In several countries, a digital signature has a status somewhat like that of a traditional pen and paper signature, like in the EU digital signature legislation. Generally, these provisions mean that anything digitally signed legally binds the signer of the document to the terms therein. For that reason, it is often thought best to use separate key pairs for encrypting and signing. Using the encryption key pair, a person can engage in an encrypted conversation (e.g., regarding a real estate transaction), but the encryption does not legally sign every message he sends. Only when both parties come to an agreement do they sign a contract with their signing keys, and only then are they legally bound by the terms of a specific document. After signing, the document can be sent over the encrypted link. If a signing key is lost or compromised, it can be revoked to mitigate any future transactions. If an encryption key is lost, a backup or key escrow should be utilized to continue viewing encrypted content. Signing keys should never be backed up or escrowed unless the backup destination is securely encrypted.

Traditionally signature with a message is used to give evidence of identity and intention with regard to that message. For years people have been using various types of signature to associate their identity and intention to the messages. Wax imprint, seal, and handwritten signature are the common examples. But when someone need to sign a digital message, things turn different. In case of signing a digital document one cannot use any classical approach of signing, because it can be forged easily. Forger just need to cut the signature and paste it with any other message. For signing a digital document one uses digital signature.

Therefore, digital signature are required not to be separated from the message and attached to another. That is a digital signature is required to be both message and signer dependent. For validating the signature anyone can verify the signature, so digital signature are suppose to be verified easily.

A digital signature scheme typically consist of three distinct steps:

1. Key generation:- User compute their public key and corresponding private key.

2. Signing:- In this step user sign a given message with his/her private key.

3. Verification:- In this step user verify a signature for given message and public key.

So the functionality provided by digital signature can be stated as follows:

Authentication:- Digital signature provides authentication of the source of the messages as a message is signed by the private key of the sender which is only known to him/her. Authentication is highly desirable in many applications.

Integrity:- Digital signature provides integrity as digital signature uniquely associate with corresponding message. i.e. After signing a message a message cannot be altered if someone do it will invalidate the signature. There is no efficient method to change message and its signature to produce a new message and valid signature without having private key. So both sender and receiver don't have to worry about in transit alteration.

Non- repudiation:- For a valid signature sender of message cannot deny having signed it.

In this report we are going to discuss different variation of digital signature. First we will describe RSA digital signature scheme and Elgamal signature scheme, along with their elliptic curve version. After covering above signature scheme we will talk about digital signature standards, and then we will cover proxy signature scheme, blind signature scheme and then we will finally talk about short signature scheme.

RSA Digital Signature Scheme

Suppose Alice want to send a message(m) to Bob. She can generate digital signature using RSA digital signature scheme as follow:

Key Generation:-

She can generate key for RSA signature scheme:

1.   Choose two distinct large prime numbers p and q.

2.   Compute n = pq.

3.   n is used as the modulus for both the public and private keys.

4.   Compute $\varphi(n) = (p - 1)(q - 1)$, where φ is Euler's totient function.

5.   Choose an integer e such that $1 < e < \varphi(n)$ and $\gcd(e, \varphi(n)) = 1$.

6.   Compute $d = e{-}1 \bmod \varphi(n)$.

Then the public key and private key of user will be (e, n) and (d, n) respectively.

Now she have her public and private key. Now she can generate the signature of a message by encrypting it by her private key.

So she can generate signature corresponding to message(m) as follow:

Signing:-

1. Represent the message m as an integer between 0 and n − 1.

2. Sign message by raising it to the dth power modulo n.

$$S \equiv m^d \pmod{n}$$

So S is the signature corresponding to message m. Now she can send message m along with the signature S to Bob.

Upon receiving the message and signature (m, S), Bob can verify the signature by decrypting it by Alice public key as follow:

Verification:-

1. Verify signature by raising it to the eth power modulo n.

$$m' \equiv S^e \pmod{n}$$

2. If m' = m (mod n) then signature is valid otherwise not.

For a valid signature both m and m' will be equal because:

$$S \equiv m^d \pmod{n}$$

$$m' \equiv m^{de} \pmod{n}$$

and

e is inverse of d, i.e. $ed \equiv 1 \pmod{\Phi(n)}$.

So, by using above algorithm Alice can generate a valid signature S for her message m, but there is a problem in above define scheme that is the length of the signature is equal to the length of the message. This is a disadvantage when message is long.

There is a modification in the above scheme. The signature scheme is applied to the hash of the message, rather than to the message itself. Now Alice have a message signature pair (m, S). So, the signature S is a valid signature for message m. So a forger (lets say Eve) cannot forge Alice signature. i.e. She cannot use signature S with another message lets say m_1, because S^e is not equal to m_1. Even when the signature scheme is applied to the hash of the message it is infeasible to forge the signature, because it is infeasible to produce two message m, m_1 with same hash value.

In practice, the public key in RSA digital signature scheme is much smaller than the private key. This enable a user to verify the message easily. This is a desired because a message may be verified more than once, so the verification process should be faster than signing process.

The RSA Digital Signature Algorithm:-

Additional instructions for RSA signature algorithm is as follows:

An RSA digital signature key pair consists of an RSA private key, which is used to compute a digital signature, and an RSA public key, which is used to verify a digital signature. An RSA digital signature key pair shall not be used for other purposes (e.g. key establishment).

An RSA public key consists of a modulus n, which is the product of two positive prime integers p and q (i.e., n = pq), and a public key exponent e. Thus, the RSA public key is the pair of values (n, e) and is used to verify digital signatures. The size of an RSA key pair is commonly considered to be the length of the modulus n in bits (nlen). The corresponding RSA private key consists of the same modulus n and a private key exponent d that depends on n and the public key exponent e. Thus, the RSA private key is the pair of values (n, d) and is used to generate digital signatures. In order to provide security for the digital signature process, the two integers p and q, and the private key exponent d shall be kept secret. The modulus n and the public key exponent e may be made known to anyone.

The Standard specifies three choices for the length of the modulus (i.e., nlen): 1024, 2048 and 3072 bits.

An approved hash function, shall be used during the generation of key pairs and digital signatures. When used during the generation of an RSA key pair, the length in bits of the hash function output block shall meet or exceed the security strength associated with the bit length of the modulus n. The security strength associated with the RSA digital signature process is no greater than the minimum of the security strength associated with the bit length of the modulus and the security strength of the hash function that is employed. Both the security strength of the hash function used and the security strength associated with the bit length of the modulus n shall meet or exceed the security strength required for the digital signature process.

Elgamal Digital Signature Scheme

Elgamal digital signature scheme was proposed by Elgamal in 1985. This is based on Diffe-Hellman key exchange. This signature scheme is quite different from RSA signature scheme in terms of validity of signatures corresponding to a message. i.e. there are many valid signatures for a message. Suppose Alice want to sign a message using Elgamal digital signature scheme, she can generate signature S corresponding to message m as follow:

Key generation:-

She can generate key for Elgamal signature scheme as follow:

- Choose p be a large prime.

- Choose g be a randomly chosen generator of the multiplicative group of integers Zp.

- Choose a secret key x such that $1 < x < p - 1$.

- Compute $y = g^x \pmod{p}$.

Then the public key and private key of user will be (p, g, y) and (p, g, x) respectively.

Signing:-

Now Alice has her public and private key so she can sign a message m by using following steps:

1. Choose a random number k such that $0 < k < p - 1$ and $\gcd(k, p - 1) = 1$.

2. Compute $r \equiv g^k \pmod{p}$.

3. Compute $s \equiv (H(m) - xr)k^{-1} \pmod{p - 1}$. Where $H(m)$ is hash of message.

Then the pair (r, s) is the signature of the message m.

Verification:-

Bob can verify the signature (r, s) of message m as follow:

1. Download Alice's public key (p, g, y).

2. Compute $v_1 \equiv g^{H(m)} \pmod{p}$ and $v_2 \equiv y^r r^s \pmod{p}$.

3. The signature is declared valid if and only if $v_1 \equiv v_2 \pmod{p}$.

For a valid signature (r, s), $v_1 \equiv v_2 \pmod{p}$ since

$$s \equiv (H(m) - xr)k^{-1} \pmod{p - 1}$$

$$sk \equiv (H(m) - xr) \pmod{p - 1}$$

$$H(m) \equiv (sk + xr) \pmod{p - 1}$$

$$v_1 \equiv g^{H(m)} \pmod{p}$$

$$v_1 \equiv g^{(sk + xr)} \pmod{p}$$

$$v_1 \equiv g^{(sk)} g^{(xr)} \pmod{p}$$

$$v_1 \equiv (g^k)^s (g^x)^r \pmod{p}$$

$$v_1 \equiv y^r r^s \pmod{p}$$

$$v_1 \equiv v_2 \pmod{p}$$

The security of Elgamal digital signature scheme relies on the difficulty of computing discrete logarithms. The security of the system follows from the fact that since x is kept private for forging Elgamal digital signature one do need to solve discrete logarithm problem.

Suppose Eve want to forge Alice signature for a message m_1 and she doesn't know x (as x kept private by Alice), then she cannot compute s(as $s \equiv (H(m_1) - xr)k^{-1} \pmod{p - 1}$). Now the only option left is to choose s which satisfies the verification. Thus s should satisfy equation $y^r r^s \equiv g^{H(m)} \pmod{p}$ as Eve knows (p, g, y) so she can compute r. So the equation can be rearrange as $r^s \equiv y^r g^{H(m)} \pmod{p}$, which is again a discrete logarithm problem. So Elgamal signature scheme is secure, as long as discrete logarithm are difficult to compute.

Digital Signature Standards

Digital signature standards define some standards to be followed. A digital signature scheme includes a signature generation and a signature verification. Each user has a public and private key and is the owner of that key pair.

For both the signature generation and verification processes, the message (i.e., the signed data) is converted to a fixed-length representation of the message by means of an approved hash function. Both the original message and the digital signature are made available to a verifier.

A verifier requires assurance that the public key to be used to verify a signature belongs to the entity that claims to have generated a digital signature (i.e., the claimed signatory). That is, a verifier requires assurance that the signatory is the actual owner of the public/private key pair used to generate and verify a digital signature. A binding of an owners identity and the owners public key shall be effected in order to provide this assurance.

A verifier also requires assurance that the key pair owner actually possesses the private key associated with the public key, and that the public key is a mathematically correct key. By obtaining these assurances, the verifier has assurance that if the digital signature can be correctly verified using the public key, the digital signature is valid (i.e., the key pair owner really signed the message). Digital signature validation includes both the (mathematical) verification of the digital signature and obtaining the appropriate assurances.

Technically, a key pair used by a digital signature algorithm could also be used for purposes other than digital signatures (e.g., for key establishment). However, a key pair used for digital signature generation and verification as specified in this Standard shall not be used for any other purpose. A number of steps are required to enable a digital signature generation or verification capability in accordance with Standards.

Initial Setup:-

Each intended signatory shall obtain a digital signature key pair that is generated as specified for the appropriate digital signature algorithm, either by generating the key pair itself or by obtaining the key pair from a trusted party. The intended signatory is authorized to use the key pair and is the owner of that key pair. Note that if a trusted party generates the key pair, that party needs to be trusted not to masquerade as the owner, even though the trusted party knows the private key.

After obtaining the key pair, the intended signatory (now the key pair owner) shall obtain assurance of the validity of the public key and assurance that he/she actually possesses the associated private key.

Digital Signature Generation:-

Prior to the generation of a digital signature, a message digest shall be generated on the information to be signed using an appropriate approved hash function.

Using the selected digital signature algorithm, the signature private key, the message digest, and any other information required by the digital signature process, a digital signature shall be generated according to the Standard.

The signatory may optionally verify the digital signature using the signature verification process and the associated public key. This optional verification serves as a final check to detect otherwise undetected signature generation computation errors; this verification may be prudent when signing a high-value message, when multiple users are expected to verify the signature, or if the verifier will be verifying the signature at a much later time.

Digital Signature Verification and Validation:-

In order to verify a digital signature, the verifier shall obtain the public key of the claimed signatory, (usually) based on the claimed identity. A message digest shall be generated on the data whose signature is to be verified (i.e., not on the received digital signature) using the same hash function that was used during the digital signature generation process. Using the appropriate digital signature algorithm, the domain parameters (if appropriate), the public key and the newly computed message digest, the received digital signature is verified in accordance with this Standard. If the verification process fails, no inference can be made as to whether the data is correct, only that in using the specified public key and the specified signature format, the digital signature cannot be verified for that data.

Before accepting the verified digital signature as valid, the verifier shall have

1. assurance of the signatory claimed identity,

2. assurance of the validity of the public key, and

3. assurance that the claimed signatory actually possessed the private key that was used to generate the digital signature at the time that the signature was generated.

If the verification and assurance processes are successful, the digital signature and signed data shall be considered valid. However, if a verification or assurance process fails, the digital signature should be considered invalid.

Blind & Prony Signature

Suppose Alice want her message to be sign by Bob without letting him know the content of the message, she can got it done using Blind signature scheme. Blind signatures scheme, proposed by Chaum, allow a signer to interactively sign messages for users such that the messages are hidden from the signer. Blind signature typically have two basic security properties: blindness says that a malicious signer cannot decide upon the order in which two messages have been signed in two executions with an honest user, and unforgeability demands that no adversarial user can create more signatures than interactions with the honest signer took place.

Blind signatures are typically employed in privacy-related protocols where the signer and message author are different parties. Blind signature schemes see a great deal of use in applications where sender privacy is important, some of them are:

1. Cryptographic election systems (e-Vote).

2. Digital cash schemes (e-Cash)

Blind signature scheme can be used with RSA signature algorithm. In RSA signature scheme a signature is computed by encrypting the message by the private key. In case of the blind signature there is one additional step Blinding the message. Alice can blind her message and get is signed by Bob, and remove the blinding factor after getting it signed. Suppose (e, N) and (d, N) is the public key and private key of Bob respectively then Alice can blind her message as follows:

Blinding the message:-

1. Alice chooses a random value r, such that r is relatively prime to N (i.e. gcd(r, N) = 1).

2. Calculate blinding factor by raising r to the public key e (mod N) (i.e. blinding factor is equal to r^e(mod N)).

3. Blind the message by computing the product of the message and blinding factor, i.e.

    $m' \equiv mr^e$ (mod N)

Now Alice can send blinded message m' to Bob. Now m' does not leak any information about m, as r is private to Alice. Any malicious user need to solve discrete logarithm problem for recovering original m from m'.

Signing:-

When Bob (signing authority) receive a blinded message from Alice (user) he will sign the message by his private key

$S' \equiv (m')^d$(mod N)

S' is the signature corresponding to message m'. Bob send S' to Alice. Alice removes the blinding factor from the signature by dividing it r and revel the original RSA signature S as follow:

$S \equiv S'r^{-1}$ (mod N)

Now Alice message m with signature S, signature can be verified using Bob's public key.

Verification:-

Now signature can be verified as usual RSA signature.

1. Verify signature by raising it to the eth power module N.

    $m' \equiv S^e$ (mod N)

2. If m' = m (mod N) then signature is valid otherwise not.

    The above scheme will work fine. i.e. (S, m) is a valid signature message tuple corresponding to Bob. Since

    $S \equiv S'r^{-1}$ (mod N)

    $\equiv (m')^d r^{-1}$ (mod N)

    $\equiv (mr^e)^d r^{-1}$ (mod N)

    $\equiv m^d r^{ed} r^{-1}$ (mod N)

    $\equiv m^d rr^{-1}$ (mod N)

    $\equiv m^d$ (mod N)

Proxy Signature:-

In proxy signature scheme a user Alice (original signer) delegates her signing capability to another user, Bob(proxy signer), so that Bob can sign messages on behalf of Alice. Proxy signature can be validate for its correctness and can be distinguished between a normal signature and a proxy signature. So the verifier can be convinced of the original signer's agreement on the signed message. Proxy signature is used in a number of applications, including electronic commerce, mobile agents, distributed shared object systems, and many more. For example, the president of a company delegates a signing right to his/her secretary before a vacation. The secretary can make a signature on behalf of the president, and a verifier can be confident that the signature has been made by the authorized secretary. The verifier can also be convinced of the president's agreement on the signed message. Typically, a proxy signature scheme is as follows. The original signer Alice sends the proxy signer Bob a signature that is associated with a specific message. Bob makes a proxy private key using this information. Bob can then sign on a message with the proxy private key using a normal signature scheme. After the message and signature have been sent to the verifier, he/she recovers a proxy public key using public information and verifies the proxy signature using a normal signature scheme.

Proxy Signature scheme is introduced by Mambo. Proxy signature scheme is based on a discrete logarithm problem. The original signer has the private key x and public key $y \equiv g^x \pmod{p}$. Proxy signature scheme is as follow:

System Parameters:-

The original signer choose k randomly and computes $r = g^k \bmod p$, and $s = x + kr \bmod p$. Now original signer send these system parameters to the proxy signer.

i.e. original signer sends (r, s) to the proxy signer. The proxy signer checks the validity of (r, s) as follows:

$$g^s = yr^r \bmod p$$

If this equality holds, the proxy signer accepts (r, s) as the valid proxy secret key.

Signing

The proxy signer signs a message m, then its signature S_p is generated. After that, the proxy signer sends the message and its signature, which are (m, S_p, r), to the verifier.

Verification

Upon receiving (m, S_p, r), the verifier recovers y' by $y' = yr^r \bmod p$ and substitute y' for y. After that, the verifier proceeds the verification phase of normal signature scheme.

Short Signature Scheme

Short signature scheme give the shortest signature among all discussed signature schemes. This signature scheme use elliptic curve and bilinear pairing. We will discuss this signature scheme starting from the basic signature scheme and then type of bilinear pairing it uses, after that security multiplier and finally types of elliptic curve used in this scheme.

Short signature scheme is in three parts, KeyGen, Sign, and Verify. It makes use of a hash function $h : \{0, 1\}^* \to G^*$. Where G is the base group and g is generator. G, g are system parameters.

1. Key Generation:- Choose a random $x \in Z^*_p$, and compute $v \leftarrow g^x$. x is the secret key and v is the public key.

2. Signing:- For a message $M \in \{0, 1\}^*$, and secret key x, Compute $h \leftarrow h(M)$, and $\sigma \leftarrow h^x$. The signature is $\sigma \in G^*$.

3. Verification:- For a given public key v, a message M, and a signature, compute $h \leftarrow h(M)$ and verify that (g, v, h, σ) is a valid Diffie-Hellman tuple.

So short signature scheme use bilinear pairing in verification of the signature.

Bilinear pairing:-

Let G_1 and G_T be two cyclic groups of prime order q. Let G_2 be a group and each element of G_2 has order dividing q. A bilinear pairing e is e : $G_1 \times G_2 \to G_T$ such that

$e(g_1, g_2) = 1_{GT}$ for all $g_2 \in G_2$ if and only if $g_1 = 1_{G1}$, and similarly $e(g_1, g_2) = 1_{GT}$ for all $g_1 \in G_1$ if and only if $g_2 = 1_{G2}$.

for all $g_1 \in G_1$ and $g_2 \in G_2$, $e(g_1, g_2) = e(g_1^a, g_2^b)^{ab}$ for all a, b $\in$ Z.

Security Multiplier: - Let a finite field F_p^l where p is a prime and l is a positive integer, and an elliptic curve E over F_p^l have m points. Let, point P of elliptic curve has order q, where $q^2!/m$. Then subgroup P has a security multiplier $\alpha > 0$, if order of p^l in F^*_q is α. We will discuss different families of elliptic curve Which are classified by the value of security multiplier.

Type 1

Let p be a prime where p = 2(mod 3). Let E be the elliptic curve defined over F_p, and equation of the curve is $y^2 = x^3 + b$, Typically b = ±1. Then $E(F_p)$ is supersingular curve, and number of points, $\#E(F_p) = p + 1$, and $\#E(F_{p^2}) = (p + 1)^2$. For any odd j / p + 1, G = $E(F_p)[j]$ is cyclic and has security multiplier $\alpha = 2$. Let | be the cube root of unity. Consider the following map, sometimes referred to as a distortion map:

$$\Phi(x, y) = (|x, y)$$

Then Φ maps points of $E(F_p)$ to points of $E(F_{p2}) \backslash E(F_p)$. Thus if f denotes the bilinear pairing, then defining e : $G \times G \to F_{q2}$ by e(P, Q) = f (P, $\Phi(Q)$) gives a bilinear non-degenerate map.

Type 2

Unlike above discussed curve this type of curve have low characteristic field. Let F is a finite field defined over 3^l where | is a positive exponent. Let curve $E^+ : y^2 = x^3 + 2x + 1$, and

$E : y^2 = x^3 + 2x-1$, over F_3^l.

when | = ±1mod12

$\#E^+ (F_3^l) = 3^l + 1 + 3^{(l+1)/2}$

when $| = \pm5 \bmod 12$

$$\#E^+ (F_3^|) = 3^| + 1 - 3^{(|+1)/2}$$

when $| = \pm1 \bmod 12$

$$\#E^-(F_3^|) = 3^| + 1 - 3^{(|+1)/2}$$

when $l = \pm5 \bmod 12$

$$\#E^- (F_3^|) = 3^| + 1 + 3^{(|+1)/2}$$

Type 3

Let p be a prime where $p \equiv 3 \pmod 4$. Let E be the elliptic curve defined over F_p, and equation of the curve is $y^2 = x^3 + ax$, where $a \in Z(\bmod p)$. Then $E(F_q)$ is supersingular curve, and number of point, $\#E(F_p) = p + 1$, and $\#E(F_{p2}) = (p + 1)^2$. For any odd $j|p + 1$, Group $G = E(F_p)[j]$ is cyclic and has security multiplier $\alpha = 2$.

Type 4

Type 4 curves are non-supersingular. By considering cyclotomic polynomials, elliptic curve with security multiplier 12 can be generated. Let $q(x) = 36x^4 + 36x^3 + 24x^2 + 6x + 1$. Let $t(x) = 6x^2 + 1$. If D = 3, then solution of CM equation will always be $V = 6x^2 + 4x + 1$. It turns out $q(x) + 1 - t(x) |$ $q(x)12 - 1$. So the value of security multiplier is 12. Following algorithm is used to generate curves:

1. Pick an integer x of a desired magnitude. It may be negative.

2. Check if q(x) is prime.

3. Check if $n = q(x) - t(x) + 1$ has a large prime factor r. (Ideally it should be prime.)

4. Try different values of k until a random point of $y^2 = x^3 + k$ has order n.

Type 5

Type 5 curve are also non-supersingular curve. Type 6 curve are ordinary curves with security multiplier 6. Order of type 6 curves is a prime or a prime multiplied by a small constant. Let a finite field F defined over some p where $p = s*q$. Where s is a small constant and q is a prime. When type 5 curve is defined over field F_{p6}, its order is a multiple of q^2.

Cipher

In cryptography, a cipher (or cypher) is an algorithm for performing encryption or decryption—a series of well-defined steps that can be followed as a procedure. An alternative, less common term is *encipherment*. To encipher or encode is to convert information into cipher or code. In common parlance, 'cipher' is synonymous with 'code', as they are both a set of steps that encrypt a message; however, the concepts are distinct in cryptography, especially classical cryptography.

Edward Larsson's rune cipher resembling that found on the Kensington Runestone.
Also includes runically unrelated blackletter writing style and pigpen cipher.

Codes generally substitute different length strings of characters in the output, while ciphers generally substitute the same number of characters as are input. There are exceptions and some cipher systems may use slightly more, or fewer, characters when output versus the number that were input.

Codes operated by substituting according to a large codebook which linked a random string of characters or numbers to a word or phrase. For example, "UQJHSE" could be the code for "Proceed to the following coordinates." When using a cipher the original information is known as plaintext, and the encrypted form as ciphertext. The ciphertext message contains all the information of the plaintext message, but is not in a format readable by a human or computer without the proper mechanism to decrypt it.

The operation of a cipher usually depends on a piece of auxiliary information, called a key (or, in traditional NSA parlance, a *cryptovariable*). The encrypting procedure is varied depending on the key, which changes the detailed operation of the algorithm. A key must be selected before using a cipher to encrypt a message. Without knowledge of the key, it should be extremely difficult, if not impossible, to decrypt the resulting ciphertext into readable plaintext.

Most modern ciphers can be categorized in several ways

- By whether they work on blocks of symbols usually of a fixed size (block ciphers), or on a continuous stream of symbols (stream ciphers).

- By whether the same key is used for both encryption and decryption (symmetric key algorithms), or if a different key is used for each (asymmetric key algorithms). If the algorithm is symmetric, the key must be known to the recipient and sender and to no one else. If the algorithm is an asymmetric one, the enciphering key is different from, but closely related to, the deciphering key. If one key cannot be deduced from the other, the asymmetric key algorithm has the public/private key property and one of the keys may be made public without loss of confidentiality.

Etymology

The word "cipher" (minority spelling "cypher") in former times meant "zero" and had the same origin: Middle French as *cifre* and Medieval Latin as *cifra,* from the Arabic *sifr* = zero. "Cipher" was later used for any decimal digit, even any number. There are many theories about how the word "cipher" may have come to mean "encoding". In fact the more ancient source of word "Cypher" is the ancient Hebrew; there are more than 100 verses in the Hebrew Bible - Torah using word "Cepher": means (Book or Story telling), and in some of them the word "Cipher" literally means (Counting)-- (Numerical description)-- Example, Book 2 Samuel 24:10, Isaiah 33:18, and Jeremiah 52:25.

- Encoding often involved numbers.

- The Roman number system was very cumbersome because there was no concept of zero (or empty space). The concept of zero (which was also called "cipher"), which is now common knowledge, was alien to medieval Europe, so confusing and ambiguous to common Europeans that in arguments people would say "talk clearly and not so far fetched as a cipher". Cipher came to mean concealment of clear messages or encryption.

  o The French formed the word "chiffre" and adopted the Italian word "zero".

  o The English used "zero" for "0", and "cipher" from the word "ciphering" as a means of computing.

  o The Germans used the words "Ziffer" (digit) and "Chiffre".

  o The Dutch still use the word "cijfer" to refer to a numerical digit.

  o The Serbians use the word "cifra", which refers to a digit, or in some cases, any number. Besides "cifra", they use word "broj" for a number.

  o The Italians and the Spanish also use the word "cifra" to refer to a number.

  o The Swedes use the word "siffra" which refers to a digit and "nummer" to refer to a combination of "siffror".

Ibrahim Al-Kadi concluded that the Arabic word *sifr*, for the digit zero, developed into the European technical term for encryption.

As the decimal zero and its new mathematics spread from the Arabic world to Europe in the Middle Ages, words derived from *sifr* and *zephyrus* came to refer to calculation, as well as to privileged knowledge and secret codes. According to Ifrah, "in thirteenth-century Paris, a 'worthless fellow' was called a '... cifre en algorisme', i.e., an 'arithmetical nothing'." Cipher was the European pronunciation of sifr, and cipher came to mean a message or communication not easily understood.

Versus Codes

In non-technical usage, a "(secret) code" typically means a "cipher". Within technical discussions, however, the words "code" and "cipher" refer to two different concepts. Codes work at the level of meaning—that is, words or phrases are converted into something else and this chunking generally shortens the message.

An example of this is the Commercial Telegraph Code which was used to shorten long telegraph messages which resulted from entering into commercial contracts using exchanges of Telegrams.

Another example is given by whole words cipher s, which allow the user to replace an entire word with a symbol or character, much like the way Japanese utilize Kanji (Japanese) characters to supplement their language. ex "The quick brown fox jumps over the lazy dog".

Ciphers, on the other hand, work at a lower level: the level of individual letters, small groups of letters, or, in modern schemes, individual bits and blocks of bits. Some systems used both codes and ciphers in one system, using superencipherment to increase the security. In some cases the terms codes and ciphers are also used synonymously to substitution and transposition.

Historically, cryptography was split into a dichotomy of codes and ciphers; and coding had its own terminology, analogous to that for ciphers: "*encoding, codetext, decoding*" and so on.

However, codes have a variety of drawbacks, including susceptibility to cryptanalysis and the difficulty of managing a cumbersome codebook. Because of this, codes have fallen into disuse in modern cryptography, and ciphers are the dominant technique.

Types

There are a variety of different types of encryption. Algorithms used earlier in the history of cryptography are substantially different from modern methods, and modern ciphers can be classified according to how they operate and whether they use one or two keys.

Historical

Historical pen and paper ciphers used in the past are sometimes known as classical ciphers. They include simple substitution ciphers (such as Rot 13) and transposition ciphers (such as a Rail Fence Cipher). For example, "GOOD DOG" can be encrypted as "PLLX XLP" where "L" substitutes for "O", "P" for "G", and "X" for "D" in the message. Transposition of the letters "GOOD DOG" can result in "DGOGDOO". These simple ciphers and examples are easy to crack, even without plaintext-ciphertext pairs.

Simple ciphers were replaced by polyalphabetic substitution ciphers (such as the Vigenère) which changed the substitution alphabet for every letter. For example, "GOOD DOG" can be encrypted as "PLSX TWF" where "L", "S", and "W" substitute for "O". With even a small amount of known or estimated plaintext, simple polyalphabetic substitution ciphers and letter transposition ciphers designed for pen and paper encryption are easy to crack. It is possible to create a secure pen and paper cipher based on a one-time pad though, but the usual disadvantages of one-time pads apply.

During the early twentieth century, electro-mechanical machines were invented to do encryption and decryption using transposition, polyalphabetic substitution, and a kind of "additive" substitution. In rotor machines, several rotor disks provided polyalphabetic substitution, while plug boards provided another substitution. Keys were easily changed by changing the rotor disks and the plugboard wires. Although these encryption methods were more complex than previous schemes and required machines to encrypt and decrypt, other machines such as the British Bombe were invented to crack these encryption methods.

Modern

Modern encryption methods can be divided by two criteria: by type of key used, and by type of input data.

By type of key used ciphers are divided into:

- symmetric key algorithms (Private-key cryptography), where the same key is used for encryption and decryption, and

- asymmetric key algorithms (Public-key cryptography), where two different keys are used for encryption and decryption.

In a symmetric key algorithm (e.g., DES and AES), the sender and receiver must have a shared key set up in advance and kept secret from all other parties; the sender uses this key for encryption, and the receiver uses the same key for decryption. The Feistel cipher uses a combination of substitution and transposition techniques. Most block cipher algorithms are based on this structure. In an asymmetric key algorithm (e.g., RSA), there are two separate keys: a *public key* is published and enables any sender to perform encryption, while a *private key* is kept secret by the receiver and enables only him to perform correct decryption.

Ciphers can be distinguished into two types by the type of input data:

- block ciphers, which encrypt block of data of fixed size, and

- stream ciphers, which encrypt continuous streams of data

Key Size and Vulnerability

In a pure mathematical attack, (i.e., lacking any other information to help break a cipher) two factors above all count:

- Computational power available, i.e., the computing power which can be brought to bear on the problem. It is important to note that average performance/capacity of a single computer is not the only factor to consider. An adversary can use multiple computers at once, for instance, to increase the speed of exhaustive search for a key (i.e., "brute force" attack) substantially.

- Key size, i.e., the size of key used to encrypt a message. As the key size increases, so does the complexity of exhaustive search to the point where it becomes impracticable to crack encryption directly.

Since the desired effect is computational difficulty, in theory one would choose an algorithm and desired difficulty level, thus decide the key length accordingly.

An example of this process can be found at Key Length which uses multiple reports to suggest that a symmetric cipher with 128 bits, an asymmetric cipher with 3072 bit keys, and an elliptic curve cipher with 512 bits, all have similar difficulty at present.

Claude Shannon proved, using information theory considerations, that any theoretically unbreakable cipher must have keys which are at least as long as the plaintext, and used only once: one-time pad.

Ciphers:

1. Block Cipher

2. Stream Cipher

Block Cipher: The same function is used to encrypt successive blocks (memory less).

Stream Cipher: This processes plan text as small as single bit. It has memory.

- One – Time – Pad (corresponding cipher is called Vernam cipher)

  $c_i = m_i \oplus k_i$

  m_i : plain text

  k_i : keystream

  c_i : cipher text

- Decryption :

  $m_i = c_i \oplus k_i$
  $\quad = m_i \oplus k_i \oplus k_i$
  $\quad = m_i$

- Assumption: is truly random.

Synchronous Stream Ciphers:

{There is a clock which is same at both the ends}

Definition: a synchronous stream cipher is one in which the key stream is generated independently of the plain text and cipher text

Encryption:

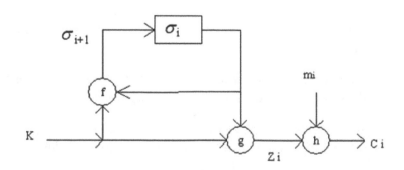

Decryption:

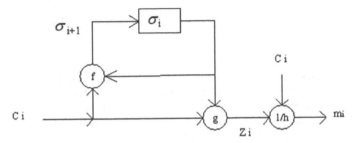

Properties of Synchronous stream cipher:

- Synchronization requirement: In a synchronous stream cipher, both the sender and receiver must be synchronized using the same key. If synchronization is lost due to cipher text digits being inserted or deleted during transmission, then decryption fails and can only be restored through additional techniques for re-synchronization. This involves either re-initialization or placing special marker at regular intervals or redundancy in plain text.

- No error propagation: A cipher text digit that is modified during transmission doesn't effect decryption of other cipher text digits.

Active attacks: As a consequence of properly (i), the insertion, deletion or replay of cipher text digits by an active adversary causes immediate loss of synchronization and hence might possibly be detected by decryptors.

Application: Stream ciphers are used for video data stream.

Permissions

Index